STAGECOACH
76

Other work by Red Cloud Wolverton

'Big Ranch Cowboy'
'To The Far Corners'
'Cowboy Coogan'
'The Devil's Garden' – (short story published in 'Tales From Cowboy Country' compilation)
'JimmyKane' (short story published in 'Good Medicine' compilation)
'A Cowboy's Ranch' and **'Hopi'** published in 'Tales From Out There' - Range Magazine publication

STAGECOACH
76

By Red Cloud Wolverton

& Margery A. Wolverton

Edited, Forward, and Epilogue

by Wendy L. Wolverton

© 2022 Wendy Wolverton all rights reserved
No portion of this book may be copied or duplicated without author's or copyright holder's permission.
Book format & layout: Wendy Wolverton

ISBN 978-1-7378192-02 softcover printed book

ISBN 978-1-8378192-1-9 Ebook

Library of Congress - Copyright

Published and printed in the United States of America.

F O RWARD

Most family road trips are the highlight of the summer, creating memorable times that bond families together. Ours was a unique experience that was more than a road trip. It was a journey through space and time. In the Bicentennial summer of 1976, we set out on a 3 month journey: to traverse 7 states in a stagecoach, to retrace the Overland Stagecoach Route.

We were all a part of living history as we lived out my father's dream. This experience would set a course for our lives. We saw the best of America, as we met diverse people, and learned lessons that would shape our life - that we are all different, but inside, we want the same things – equality, peace, happiness.

For my parents, my 9 year old self, my older brother Kip, and my sisters Tammie and Holly, and the friends who joined us, this was the trip of a lifetime. The close friends who accompanied us are all named throughout, but the main ones were Joe and Pearl Herin, the Jack Thompson family, and the Dick McCombs family. These people were a part of our daily lives and became family to us. Many others contributed along the way and made the trip possible; including the wonderful people of every small and large town who welcomed us with open arms.

This was my parents' dream, and we were all captured in it. This is a story about hope and heartbreak. It is about tragedy and triumph. It is a story of family and friends; overcoming obstacles, and achieving dreams. This is told through the journals of my father Red, and mother Margery. From their point of view, we are all reflected. Each one of us in life can see through their eyes, as we dream, strive, fail, and through persistence and sheer grit, succeed in our endeavors. This book publication, like the stagecoach trip, took many years to come to fruition, and its completion is an achievement to honor and say Thank you to Red and Margery. It is dedicated to our family.

TABLE OF CONTENTS

PAGE 5	FORWARD
PAGE 8	PROLOGUE
PAGE 11	CHAPTER ONE – HOW IT ALL STARTED
PAGE 21	CHAPTER TWO – TRIALS AND TRIBULATIONS
PAGE 37	CHAPTER THREE – WILL WE MAKE IT TO ST. JOE?
PAGE 45	CHAPTER FOUR – THE START
PAGE 73	CHAPTER FIVE – NEBRASKA
PAGE 95	CHAPTER SIX – NEBRASKA PARADES
PAGE 119	CHAPTER SEVEN – ON TO COLORADO
PAGE 137	CHAPTER EIGHT - COLORADO HISTORY
PAGE 153	CHAPTER NINE – WYOMING
PAGE 171	CHAPTER TEN - NEW STAGECOACH 200 YEARS
PAGE 207	CHAPTER ELEVEN – UTAH
PAGE 235	CHAPTER TWELVE – NEVADA
PAGE 267	CHAPTER THIRTEEN – EYES ON THE HORIZON
PAGE 281	CHAPTER FOURTEEN – THE WESTERN SLOPES
PAGE 307	CHAPTER FIFTEEN – THE END OF A JOURNEY
PAGE 329	EPILOGUE

PROLOGUE

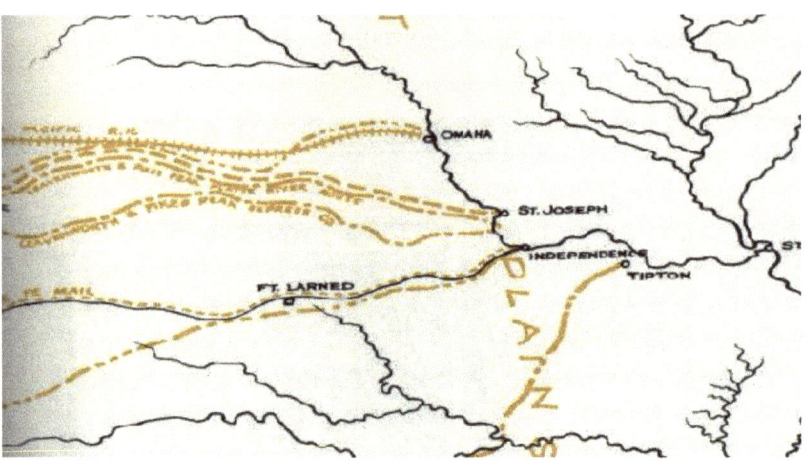

"The trip was driving an authentic Concord stagecoach and six horse hitch out of St. Joe, Missouri, heading for Sacramento, California. Due to the change in the times, things such as modern highways, fences, and private property, it was impossible to follow the exact trail. We were able to start from the Pony Express stables in St. Joe, which were only a couple blocks from the original stage station. It was a most thrilling experience, as a Bicentennial project to be able to hitch our stagecoach up there near the original starting point, and to load up and drive out of St. Joe across the mighty Missouri River, over that high, shaky steel bridge, and head out on the original Overland Trail for California."

At times to me as the driver, it was a deep emotional thrill. More than several times on the trip, as I drove up to where an original station stood, *I would get the feeling that I'd been there before…*

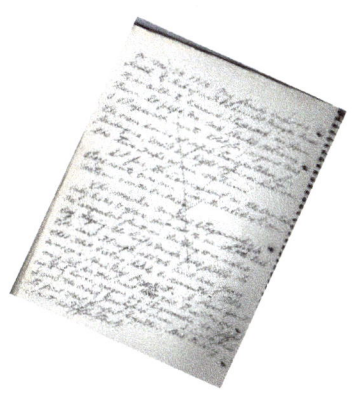

** Dad always said he was born 100 years too late.

When I topped the last rise, and let out my hitch to take the slight down grade across the draw, and then roll up to the log station at a full gallop at Virginia Dale, I could almost see big Jack Slade standing there nodding his approval of the proper way to roll into an important station like his was.

Virginia Dale Stage Station and Jack Slade's Cabin.

There were lots of long hard days the first month of the trip, but the most difficult part was behind us. That was the months and days and years of preparation that it had taken us to put all this together.

CHAPTER ONE
HOW IT ALL STARTED

"**Romeo! Rebel! Get up!**" With those words, we started a journey... that had taken a lifetime of dreaming and preparation to get underway.

The desire on my part had been with me for a long, long time. It all started ages ago, when I was pretty young. I helped form an outlaw band that had but one thing in mind – to rob the stagecoach when it rolled into town for the annual 4th of July celebration. We had a large outlaw group and I'm sure we would have gotten away with our escapade, but like a lot of organizations, we had a rat amongst us. One of our group squealed to the Sheriff's Posse what we were planning on doing, and after a successful hold-up, and while we were making off with the loot, we were ambushed on the off side of the Courthouse Square by mounted posse men that galloped down on us from every direction.

We just didn't have a fighting chance so we surrendered peacefully and were led off to the log stockade and drug before their kangaroo court, and sentenced by the "hanging" judge to take part in the western ceremonies for the rest of the day. Our sentence was to ride our horses up and down the main street and to rope and drag, if necessary, to the log stockade, any person found not wearing western attire.

We had a lot of fun and the day ended all too soon, but that was how my interest in stagecoaches was born.

It was a reenactment of history, from June 1st, 1858 through May 10, 1869 - a time when the goldfields of the Sierras were brought closer to the banks of the East by the stagecoach. The driving of the Golden Spike at Promontory Point, Utah in 1869 ended the most dramatic era of stagecoaching that ever existed.

For 11 years, men such as Ben Holliday, Bob Spotswood, Hank Monk, Frank Root, and even at least one woman such as Charlie Parkhurst owned or drove the stagecoaches that crossed our nation day and night, winter and summer, rain or sun, in a continuous stream.

Those were times of great hardships and heroic feats of both men and horses.

I was ranch raised and had driven horses and mules on all types of farm machinery, wagons, and chuck wagons, but every time I ever saw a real live stagecoach or even one on the movie screen go rocking along in a good trot or gallop, I would perk up like an old fire horse when he heard the alarm. **For years I knew and dreamed and worked for the day that I would have a spirited six horse hitch and stagecoach of my own.**

In 1962, I managed to scrape up a few thousand dollars, and was able to form a small corporation to buy a ranch in Central Oregon. Those mountain-desert ranches don't actually have to run very many cows to have quite a few acres, or sections, or even townships in them. They are large and rough enough that you do your work horseback, and it takes quite a few good tough horses to run even a small ranch. Most of the old, big chuckwagon ranches in the northwest that I had punched cows on had quite a bit of Morgan horse blood in their saddle horses, and that was sure a horse to ride across the desert on.

Finally, I have lived that dream.

When we started ranching I wanted to raise our own horses, and I wanted saddle horses that could double as light harness horses. **I had that stagecoach thing in the back of my mind all the time.** We found a two year old Morgan stallion, which had the size and disposition we liked, so we bought him, and then proceeded to pick up a few registered Morgan mares. Stagecoach horses need to be four or five or preferably eight years old to be really good, so it takes quite a while to raise and break a good stagecoach hitch.

We knew several years before the Bicentennial year of 1976 arrived that we were going to celebrate our nation's birthday with our horses and stagecoach, long before we settled on exactly what route we wanted to take. Two years ago my wife Margery was with me in our truck hauling a load to Pasco Washington. We were up in Wyoming, out in the Red Desert area, heading west. We'd been talking about the horses and what to do for the Bicentennial, when suddenly she looked towards me, her eyes all lit up and a big grin over her face. "I just figured out what we should do for the Bicentennial", she said. Between shifting gears, and watching the highway, I managed to ask her again to let me in on the good news.

Two of the leaders — Rebel and Rosiene.

"We'll retrace the Overland Stage route", was her reply. I didn't say anything for a few minutes, and when I looked at her again, I must have had an odd look on my face, as she asked, "Well, what's the matter. Don't you like it?" That wasn't the reason. I had driven all but the last 100 miles of the route many times, and so was calculating the problems it would present. I immediately thought of the steep, narrow, high steel bridge across the Missouri River coming out of St. Joe, and the miles of winding, heavy traveled highway 36 out of Kansas. The heat and storms we might encounter in Nebraska reminded me of the flash floods we might run into in Colorado. Wyoming might be hot and windy, or it might be cold and windy, but it was almost certain to be windy. Wind or no wind, I like every square foot of the state.

After all, the stagecoach was one of the most important links in transportation; that is in passenger service, mail, and light express, bullion and money, in the western United States from the 1850s to clear into the early 1920s.!

So what would be more fitting as a heritage project than to rerun the 'Great grand-daddy stage line of them all'!

The one that brought the California gold fields closer to the end of the rails and the East -

The one that served as the rapid transit line for eleven years in the height of the gold boom and war years –

The one that has been ignored by too many history books –

-The Overland Trail mail stage route from St. Joe to Sacramento.

Next in thinking of Utah, my first thought was maybe we'll get time to take another swim in the Great Salt Lake, and that in turn reminded me of the salt flats, and how rough they can be at times. I've seen the winds die down at sundown on the desert may times, as if things went right maybe we could cross the salt flats at night, which brought me to my beloved state of Nevada. I've spent some summers buckarooing in Nevada, so no one had to tell me any wild mesquite stories to convince me how rough they can be at times.

I was brought out of my vacant stare by Marge asking me, "Well, what's wrong with the idea?" It didn't take me long to answer that **I thought that was the best Bicentennial idea that I had yet heard of, and that we'd do it if there was a way, and that we'd figure out how to do it even if there wasn't a way.**

I could see that a trip like this would take a lot of preparation time. We had a good six horse hitch of horses pretty well broke, but we'd need at least two hitches and probably three to be on the safe side.

There aren't many places you can buy a well broke six horse hitch anymore, and it takes a year or so to get a bunch of desert raised horses in shape to be safe to drive through towns and along today's modern highways. I never had any doubts as to the fact that I could drive the stagecoach every day all the way by myself, but I decided I needed to be prepared for the unexpected. Without a relief driver, I could think of a hundred reasons why the trip could be held up or maybe even completely cancelled enroute if something happened to me.

I had an old cowboy friend that I'd worked with on the ZX Ranch at Paisley, Oregon. He'd worked horses a lot when he was young, and he'd sold his ranch recently and wasn't tied down. We stopped by Redmond, Oregon on that trip and visited Joe and Pearl. It took him about as long to make up his mind to go along as it had taken me.

We had an old mudwagon stagecoach and enough extra unbroke horses to make the trip, but after studying it over, **we decided we'd need either an original coach rebuilt, or a new one for the trip.**

We finally located a 1968 Frizzell coach that had been built to the exact Concord specifications of one hundred years ago. **It was priced at $17,000.00 cash which almost floored us. We decided to chance it, but before we could get the money together, another fellow bought it.**

We had started writing to prospective sponsors with the Wells Fargo Bank of California as our main target. This trip would have been a natural for them, and besides we thought they might have a stagecoach they'd like to lend us. They did say they thought the trip sounded very worthwhile and they wished us the best of luck, but they didn't wish to participate in it financially in any way. However, they did send us an official document granting us permission to use the Wells Fargo name and emblems on our stagecoach and strongbox.

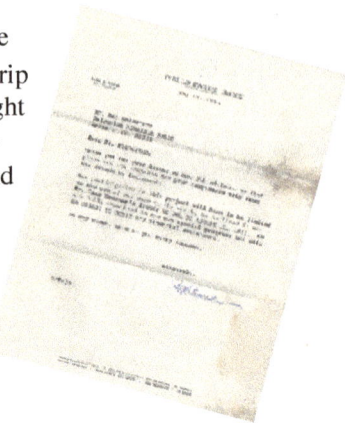

In the spring of 1974, we were living in the mountains near Wetmore, Colorado. We had ten head of horses broke to drive, and enough young unbroke horses to put us in pretty good shape by the Centennial year. But then I pulled a boo-boo. Art Foss offered me a foreman's job on the GI Ranch one hundred miles out on the desert from Bend, Oregon towards Burns. I told him we had twenty head of horses we didn't want to part with. He said to bring them; that they had plenty of room and work for them.

We decided if we had to finance it ourselves, we would use our own name. It looks pretty good on the coach.

I sure thought it was the thing to do. Things worked out for awhile. Our stagecoach horses are all broke to ride; so we put them right to work punching cows out there on the desert. We even found time to drive the six head occasionally. That fall we took the horses up to the Pendleton Roundup and pulled a large band wagon with a Navy band in it in their parade. We had a good time and enjoyed the Roundup. Cow prices dropped that fall and the GI Ranch, like quite a few others, had to cut expenses drastically.

It was a long ways to school out there. At Christmas, we were notified that they wouldn't send the school bus out to the ranch any more, and that we would have to haul our kids twenty-five miles to meet the bus.

When a doctor offered me a job on his purebred Angus Ranch three miles from Prineville, it sounded so good to us that we moved again. **The only problem was he didn't have room for our horses**. We shifted them around from one temporary spot to another for six months. **I had already gotten disgusted and sold some of the young horses that we needed later to have for the trip.** We finally decided we were going to have to return to our place in Colorado so we could devote more time to breaking our horses to work, if we were going to be able to make our trip. The last of August we packed up again and headed back to Colorado.

We got back to Pueblo in time to show our old mudwagon coach and six horse hitch in the Colorado State Fair Parade. It has always been a thrill to me to drive a six-horse hitch in a parade.

> The kids and young people seem to appreciate it, but it is the older people that repay me for our efforts. They really enjoy the sight.

Twenty years ago Marge and I scraped up enough money to make a down payment on 120 acres in the mountains south of Wetmore, Colorado. It's one of those places that is close to civilization, but is real isolated. It is just two miles to the

telephone, electricity and a paved road, ¾ of a mile up a 16% grade, and then down 1¾ miles of side hill, winding road into a timber covered basin of national forest land, just 120 acres in the bottom of a basin of several thousand acres of national forest. There used to be lots of deer, bear, mountain lions, turkeys, and all kinds of birds. It always has been a place that is hard to get in to, but once you're there, you hate to leave.

Our place is known as Babcock Hole, after a gang of outlaws named Babcock that settled the valley first in the old days.

There was an old house on the place when we bought it, but it was pretty much rat infested, worn out, and right out in the path way of the fierce winds that blow down the valley at times. Once after spending a night in the old house when we had withstood one shuddering blast after another, we decided if there was a place that the wind didn't hit so hard, we would rebuild there. The fierce wind was still howling down the canyon when daylight finally crept in on us; so we went shopping. About 200 yards up the canyon in a pretty grove of pine, that wild wind was hardly rustling the pine needles. We decided right then that was where we would rebuild.

We didn't have any money so decided we could tear the old big house down and salvage the good lumber, nails, windows, and doors and build us a smaller cabin in the clearing in the pines. We could always add onto it as time and finances permitted. We got a 12 by 24 foot cabin up in no time and were able to move into it for a while before we had to leave to go to the outside world to replenish our finances. For the past twenty years it seems that is what we have been doing over and over. Going out and working and building up a good stake, then returning to the "Hole" until it was gone again.

It takes a lot of feed to keep twenty head of horses, especially when you have to buy it, so I had to work part time. I had my diesel truck-tractor; so I'd haul a load or two of steel, then come back to the Hole and work on the log addition until our finances ran low; then I'd have to go out again. It sure was hard to leave the peace and quiet of the 'Hole' and head back to the hustle of a long haul steel hauler.

CHAPTER TWO
TRIALS AND TRIBULATIONS

On one of my trips to Oklahoma City, I stopped in at Frizzell's Coach & Wheelworks for a visit. Lo and behold, there was the Santa Fe coach in for repairs, that I had tried to buy the year before. It was on its way to Oregon. When I climbed up on it and tried it on for size I never had the slightest thought that I might drive it proudly out of St. Joe, across the mighty Missouri, and west for 600 miles before our own coach would be delivered. **I decided that night while talking to Mr. Frizzell that we should have a 12 passenger coach for the trip. They were the ones used on the main line where the passenger traffic was the heaviest.**

I got a price quoted right away from Frizzell at $27, 250.00 to build the coach. Also he informed me that he wouldn't accept the order to build it unless the order was accompanied by a 50% cash deposit. We were negotiating with several large advertising firms to sponsor the trip at that time. We'd also applied under what appeared to be very favorable conditions to the Colorado State Bicentennial Commission for $20,000.00 to help finance the trip. **Things really looked good at that time so ...**

> ...we decided to use our ranch, the 'Hole' for collateral to borrow the money from the bank to pay for the coach.

The first bankers we approached were very impressed and implied they could see no problem in lending us the money we needed but they had to think it over. Come back next week was the runaround they pulled on us for two months before they politely refused to lend us any money what so ever. The second bank we went to said sure they'd lend us what we needed, but immediately limited it to $18,000,00. We hadn't been turned down by all the advertising firms and Centennial Commission at that time. **The stagecoach builders said they needed six months; so we decided to take the risk so we could get the stagecoach ordered.**

Breaking horses, and stagecoach tongues...

It takes lots of work and training to shape up fifteen head of mountain-desert raised horses to make them fit and safe to drive in towns through crowds of people. The only way you can give that many horses the work and training they need is to spend full time; so I quit the trucking and went to work on them. **The Colorado mountains, at an elevation above 6,000 feet, are a pretty tough place to work horses in January and February, but we didn't have any choice except to get right with it.** We spend a lot of time driving our young horses in single harness afoot before teaming them up and starting them on a wagon.

Tammie was a senior in high school and had a short day the last semester. She'd pestered me to let her drive her pickup to school; so I finally agreed that she could, and I'd pay the expense if she'd come right home and help with the horses. She'd rather work with the horses than almost anything else, even chasing boys. She spent many a mile behind the horses before we got the hitches put together. When I'd hook a team together on a **wagon she'd get a break and come along on her saddle horse, Max Brand,** as my hazer. Quite often I needed her too. We had several good runs and chases and mess-ups and pile ups.

One of the worst wrecks we had occurred one evening... when I told Tammie to come ride on the coach with me *instead of saddling her horse. I had worked the six horses in separate teams on the wagon all, and thought I had them all pretty well settled. It was a brisk, cold cloudy March day. The horses were pretty edgy, but I thought I could handle them together in a hitch. The first hundred yards wasn't any problem. The horses were stepping right out and responding to the lines real good, but then when we dropped down a bank to cross the creek, things changed quickly.*

The coach rolled and boogered a wheel horse. That near wheeler looked back up over his right blinder on his bridle and saw the coach coming after him. He immediately lunged ahead to get out of the way. He jumped so hard coming up out of the creek that he slammed the double trees into the swing horses, spooking them enough to cause them to lunge into the lead team. I had the brake lever crammed as far ahead as I could push it, and I had plenty of leverage too, as I was hauling back on all six lines with all my might. By the time we were on level ground, we were going as fast as six horses could run. We had about 100 yards of level ground before we dropped into a left hand bend of the valley that was rocky and narrow. There was an opening in the valley that swung towards the right side up a pretty steep grade. It was pretty well clogged with oak brush; so I figured if I could swing up that way I might pile into the brush and get stopped. I never got turned up the draw.

Tammie had been practicing barrel racing previously and had been using this flat for her arena. She just left the barrels on the flat when she got through. They were still there. We made it between the first two barrels, but it didn't seem to make much difference which set of lines I hauled in on. My lead horses both saw that barrel quite a ways ahead, and they each decided to go on the outside.

Two or three times I almost had one leader yanked over to go past the barrel on the inside, but finally right at the last, they instantly swung wide and straddled that barrel as hard as they could run! I was pulling with all my might, trying to turn the hitch to the right to get away from that barrel before the coach got to it, but those horses sure seemed programmed to stay astraddle of it. Either the lead bars or the front end of the swing pole knocked it over, and for an instant I thought I was going to get to the side away from it, but the wheel tongue knocked it the same way the horses had lunged to clear it. All it did was to spin the barrel crossways right in front of the off front wheel. Even then I hoped it was going to spin off to the side and get away from us. Instead I think it just squatted down and dug in right square in front of that right wheel. **That old coach leaned so far to the left I shore thought it was going over!**

I pushed the lines ahead and squalled at the horses. As if loosening up wasn't enough, when I let up on the lines, the horses even seemed to hit it harder and just jerked that old coach right back down out of the air right on the ground. I just about had time to fall back on the lines again before the rear wheel played the same tune on us. Tammie said afterwards that when that rear wheel went over that barrel, that her side of that high seat dipped so low that she could have reached out and scooped up a handful of dirt. I throwed the slack at those horses' heads again and squalled, and danged if they didn't jerk it back to the ground again. By this time those six horses were really stretched out and making that old coach rattle. We'd already got too far to turn up the right hand valley, and that rough rocky lift bend of the trail was fairly leaping towards us.

There was a narrow brush filled stock trail that went up straight up a steep bank right at the start of the bend. Those horses had used that trail a lot as a short cut to the meadows up above; so they didn't hesitate when I hauled them into it. They just crowded together and tried to plow up it. That thick brush sure makes a good rough-lock, if you don't get whipped to death by it. We almost slid to a stop after turning up it.

We finally got the horses quieted down and straightened out and backed down the trail far enough to be able to swing them around and continue on our way. I held them to as slow a walk as possible, and we were doing pretty good until something happened that I never did figure out. I guess about the time a wheel slid sideways off a rock, that spooky wheel horse looked back around at me again, snorted, and quit the flats right there. His commotion was all the other horses needed to set them off again. **In the wink of an eye, I had six broncs pounding down the valley hell-bent again.** We made it out of the boulder patch and had about 15 yards of good smooth valley that curved to the right before we would come to a bad wash which I knew was too rough to cross at stampede speed. There was lots of oak brush all along our right but I couldn't pull the lead horses into it. We still had about 50 yards to go when I yelled to Tammie to grab the lead lines out of my hands and to hold the leaders as close to the brush as possible. **I'd showed her several times how to grab the lead or wheel lines out of my hands to help in case of a run-away if I needed it.** She did a good job this time and was able to hold the leaders right against the brush. I really put the pressure on my swing team and was able to jerk them right into a large clump of stout oak brush.

We were almost stopped when the off swing horse fell down! It knocked us back out of the brush and back in the open again. The horses were really spooked now and trying to get away, but that swing horse just got more tangled and fouled up, the harder he tried. He finally flopped over the swing pole and broke it just as we got everything stopped. It was a sight! I had a time getting Tammie in motion. She just couldn't get in gear to jump down and help untangle them. Since the swing pole was broken, we just had rigging enough for four horses; so we moved the lead bars back to the wheel tongue, and tied two horses onto the rear of the coach. Hooked four head back together and continued on with our driving. The afternoon had turned so bitter cold I could hardly finger the lines, but we went ahead and worked the horses until dark. Tammie said she'd had enough of riding on the coach with me. If I wanted her help she'd gladly go along horseback, but no more stagecoach rides for her. She finally consented to ride inside once in the summer, but never climbed up on the driver's box with me again until after we'd returned home in the fall.

We used our horses working at the ranch on quite a few pieces of equipment, like hauling wood on a freight wagon, pulling the road grader over the hill to plow snow when it got deep, cleaning the corrals with the hay rake, and feeding with the hay wagon. I made a deal with Dick McComb to move into the Horseman's Arena at Pueblo West to continue their training.

We talked my Wetmore neighbors into helping, so we moved our horses and equipment out of the Hole to George Draper's ranch. On the morning of March 18th, we started to Pueblo West, with six head on the coach in the lead, four-up on the hay wagon with George and Buddy Draper driving, and Jim West had a team of bald-faced mares on a doctor's buggy. We had quite a parade of our own, driving half way to Terry Everhart's corrals where we spent the night. The Pueblo newspaper really gave us a lot of good coverage and publicity, and we really appreciated it.

The next day was a real cold day with a knife-edge wind blowing out of the northwest. It wasn't so bad as long as it was quartering to our backs, but sure became unbearable when we faced it. It is difficult enough to drive a hitch down the road when a hard cross wind is blowing and the weather is warm. When the thermometer is shivering around 20-25° and then the wind is blowing 35-50 miles per hour, it really starts to toughen up. There is about 30 feet of lead line grabbing at every change of the breeze, and with each different pressure on the line, the lead team thinks you are trying to turn them one way or another. You are constantly pulling in or slipping out slack to try to keep them going in the general direction. On top of everything else, it is hard enough to keep your hands warm with a fist full of lines in each hand on a cold still day, but it sure makes me sympathetic to those old time skinners.

We rolled in to Pueblo West at about 2:00 P.M. There was a large crowd awaiting us in front of the Inn. One of our friends in the Gunslingers Club had met us down the road with a crew of local dignitaries to ride the rest of the way in on the stagecoach. They wanted the hay wagon to circle around and come to the Inn from another direction, and they had an old-time "doctor" to ride with Jim in the buggy. I finally got the signal to gallop on up to the Inn where we were met by the hay wagon loaded with masked hombres who immediately proceeded to hold up the stage. Some of my passengers were expecting just such a shenanigan; so they had their sidearms under their coats. A heck of a bang-up gun battle ensued right there, and wound up with fellows plugged all over the landscape around the coach. I guess the outlaws outnumbered us.

As the smoke cleared, they could be seen running to the hay wagon with the strongbox and making their getaway. It was a real relief to get the robbery over and get to the horse corrals to put up the animals, and then get in out of the cold. **That day must have set an example for our trip as we were held up a good many times, and the robbers always made off with our strong box. Someday maybe I'll have a cavalry or cowboy escort along when those robbers hit me. I'll bet we play a different game then.** The area around the Horseman's Arena at Pueblo West was a real good place to work our horses. There are lots of uncongested dirt roads, and the country is flat to gently rolling.

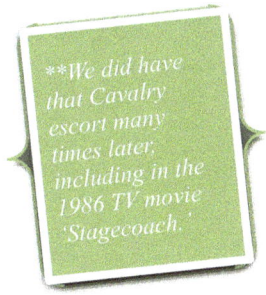

**We did have that Cavalry escort many times later, including in the 1986 TV movie 'Stagecoach.'

There is plenty of room in the arena area to hook up and head out. After we'd been there a couple weeks, Joe and Pearl rolled in with their camper. I'd told Joe he should come and spend a month driving the horses every day, both for his practice and to get to know the horses. Joe had driven horses a lot when he was young, but he didn't realize handling six head of frisky stagecoach horses at a gallop was quite different than driving a freight team in a walk with a load of wheat.

It takes a lot of practice after you've been away from it for years, to get the feel of the lines, and to turn the blisters between your fingers into calluses. It takes a lot of finger and shoulder exercise to get into shape for steady driving. Joe didn't stay and drive as much as I hoped he would. He was just beginning to get the feel of things when he had to return to Oregon to get his affairs in order to make the summer's trip.

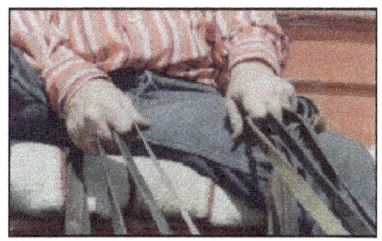

Making a good stagecoach horse – Movie prep

About that same time, George phoned and said a Charles Bronson movie * was being filmed up near Canon City, and they needed six teams and could I furnish them? Well, we had the horses, although we'd been working them as six horse hitches instead of teams. We had a few days so we got right after them, working them in two's to get them lined out. To start with, they just wanted one team; so I took up Bandito and Houlihan, one of my wheel teams.

The movie company was to provide the teamsters, but I had to drive the wagon up a couple miles from where we hitched up to get to the set. When they sent a fellow over to take my wagon, I said I would stay up on the wagon until I saw how he did. **It would have been comical if it hadn't been so disgusting.** When I handed this bird the lines and said, "Give her a try", he never even knew about the brake.

He just took both lines and held them in his two hands together out in front of him. Then with a couple of forward jabbing motions, he says to the horses, "O.K. Go! Go!" We were setting on a hill, and I had the brake kicked on real hard and locked in place. I didn't get a chance to boot him off the driver's seat. Before I could get a word out, Rudy, the stock contractor, yelled, "Get that dude off there! Damn! I thought you said you had some teamsters." Turning to me, he said, "Red, you drive your own wagon." It didn't take the make-up man long to get me ready. I had on my everyday work clothes, and the only fault they could find was my neck rag was too bright colored, and my clothes were too clean. They gave me a black "wild rag" and throwed some dust on my Levis and I was ready. The movies are great. You spend all day shooting the same scene over and over, to make a five minute part, and then chances are it's cut out in the end.

* 'THE WHITE BUFFALO' starring Charles Bronson, filmed in Cañon City Colorado - 1975

This was a normal day. I did get a kick out of one of the last runs I did. It was a covered wagon scene, with a man and wife, and a whole passel of kids, not to mention all the trunks and other paraphernalia that were loaded on. We were supposedly heading west to the Promised Land when the scout gallops by and yells that Custer has found gold in the Black Hills, and we should light a shuck up that-a-way. At this point, we are supposed to pull a 90° right hand turn and head for the hills. The first time was a rehearsal. The second time, the director decided I should lope right out and pass the other wagons. **Then he asked me for a little more action.**

The last time we shot that scene, when I turned and started towards the Black Hills, I squalled at my horses and threw them the slack in the lines. We were going right across the bunch grass and it was quite a ways from being smooth. I really had that old covered wagon bouncing, and my passengers thought we were having a runaway. She and the kids went to yelling and carrying on, and my team thought that was to encourage them. I really hated to pull them up when we got down to the bottom of the draw and out of the view of the cameras, but the woman and kids were sure glad to get out of that wagon.

I went back to Buckskin Joe with the movie crew for a few days, with 12 head of horses. Then we finished up down at Chama, New Mexico with two teams and a single horse on a buggy. I used one of my blaze-faced lead teams and the wheel team out of the same hitch, at Chama, which was supposed to represent a Cheyenne Wyoming railroad scene in the movie. It was really some experience for those horses, and I'm sure helped greatly preparing them for our summer's trip.

One time in particular ---we were in the train yard with the horses right next to the tracks. I had Houlihan on the train side and it passed closer than five feet. Bandito was as unconcerned as if he'd been around trains all his life, but Houlihan was a little different. When that thing came by, he knew it was a fire-breathing monster out to devour him. It hissed, and he jumped. Right straight up! If he'd had wings, he'd of kept on going. I'd known beforehand that something might happen so I'd already talked to this fella who was close by me on the set to come help if I needed him. When Houlihan jumped I hollered at him to grab him. It turned out that he was as scared of Houlihan as Houlihan was of the train. I guess misery loves company alright, because I was able to soft-talk both of them into settling down and they took right to each other.

Right down along the railroad tracks for 50 or 75 yards was a great long pile of buffalo bones piled 12 feet or higher. I was driving a big high sided wagon that was loaded to spilling over with some of these bones, and was parked between this bone pile and the train tracks. When the cameras were pointing our way, this fella and a Mexican worker would climb up on the wagon and start to throw the bones off. We shot that scene over 10 or 20 times. Between takes we had to reload all the bones that were thrown off while the cameras

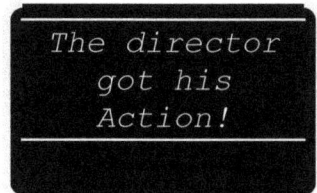

The director got his Action!

were running. This was just background for the main scene, but they shot it over so many times, we 'pertner had those old buffalo bones trained to crawl back on the wagon by theirselves.

On our summer's trip, we drove mostly wherever we chose with the stagecoach. The interstates were real good to travel; straight, big and wide, and only one way traffic to worry about. What I really preferred was a good solid dirt frontage road. The horses do better on dirt, and if it's solid the coach feels better on it. **The interstates have lots of problems;** like in the livestock country, they are fenced and have cattle guards on all exits and on ramps and mostly they don't have any gates.

> With all the commotion, movies are good preparation for whatever may come.

We solved the cattle guard problem without much trouble. We packed two sheets of two inch 4ft. x 8 ft. plywood panels which we hauled in our pilot-car pickup. We'd put these sheets of plywood down over the cattle guard and drive the horses and stage right across. After the first few times, the horses didn't pay much attention to them.

Nevada has real good highways, but most of the interstates end a mile or two outside the towns. One such place is Carlin, Nevada. Coming in from the East, the interstate ends about 5 to 7 miles out. From there on to town there is just a little narrow two-way highway, with hardly any shoulders on the side.

Just before the freeway ends, you come to a tunnel cut through the mountain ¾ mile or more. The old highway is still there circling the mountain, and it is one place where there's a gate, but the Highway Department keeps it locked. Luckily I knew all this ahead of time, and was able to talk the state patrol into unlocking it for us. The Carlin police knew when to expect us in town. Much to my pleasant surprise, they were waiting where the old road circled around the freeway which ended about there, and would escort us into town. We only had to travel the main road about ¼ mile to where we could pick up a good dirt road for a mile or more. The officer said he'd meet us where the dirt came back to the asphalt. On the way, I noticed ahead what appeared to be a dirt road down next to the railroad tracks. When I asked about it, the cop said, "Yeah, that would be a good one. It will take you all the way into town." The farther we went, the closer the dirt seemed to get to the tracks, and the higher the sagebrush got on the other side.

The cop had said that about half way to town, we'd come to a slough and that the dirt road crossed the bridge over the highway, then returned to the tracks on the other side. He'd wait for us at the bridge to hold up traffic. I could see the slough up ahead, and the train was catching up behind. It looked like if I'd lope the hitch a bit that I could time it so the train engine would have a chance to pass us while we were away from the tracks. After getting across the bridge, I slowed to a walk. The horses didn't seem to pay any attention so we proceeded on down the dirt road parallel with the train. We moved out at a right brisk trot. Before the whole train had passed us, it started slowing down for the town. Pretty quick we were traveling as fast as it was. Then we gained on it.

We ran right beside it for a couple miles. Up ahead there was a side track to the right of the main line. The dirt road forked, with the right hand fork going back out to the highway. The left fork crossed the siding tracks and ran between the two sets of tracks all the way into town, which was about another ½ mile. There was a string of boxcars setting on the siding, and that road between the moving train and those boxcars sure looked narrow. It was like looking down the "devil's slide". I decided to take my chances on the right hand fork to the highway, in spite of the fact the truck traffic on that narrow two-lane had been real "hairy". Just before we got to the forks, our cop showed up, coming up the road between the two tracks. "It's all clear. You can make it down that road, and it'll take you right on into town. I'll see you there where the mayor's waiting."

I just didn't have the heart to tell him with all of his confidence that I'd already decided to take the other road; so I waved a hand full of lines at him and said, "Thanks, we'll see you in town."

> *Marge was on the box with me, and Wendy was riding on top. I think she was kind of worried about being so close to the tracks because she spotted an approaching train several miles back, just as soon as it poked its engine out of the tunnel near the mountain.*

With a slight pressure on my lines, we swerved across the tracks and into that moving, grinding metal funnel. **It was really comical to watch those lead horses, Romeo and Rebel.** They never hesitated or gave the slightest hint of trying to turn back, but they were both concerned. Each was sure he was too close to the train on his side. With necks arched to the outside so they could watch the train with both eyes, they pressed their bodies together, and each tried to trot down the middle of the road.

For a long ways, it seemed the trains were so close that we could have reached out on either side and touched a train. I was sure proud of that hitch when we poured out the other end of that funnel, into the waiting group of people. We stopped and loaded up, and make a grand entry through town and on into the park, where we spent the evening as special guests at their community supper. Guess those trains at Chama had really given those horses their homework.

Scheduling the trip...the ups – and the downs.

By late in the fall of 75, we had our trip schedule all figured out. We originally planned on leaving St. Joe on the 2nd of June, which would allow the kids to finish school before we pulled out. The reason we moved the date up a week to May 25th, came about because of the State of Wyoming. I had written to Mr. Pat Hall, the head of the Wyoming Bicentennial Commission, about our trip and plans, and asked Wyoming to recognize it as a Bicentennial project. He liked our plans and went to his Board for endorsement, but they refused it. However, he liked the idea so much that he came up with a plan of his own. The Wyoming Commission would sponsor a stagecoach trip to run from Cheyenne to Deadwood, South Dakota, in conjunction with the Cheyenne Frontier Days. The Deadwood rodeo started about ten days after the first day's parade in Cheyenne, so the run would bring publicity to both shows. It's slightly over 400 miles between the two towns or about 40 miles a day, which is a pretty tough schedule if you don't have several changes of horses. Well, we had several more horses available at that time, and we had the "celerity" or mudwagon type of coach, which was the type commonly run on the Deadwood route for eight or nine years.

When I heard of Mr. Hall's plans, I went up to talk about us making the run right along with our regular cross country run. This meant we would be running the stagecoach 80 of our 94 days instead of 70, but I felt we could do it. I offered to make the Deadwood Run at a cost which I had calibrated at $3,000.00. Monty Montana had offered to do it for about $20,000.00 so I understood. **After we had rescheduled our trip to leave St. Joe on May 25 in order to allow the extra 10 days for the run, Mr. Hall notified me that the Commission had rejected our offer; so the Deadwood Run was canceled.** Maybe we can make it some other year.

This wasn't the only cancellation we had.

> **We had decided we needed a new authentic Concord stagecoach to make the trip in, and after a number of sponsors refused, the hand writing was on the wall. It was plain to see. "If we are going to make the trip, we will have to be prepared to do it all on our own.**

The first bankers I talked to about our plans were extremely interested but they felt before they lent any money they would have to have more than security to lend on. They wanted a concrete plan of repayment before they would get involved. The second banker was a man I had known for twenty some years. He was willing to lend some on our property which was just enough to get us in over our head, but not enough to guarantee financial backing for the trip.

> We still don't have the money for the trip…

The date was getting late, and we needed the money to get the stagecoach people to build our coach. We still had our trip plans being studied by several large companies; so we held our noses and dove right in, clear up over our ears. **As time went on all of our prospective sponsors backed out.** They all thought it had lots of advertising possibilities but they felt sure it would cost them more than their return from it. One very large corporation was so interested that I flew to Salt Lake City to their head office to discuss it with them. They had spent over a half million dollars for advertising the year before. When they offered me just one thousand dollars to put all their signs on our trucks and stagecoach and to spend an extra day at each of their stores in the ten towns we would pass through, and keep the signs on for a full year, I told them to keep their money.

We were turned down many times and places and ways for help, but we just kept going ahead with our preparations. We kept working our horses and getting our outfit together. I have pretty much believed what my old Dad used to tell me, at least as far as able bodied men are concerned. "God helps those that help themselves. He isn't going to give you something because you have prayed for it, but if you work hard enough, He might arrange for the pieces to fall into place if you stay with it long enough." I don't know what guided me, but I went in to see another banker that was a total stranger to me. We sat and talked for awhile. I told him of our plans, and when he asked how much money I needed, I was almost scared to speak for fear I might be sleeping and wake up. I really knew I was dreaming, when he handed me a personal note to sign for the money we needed.

With the financial problem solved, the labor situation became number one on the list just before shove-off time. **All our help except Joe sent word that things had changed and they wouldn't be able to go along.** I still had an ace in the hole though. My good friend Jack Thompson that owned the trucking company I'd worked for, was an old Kansas farm boy that hadn't ever gotten 'all of the country out of the man.' I still smile at the amount of time it took him to make up his mind the day I went in to see him. I says, "Jack, there's something I would like for you to do for me." "Yeah, what's that?" he answered, looking quizzically up from his disarranged desk full of papers. "Jack, I want you to come to St. Joe and ride shotgun on our stage trip as much as you can.", I said. He asked, "What day are you leaving St. Joe? He was all enthusiasm if I ever saw it.

We still had about two weeks before time to leave. Jack and his boys came out to the arena almost every day or evening to help shape things up and to learn the horses. His number two son, Keith, who was a senior in high school then, came out and painted our horse van and stenciled the words, "STAGECOACH 76" on the sides of it. It doesn't sound like much of a job to paint a horse van until you consider the size of it. It's 40 feet long and 13 feet high. It was quite a job.

*CH*APTER THREE
WILL WE EVEN MAKE IT TO ST. JOE TO START THE TRIP ?

About this time, **we were faced with an even bigger problem**. Mr. Frizzell called me from Oklahoma City and said that they couldn't possibly finish the stagecoach in time for us to start the trip. **Like some of our other problems, an answer came up at the same time as the problem.** The fellow who had bought the "Santa Fe" coach wanted to send it back to Frizzell's factory for some repairs, and he wouldn't be in any hurry to get back. When Mr. Frizzell asked him if he would consider renting or lending it to us, he replied that he'd be happy to lend it to us if he could go along with us. Also, if we wanted to use it, we would have to come to Oregon to get it. This was on Monday, eight days before we were due to leave St. Joe on May 25. It was a case of move quick or not at all. Mr. Frizzell's son flew to Oregon, rented a truck and hauled the coach back to Pueblo so we could take it on to St. Joe with us. Things worked out pretty good.

John got in to the arena about 11:30 P.M. Friday night. We had supper, unloaded the stagecoach, and then I tried to get him to sleep at our place, but he said he wanted to go to town so he could turn the rented truck in, then catch a ride to Colorado Springs and get the first plane to Oklahoma City in the morning. It was late when I got to bed, and I was almost asleep when the stillness was shattered by the ringing of the phone. It was John. He said he couldn't find a room, and if the offer of the bed was still good, he'd be right back out. I told him it would be ready by the time he got back out there. Needless to say, it sure didn't take very long after we'd all hit the sack to spend the rest of the night. Right there I think another example was set for much of our trip as it was some time before I got another good night's sleep.

We never were able to find a sponsor for our trip. We applied to the Colorado Bicentennial Commission and were turned down. The only reason we ever heard was because we didn't have any of our own money invested in the project! Of course we had raised the horses and broke them ourselves so they didn't cost us anything.

Has anyone bought horse feed lately? I already had the big diesel truck and trailer to move our equipment in so likewise that didn't cost extra. The stagecoach only cost us $28,000.00 but we were going to buy it whether or not the Commission helped us and even if we weren't able to make the trip; so I guess it didn't count either!

Of course their refusal wasn't new, as we **had had to apply three times to them just to be recognized as an official heritage project.** The first time, they suggested we acquaint ourselves with the problems of handling horses on cross country trips and they advised we join the Wagon Train. *(Bicentennial Wagon Train heading east.)*

The second time, they just said **we did not "fulfill the criteria for a heritage project".** The third time, we received a begrudging recognition, but only after we got some people to apply a little pressure. Our local county group did their best to help us. They went in hock several thousand dollars to have **300 silver and 300 bronze medallions made for us to take along on the stagecoach in the strong box**. If we had been able to sell them we could have realized about $1,000.00 profit for our share. We only sold a few all summer, **but they did lend a very western atmosphere to the trip.**

> **It was really a western stagecoach scene to drive up in front of a local bank in the evening, and hand down the strongbox containing close to $10,000.00 worth of silver in it to be locked up in the bank overnight. Then in the morning, we'd drive the coach and horses back to the bank to pick up the strongbox before heading out on our day's run.**

> One of the most comical things that happened to us all summer took place due to the strongbox being deposited in a bank for the night.

The evening I drove the stagecoach into Hiawatha, Kansas, it was raining lightly and somehow, somebody got their wires crossed. I didn't know which bank we were scheduled to leave the strongbox in. We planned to spend the night camped at the auction yard on the west side of town. We were clear out there before our police escort got it straightened out over their radios which bank we were supposed to go to. We decided when we got camped that Keith would take the strongbox back to the bank in the police car; then in the morning we could drive the stagecoach back through town to retrieve it. By the time we unhooked and Keith left with the strongbox, it was full dark. Things went OK, and they got it to the bank, and returned
to camp.

We spent the night, and got hooked up in good shape the next morning. Since we had to come right back by the sale yard on our way out of town, we all piled on the stagecoach for the trip to the bank to get the strongbox. Things went just fine until we got downtown and asked Keith which bank he left it in. He looked around. Then he got the funniest look on his face. He couldn't remember which bank he'd gone to. It looked a lot different in daylight than it had in the dark!

We made quite a circle around town hoping to refresh his memory, but he didn't see anything he could recognize. Finally we stopped the coach after I noticed a pickup behind us that had followed us from the sale yard. I asked the driver if he knew all the banks in town. He said he did so I explained our predicament to him and asked if he could haul Keith around to all the banks in hopes he'd recognize one. He really got a kick out of it, and said he'd be glad to help. So that's how we finally found the bank with our strongbox in it. We had several good laughs and ribbed Keith no end over the deal.

{ *The old stagecoaches lost a strongbox every once in awhile. We lost the bank.* }

In 1976 it took a different kind of stagecoach horse than it did a hundred years ago, at least in some respects. Back in the old days, the stagecoach companies tried to keep their horses grain fed for the reason that they could pull a coach hard for a half day or so, and then still outrun and outdistance a band of grass fed Indian ponies time after time.

We only had two hitches and a couple extras, which meant our horses each worked one half of each day. We needed fit horses for our summer's trip, but they also had to be the type that could stand quietly in a crowd or in traffic. They had to be content to drive and handle quietly when hauling the loads of kids around towns. **You need horses with natural gentle dispositions to start with, and then it takes a lot of training and handling to get anywhere near this type of stagecoach horses. I believe our horses were just about as close to this type as any could be**.

> We always drove hard, either in a trot or gallop, most of the time covering 20-24 miles in around three hours.

In the whole summer, nobody got kicked, bitten, or even stepped on by any of the horses, even the crew members. **There were several times when a kid would come up and grab a leg of a horse before one of us could get to him, but the horses paid no mind to it.** One time a little kid wanted on the coach and crawled between the hind legs of a wheel horse and his singletree before he was noticed. The closest crew member reached over, put a hand on the rump of the horse, picked up the kid, and set him up on the coach. The horse was Bandito, and he just stood there watching all the time.

One day this summer, coming out of Green River, Wyoming, I drove my hitch 33 ½ miles in about 5 hours driving time. The horses trotted up the last hill for a mile or more without any urging from me. The following day in Lyman, Wyoming all the kids in that corner of the state came down to the rodeo grounds and got a free ride on the coach, pulled by that same hitch. One of those loads had so many kids on it that I asked to have them counted when we got back to the rodeo grounds. **We made a record that day**, for ourselves, and I think probably for all time.

There were 54 kids in and on the stagecoach.

Big John Frizzell delivered the Santa Fe coach to us in Pueblo West on Friday night, May 21. We were scheduled to start the trip out of St. Joe Missouri on May 25. It's about 650 miles from Pueblo to St, Joe. I figured if we left Pueblo West Sunday afternoon around 4 or 5, that we should make it into Troy, Kansas, 12 miles from St. Joe, by no later than Monday evening. That would give us a night's rest, and time to get unloaded and squared away; so we could be into the Pony Express Stables by around 10:30 A.M. on the 25th without any problem. **To mention that things don't always go the way they're planned would be the understatement of this trip.**

On Saturday, we found time to hook the horses up to the Santa Fe coach, and to make the proper tongue and harness adjustments that were necessary. I would like to have been able to have worked all the horses for several days on this stagecoach before starting the trip, but I guess we were lucky to get what we got. **Saturday we got a jillion things finished we'd been worrying on.** Keith finished painting the horse van. I got the old sign painted out, and he touched up some places where the paint had flaked off, and then got our name across the top of the coach. Marge and Tammie spent the day washing and polishing horses, and packing and moving as we had to have the house emptied as well as getting everything else done. They were also packing the camper which we had just bought the day before, and getting it ready for the trip, as well as trying to finish some sewing on Marge's dresses and on Tammie's clothes for her high school graduation the next day.

Sunday, Jack showed up early with his crew to help load and hook up the camper trailer and stagecoach trailer. It sure looked like we were going to get started out in good time since we were ready to load the horses as soon as we got back from Tammie's graduation on Sunday, about 4:30. **After that we had one setback after another**, and it was 11 P.M. before we left the truck stop out at the edge of town. We made it to Eads, Colorado by about 2. A.M. Everybody was so tired and give out, we decided we'd better stop and camp for the rest of the night. We just left the horses in the truck as we didn't plan on being there long enough to bother about unloading them. We got away from Eads early that morning, but my 20-20 hindsight vision indicates that I might as well have stayed in bed and got a good sleep. **The farther we traveled the more hectic our trip to St. Joe got.**

PIONEER DRESS
Mrs. Margery Wolverton (right) and her daughters Wendy, 9, and Tammy, 18, model pioneer attire they will wear on their stagecoach trip which begins Tuesday from St. Joseph, Mo. to Sacramento, Calif. The dresses, made of fabrics ranging from calico to double knit, were designed by Mrs. Wolverton. The three are members of the Ivan "Red" Wolverton family of Wetmore. —Staff photo by W.H. Hawkins

We were in western Kansas when Jack came in on my C.B. wanting to know where a good cut-rate gas station was as he and Tammie were both getting low on gasoline. I knew of one up ahead where I'd bought diesel a good many times. Gas was five or six cents a gallon cheaper. On three rigs that each hold 30-40 gallons that mounts up. I really didn't need any diesel, but since we all were stopped, I decided to fill up. The station man told me they had just run out of diesel, but there came the supply truck up the road. It only took about 32 gallons to fill up. There must have been moisture in the tank. Before I got very many miles down the road, I started having trouble.

I stopped and changed fuel filters a couple times, and finally limped into Salina where I got a mechanic to work on the truck. He finally got it to running pretty good way late in the night, so we started on, but it wasn't long before I was having trouble again. I didn't know where there was a diesel mechanic for a 100 miles or more; **so I decided to keep going as long as it would keep running.**

I pulled into Troy, Kansas up the hill to the fairgrounds just as the sun was coming up, **Tuesday morning the 25th**. The hill was a real steep one and I'd lost so much power that we had to hook Tammie's pickup on to the front of the truck to make it up the last grade. Joe and Pearl's camper was parked there at the fairgrounds, and it sure was a welcome sight to see.

**DAY ONE
MAY 25th**

CHAPTER FOUR
THE START! MISSOURI AND KANSAS

Day One
May 25th

This is the day we've waited for!

By the time I got the truck parked, there were some of the town officials showing up to help us get prepared for the day's events. I had phoned Mr. Richmond in St. Joe the night before, and informed him of our troubles, but that we would still make it into St, Joe in time to hook up and pull out on schedule. The Bicentennial chairman at Troy pitched in and really helped us out. He knew a man that had a large truck that would be glad to haul our horses into the Pony Express Stables. He also knew of a good diesel mechanic we could get to work on the truck and have it ready that day so we wouldn't be held up any on account of it. Jack's wife, Geneva, had breakfast ready for us by the time we got our horses unloaded, fed, and watered. The horses looked pretty good for having been on the truck for 40 hours, but they sure were glad to get out of the truck and be able to lay down and roll. We could unload or load all twenty of the horses out through the side door of our horse van without a loading dock, but the truck we got to haul us on into **St. Joe** was a bob tail and had to have a dock.

Charlie showed up in Troy that morning with his horse trailer and two horses so we had quite a caravan moving into the Stables. Jack was pulling the stagecoach on a trailer behind his motorhome, and both Tammie's and Joe's pickups were rigged with flashing lights for use as pilot vehicles. There was a large crowd at the lot waiting for us.

We had a lot of help unloading the coach and rigging the tongue and doubletrees, unloading the horses, sorting the harness and collars out and getting everything in its right place. It was a wonder we got it all hooked up proper since Tammie and I were the only ones that knew what went where. I was busy trying to sort out harness and point out which horse it went on.

Leaving St. Joe Missouri

MARGE'S JOURNAL:

5/25 ST. JOE to TROY KS.

Hitched up at Pony Express Stables.

I know what Red and I felt that morning must have been the same feelings shared by our ancestors 100 years ago.

A thrill of anticipation, a wonder of the unknown that lay ahead of us, a strong faith in God, and a determination to see it through,
come what may."

The TV and newspaper people were trying to get an interview. I had to tell them I sure appreciated their interest, and I'd be glad to cooperate if they could just follow me around and get what they wanted while I was trying to get the outfit rigged up.

Somehow we finally got hooked up to my satisfaction. I was on the "box" with the lines in my hands. Jack was ready, riding "shotgun" beside me. Marge and Wendy were in the coach. Joe, Charlie, Keith, and Tammie were ready with their saddle horses. The boys, Kip, Eddie, and Dickie, were on top, **so we were ready to start** -- to drive up in front of the Pony Express Stables to pick up part of our passengers. **We had a good start even though the tension and pressure were great.** That bunch of horses always has liked to perk up and strut a little when there was a crowd around. **Even though they had had a long hard truck ride, they seemed to realize this morning was something special. As soon as I called out to my leaders, "Romeo! Rebel!", all six head were right up against the bits.**

"That was one of the rare days I rode inside the coach. I still remember it. What a thrill"

We had sort of a bad place to start out from. We were in a narrow vacant lot, heading west, and we needed to be on the street parallel to where we hooked up but headed in the opposite direction. We had to make a U turn through the alley into the street. The street was pretty narrow there, and since there was a big parking lot across the street, I decided to pull into it and then make the swing to the east. When I first looked across the street, I laid out a trail around some busses that had a gentle curve and a good open way back to the street. My outriders ducked down a narrow lane between parked cars that didn't look good at all to me. The stagecoach horses were a little nervous, and felt they wanted to follow the saddle horses, but I was able to hold them to my chosen route until I got the outriders back in front of me where I wanted them. We then proceeded on up to the Stable without any trouble.

We had deposited our strongbox at the Park Bank, which was right on up the street in the next block. Jack did a good job of jumping down and going after the box. **He hoisted it right up on the front of the coach in true stagecoach fashion;** and we were on our way again to the **Patee House Museum,** where we picked up the rest of our passengers, **with a fitting ceremony for starting a 2000 mile stagecoach trip to the west.**

The horses seemed to be getting more nervous with all the excitement. The best medicine I know for that is to let them trot right out for a few miles, but that's difficult when you're in town and being escorted by the police. They seem to know better than I do what speed we should travel. They kept trying to hold us back to slow us down as we approached the **Missouri River Bridge**. The St. Joe police were quite worried about us crossing it. They had asked me several times if I had any misgivings or doubts about the crossing. They didn't seem to trust my judgment when I kept telling them we wouldn't have any trouble. I had mentioned that we would appreciate it if they would escort us across so the motorists wouldn't try to pass while crossing. I finally figured out they

planned to hold up all traffic on both ends of the bridge until we got clear out of the way. Later I learned why they were so concerned.

It seems a year or so ago some people with horses and wagons were crossing the bridge when their horses got spooked and whirled and ran through or over the railing. One person was killed and another seriously injured.

Our horses were doing real good until our escort stopped suddenly right in front of us just as we were coming up the on ramp to the bridge. I almost wasn't able to get them stopped. The police were waiting for one last truck to get off the bridge before letting us on. I hollered at them and said, "Come on, let's go. We're OK."

I had Romeo and Rebel out there in the lead, and I had practiced quite a bit with them crossing bridges. Every chance I got for the last couple years, I had held Rebel, the off leader, as close to the bridge railing as possible. He seemed to enjoy looking over the edge. He'd arch his neck, turn it out to the right slightly, cock both ears forward, and act like he really got a thrill out of being where he could look down on things. This day crossing the Missouri River, he stepped right out with all of his usual signs of interest.

The bridge was built, I suppose, so large boats could pass under it, for it was sure steep on both ends and high in the middle. **It was something to see! That big muddy river, rolling and whirling under us.** When we started down the west side, I discovered the brakes on the coach weren't holding the rear wheels as good as they should be.

The only way I could see to make them work better was to press harder on the brake lever. I was already pushing with all my weight. The only way I could push harder was to run a seat belt type strap across my lap from the side railings. We had an extra large strap handy, and I had both hands full. I asked Jack to fasten the strap in place for me. After he got it fixed, I was finally able to get enough leverage on the foot lever to hold the coach back enough to keep it from running up on the horses. **Nobody but Jack and I knew we had any trouble holding back, coming off the west side. It was a real thrill to drive the stagecoach over that bridge.**

Bert, the reporter from the Kansas City Star, rode on the front seat up on top of the coach, right behind me, where he carried on an interview all the way to Wathena, Kansas. I didn't have time to stop and visit before we left so I had told him to come along. That way he'd not only get the interview but would also get a real bird's eye view.

From the Pony Express Stables we drove to the Patee House. This building was built in the 1800's. We picked up dignitaries who presented us with a bronze Pony Express Rider and a key to the city. From there we stopped at a bank where we picked up our strongbox full of $7000 worth of silver and bronze medallions.

We headed for the old bridge across the Missouri. This bridge would be one of the biggest danger spots on our whole trail. The leaders pointed their ears and stepped right out as if they'd been over it a hundred times before. Red guided them skillfully alongside the iron railing and I could see out the window as Rebel arched his neck and looked down.

Not a misstep was made and we picked up speed as we started down the other side. As we cleared the bridge, we saluted our police escort and started west across Kansas.

A good many similar interviews were carried on throughout the summer that way.

The town of **Wathena** was expecting us, and had invited us to have lunch in their good restaurant as their guests. We stopped in the park and tied our horses up. Part of our group had already gone in to eat. The rest of us were getting ready to go when Joe decided Tammie's horse, Max, wasn't tied up properly so he thought he'd move him and hobble him. That should have worked out OK, but it didn't. Max has his own ideas about how he should be tied, and as to hobbles? Unh-unh! As soon as Joe got him hobbled, he whirled and ran, heading right for the stagecoach horses.

Jack happened to be close enough to run out in front of him. He got Max stopped, but in the process he got knocked down and rebroke a finger which he had broken before we left. Without any further trouble, we went in and had a good meal; then headed on west to Troy.

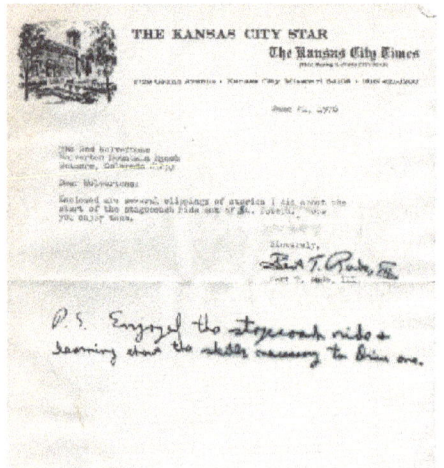

The country gets right hilly as soon as you leave Wathena. It was on one of those hills that we had **the only real difficulty of the whole trip with passing motorists.** We had started up a long hill and were running pretty much on the highway shoulder so the traffic could go by us. We were doing real good until we came to a strip about 150 yards where we had to stay on the pavement. The hill was steep enough that it was about all six horses could do to pull it in a walk so I was content to do it that way.

About two-thirds of the way through the strip, the traffic had piled up behind us pretty far. About three or four vehicles back, a fellow in a truck stuck his head out and yelled in a very foul manner to get off the road and out of his way. **His talk was loud and foul enough that our male crew members immediately thought they should go back to his truck and shut him up.** I had an awful hard time persuading them to pretend they didn't hear anything. His next outburst was pointed right at Tammie who was leading our outfit. Tammie galloped her horse up ahead to our sheriff's escort, and what she said I don't know.

About that time, I was able to get out of the highway so the traffic could pass. When "loud-mouth" got to the sheriff's car, he was stopped and told by the officer to cool off. When he got on his way again, he called one of his buddies on his CB and asked him to bring his big truck out, and the two of them would wipe us clear off the road.

The Kansas State Patrol had answered my letter telling them about our proposed trip. They wished us well, but they couldn't give us an escort across the state; however if we had any trouble to give them a shout on the CB as we had one in both the truck and our pilot car pickup. We didn't call them that day. We didn't have to.

They must have been listening to what was going on for it wasn't but a short while until there was a State Patrol car working in our vicinity as we traveled on. That night, the kids heard from a deputy that the police had been watching "loud-mouth" for quite a while, and they picked him up shortly after. We didn't want to cause any trouble or get in a fight of any kind, but sometimes it is real difficult to turn the other cheek.

Troy is a nice little town, and it sure has a whale of a Lions Club. They put on a community pot luck meal for us that night that we still remember. When we walked in that building we saw the most tremendous amount of food we've ever seen in one place at one time. There were three long wide tables that ran the entire length of the building, and all covered with the prize recipes of the community. It was topped with a stagecoach centerpiece with vases of the biggest and most beautiful assortment of peonies imaginable. After the dinner that followed, Marge was delighted when the ladies presented her the peonies to take along on the trip.

When we came into Troy that afternoon, the city police escorted us through town before heading to the fairgrounds. The downtown area is sort of on the top of one hill, and the fair grounds are on the next one to the west. The valley between them isn't big, but the road goes straight down one side and right straight up the other. It was steep enough going down that I didn't try to hold the coach back. Instead I kicked the horses out and tried to talk them into outrunning the coach to the bottom. We made it in good shape, but I could see if we made it all the way up the other side, we'd be lucky. The street here was blacktop of the sticky tar type, and it sure looked steep. I kept the horses running as far as I could. We broke over the steepest part just as we pulled down to a walk. They were starting to slip a little, but I had noticed that the left hand side of the road was of a rougher surface. I pulled them over to that side, just barely in time, so they could get enough footing to make it on over the top of the hill.

The Way-More Feed Company had furnished us with several sacks of feed, and said they would like to get some pictures. They had a large sign in the back of their pickup which they parked by the stagecoach for a back drop. We got Kip and Wendy by a sack

---

Sidebar:

Charlie Johnson almost got bucked off his horse. Joe rode Buddy and he was prancing.

Had a welcome committee at Wathena. They took us to a café where we had a smorgasbord lunch. Mayor's daughter sat opposite us. It was delicious. City paid for it.

Left my purple bonnet at café, and one of the ladies went back for it.

No problems on way to Troy. Mayor and others rode into town with us. They had a big potluck at 4 H Grounds. Three long tables of food. What a meal! Sat and visited with people afterwards.

of feed feeding Muskrat and Bandito in the foreground. One of the horses had a nose bag on, and the other one was eating out of the pan.

Everybody was excited over our trip. We had lots of company that night. The folks from Highland (our next day's stop) were there, and they were planning quite a program, and were up checking to see what time we'd be there. Finally after 11 o'clock, all I could say was, "You guys will have to excuse me. I just can't stay awake anymore." This was Tuesday night. **I hadn't had over three hours sleep since getting out of bed Sunday morning.**

DAY TWO
MAY 26th

It was Joe's turn to drive this morning. The horses were showing signs of the hard trip on the truck; so I decided to just use four head on the coach that morning. Joe hadn't driven for over a month so I took his hitch around the infield for a couple turns before I gave them to him. He got started out OK until he stopped, coming up a steep grade right at the edge of the road. When he went to start again, the horses wouldn't pull for him. We finally had to get Charlie on Mojo to hook onto the end of the tongue with his lass rope to get started again. I guess they had to hook Mojo to the tongue a couple times more when they tried to start up after stopping for a rest.

I loaded the extra horses in the truck and drove to **Highland** where I met the town officials. We went over the last minute details of our first parade of the trip. I'm not trying to turn state's evidence, but **I also helped to plan the stagecoach robbery; the first of many to follow as the trip progressed.** Due to that wonderful invention called the CB, the whole town was ready and waiting when Joe came trotting into town. Jack and I swung up on the coach, and the rest of the parade units that were waiting fell into line.

Our parade proceeded right on up the thoroughfare. *We just barely got through the center of town, when a whole group of masked desperados swarmed down on us and demanded our strongbox.* Outnumbered the way we were, we handed it over without a struggle.

5/26 – TROY to HIGHLAND

Hauled Mayor Gilmore into Highland at head of parade with Saddle clubs.

Got "held up" in the center of town, gave them Fritz's strongbox full of paint. Wished I'd taken a picture of bandits coming at us.

Drove to ballpark and unhitched. Had potluck the ladies fixed. Another wonderful meal. Flag dedication ceremony and Red gave a speech. It was better than the Representative's.

Headed for Hiawatha. Stopped at auction yard for night. Supper in camper.

We had a lot of fun and didn't come out total losers either. While the scoundrels were holding us up, Charlie slipped up behind one of them and slipped a rifle out of one outlaw's saddle scabbard and made off with it. **Later on at the ball park, we were able to use it as trading material to get our strongbox back.**

The town had planned their bicentennial celebration to take place on the day of our arrival. They had a real good program with several state legislators and Bicentennial officials as speakers. The town was presented with their Bicentennial flag; then I was asked to make a little speech and introduce the crew. They topped off the ceremony with one heck of a good community potluck meal. I ate a whole plateful of just desserts afterwards.

I had been so busy for the last couple weeks in Colorado that I had only been driving the hitch that I planned to use coming out of St. Joe. Two of the horses that I hadn't been driving were pretty bronky to start with when they were driven regularly. Out on the ranch, I usually work the spooky horses in fours before hooking them up in sixes. That sure seemed like the smart thing to do there in Highland that afternoon. Especially since they were still a little stiffened up from that long truck ride. We had plenty of help and were careful; so after a small fit of rearing and bucking, I got them lined out pretty good. The weather turned cool and cloudy so I let those old ponies step right out. We'd trot on the level, slow to a walk on the steep part of the hills, then gallop down the next one. We made it to **Hiawatha** in about three hours. We were a little disappointed that the town didn't have any celebration planned, but it sure felt good to get to bed early that night. **Hiawatha was where we lost the bank with our strongbox in it.**

DAY THREE – MAY 27th

DAY THREE MAY 27th

As Joe was driving this morning, when we came to the sale yard, I dropped off the stage, loaded up the relay horses and moved on up to **Fairview**, where we met some very wonderful people. Mayor Dierking acting as our official host, met the stage at the edge of town, and rode into the city park where we had our noon stop. He escorted us to the local restaurant for lunch, where they sure lived up to their reputation for good food, especially the pie. There were probably a couple hundred people that came by that afternoon to look the coach and horses over. We felt highly honored when the mayor brought **Mrs. Rogers, the mother of General Rogers, Chief of Staff of the United States Army,** down to visit the coach. Due to the generosity of the mayor, we now have a very good picture of Mrs. Roger, the mayor, Margie, Max, and myself standing in front of the coach, with Wendy perched on top.

5/27 FAIRVIEW to SENECA
Fairview, Kansas. Mayor Dierking and his party rode in with us. Unhitched at a lovely green park.

Went to Cozy Café for dinner. Had hot beef sandwiches and delicious pie. The mayor picked up the tab for us.

Had our pictures taken with General Roger's Mother. She's over 80 and looks about 60. Reminded me of Aunt Vera.

Seneca, Kansas. Stopped at 4H Building. Lots of people came out to see us.

Dr. Berchley came over and decided to send some horses with us.

That afternoon I drove the six head on to **Seneca**. **It was a good afternoon to be alive out in Kansas.** The country was beautiful; Kansas in late spring is a land of green fields, with grass and wheat belly high to a horse. Big square farmhouses sit contentedly among huge old trees, flowers are blooming everywhere, and creeks and rivers criss-cross the land. Farmers at work in the fields waved to us or came over to chat if we stopped. Birds sang from the trees and fenceposts, and the days were sunny and warm. I can still hear the June bugs singing in the low places as we clipclopped along.

We had been informed that Seneca would probably be a high spot in our journey across Kansas. We had invited the governor to ride with us. His answer was that he couldn't make it, but that a personal aide from his office would meet us in Seneca to present us with some official documents recognizing us as an official Kansas Bicentennial project, and then take a ride with us.

We had made written arrangements to stay overnight at the fairgrounds; so when no town officials met us, we drove on to the fairgrounds and set up camp. I was in the back end of the horse van, when a fellow drove up, got out of his car, and came over. Asking if I was Red, he introduced himself as one of the town officials. He said he had heard from the Governor's office. **Seems they had decided we weren't a non-profit organization.**

They couldn't recognize us as a Bicentennial project and didn't care to participate in our activities. My first reaction was to ask the man on what they had based their decision. His answer was that since we were hauling mail and passengers, and had brought bronze and silver medallions for sale that that put us out of the non-profit category. **I think that was one of the few times on the entire trip that I lost my temper.** I blew off and exercised a whole string of cuss words, of which I have quite a vocabulary. Afterwards I felt sorry for the fellow who brought me the message, especially after I learned he was quite religious.

It was rather infuriating though. **We had been able to get no financial help from anybody or any place.**

Here we were, trying to do something as individuals to celebrate our country's birth that we could share with thousands of people.

Something that had played as great a part in our country's history as anything I could think of, and something that you might say really started in and originated out of Kansas for a good many years.

Since I was born in the state of Kansas, I really felt let down.

** It is true, our stagecoach trip started in Missouri, like the first daily overland mail stage, but a few months later in 1858, the starting point was moved to Atchison, Kansas. There were all the other lines, too, that ran west or southwest out of **Atchison or Leavenworth.**

We really felt that Kansas should be proud of its stagecoaching history, and that they should be pleased when they heard we were trying to reenact that period of time

Red Wolverton's "Stagecoach 76" stopped in downtown Seneca Friday morning before leaving for Baileyville. The crew spent the night in Seneca and planned to have lunch at Baileyville. A stop at Marysville was planned for Friday night.

I must have convinced the town official that we were sincere. He said he guessed it was too late to do much that evening, but if we would care to take the stagecoach back up town the next morning, he would get a group of the town officials to ride with us, and get some newspaper shots in town. Everybody seemed to enjoy the tour the next morning down through town. Later in the summer, we received a copy of the local paper with our story in it.

DAY FOUR
MAY 28th

Baileyville wasn't very far up the highway. It was an old town, proud of the fact it was close to the Overland Trail. The local people had a community noon meal planned in the basement of the Catholic Church, in honor of our passing through.

One of the good people we met there, Mr. Feldkamp, was so interested in our journey that he called his daughter in Sacramento to tell her of our trip and to keep a look out for us. Later she saw us on TV coming into Reno, Nevada, and again when we rolled into Sacramento. She tried to find us at the California State Fair Grounds, but was unable to; *but I'll tell you all about that later on.* While in Baileyville, Marge visited with some of the descendants of early day pioneers, who gave her pictures and clippings about their ancestors and the history of the area.

> One of the interesting stories was about the old stage station of Ash Point. It was established by "Uncle John" O'Loughlin, as he became known from St. Joe to the Pacific Coast. **

5/28 SENECA to BAILEYVILLE

Held a dinner for us in the Catholic Church, and a variety of religions all mixed happily in the American tradition, as all the questions centered on the item of interest – our stagecoach and six-horse hitch.

Many questions were the same in every state. Who were we? How did we get the idea for the stage-coach trip?

Doc rode with us part way. Mayor Feldkamp rode into Baileyville with us. Ladies of Sacred Heart Church provided dinner for us. Ham and roast beef, corn, mashed potatoes, gravy, kole slaw, rolls, ice cream and cake. Good.

Took a whole load of kids down the street.

** He built a hotel, general store, and post office, as well as a large barn to house the horses and mules for the Overland Trail traffic. He was highly respected, not only by the white people, but by the Indian tribes of the area also, who called him "White Brother." In August of 1874, Ash Point received news of an impending plague of grasshoppers. The community hurried to harvest all the crops they could. By mid-afternoon the sun was blotted out by the clouds of grasshoppers which devoured every growing thing. Next morning there were even holes in the ground where the bugs had dug out and eaten the onions. With the loss of so much of their food supply, the people had a very hard winter that year.

Ash Point had the only well on the trail after leaving Seneca, and was ideally situated to be the noon stop for travelers. It was never bothered by the numerous Indians around. Travelers continued to use the old trail, and stop there, long after the railroad was built. The town of Baileyville started out known as "Haytown" for the enormous quantities of prairie hay that were shipped out. **Some of the early settlers were Bert Rice, the Rasps, and, of course, the Baileys, one of whom later became the governor of Kansas.**

According to the stories, one of his campaign promises was to get married if he was elected. After winning, he received many offers, but he had already made his choice, and was quietly married the day before moving into the governor's mansion. Another interesting story concerned the early religious meetings. All faiths met in the schoolhouse. At one such meeting, the pastor was unable to be there, and there was no Bible among the gathering; so they quoted Scripture from memory. Following that, they raised a collection, each member donating 25 or 50 cents, for a total of $8.00, with which they purchased a Bible that was to be left at the school and used by all denominations. It later became the property of the Baptist Church, which apparently still has charge of it.

These historical articles were given to us through the courtesy of Mr. Hay and Mr. Feldkamp.

We hope we have done them justice as we certainly appreciated receiving the material.

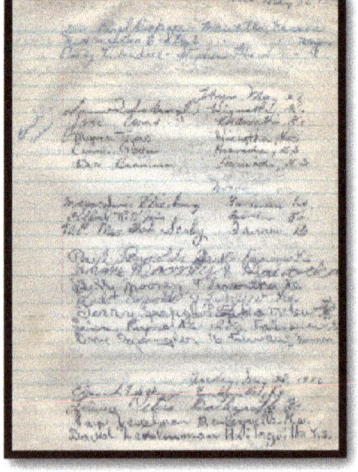

Meanwhile, back at Baileyville, things were happening. Several of our horses had picked up a cough and a slight runny nose. I was sure they just had a cold, but when out in public, sometimes it is necessary to do things different than you do at home on the ranch.

I called the vet that morning early at Seneca, but he didn't catch up with us until at Baileyville. After checking all the horses, his diagnosis was a straight case of shipping fever, which just amounted to a common cold. He advised me not to use a couple of the worse ones for a few days. I told him they didn't look near as sick to me as what I had been a good many times, without missing a lick of work. I proposed using those horses right in their turns because I felt they were just as tough as I was. He looked at me and grinned. "You're probably right. I doubt if it'll hurt them." We kept them on combiotic for a few days, and never had any more trouble for the rest of the trip.

Baileyville wasn't near half way to **Marysville** from Seneca, but there was a highway rest area on up the road just shy of half way between the two towns. I had decided earlier that Joe could leave his hitch harnessed up at Baileyville during noon, and then drive them on up to the rest area, where I'd take over and drive my hitch on into Marysville. I didn't realize I had stopped the truck on a slight uphill grade in front of the school. The way I was parked it was real easy to stop the stagecoach heading the same way. After we'd eaten, and were ready to move on, we talked all the town kids into getting on the coach for a ride out of town. It made a pretty good load. The ground was pretty soft, and the horses hadn't really got used to Joe yet, and weren't starting out very good for him yet. **When he called to them to "get up", part of them did and part of them didn't. Then the ones that didn't, did, and the ones that did, didn't.** Then none of them did, and wouldn't. **There Joe was, with a loaded coach, and six head of horses that wouldn't lay into the collar.** Tammie was there on Max; so I told Joe to hold it a minute.

I got my long nylon lass rope out of the truck, hooked it to the end of the swing pole, and run it up between the leaders, borrowed Max from Tammie, cinched the saddle down tight, then stepped on him. I took my turns on the horn and started out. My rope is about 60 feet long so I had several coils in my hand. Max laid into the pull good, but I still let the rope slip, took another turn as he was stretching out and getting lower to the ground; and when I felt he was really laid in with all his might against the pull, I took another turn and held it tight. We just kept right on moving, and Max started that whole loaded coach out all by himself from the saddle horn. After it started to move, Joe's horses came with it several steps before they laid into the collars and took over the pulling. **We were all mighty proud of Max that day.**

Somewhere along the line, a fellow that was running as an incumbent in the election to state legislature, heard about the governor snubbing us. He met Marge and told her he'd give us a $100.00 bill if we'd let him put his sign on the back of the stagecoach and ride into Marysville with us. That sounded OK to me, so that afternoon

Larry Rogers, running for state senator, caught us at the rest stop and rode with us to Marysville.

Put his sign on back of coach. Was quite upset at the rebuff, the governor's representative had given us.

Rode into Marysville and parked at the Armory for the weekend.

Had steak and shrimp at a good restaurant.

we met him at a stop a few miles out of Marysville and hauled him into town. We all had a good time, and he got several rolls of pictures to use in his campaign. **I haven't heard if he got elected or not, but I wished him luck.**

We got into Marysville Friday afternoon of Memorial Day Weekend. We didn't want to do any stagecoaching on the highway over the holiday so were glad to hole up for awhile. I treated the crew to a restaurant meal that evening, to the tune of about $ 60.00, and figured we'd put the political money to good use.

DAY FIVE
MAY 29TH

DAY FIVE
MAY 29th

We had plans for downtown Marysville at the Pony Express Stable the next day so we checked its location out on the way back to camp. The plan was to haul the officials from the Stable to the County Courthouse for a Bicentennial ceremony and flag presentation. We spent Saturday morning polishing up the horses and harness. We were downtown by noon, a little early, but we wanted time to look around and take a few pictures of our own. We finally got our passengers loaded, with the **Attorney-General of the State of Kansas, on the seat on the top front end of the coach,** right behind me.

It was about a mile up to the Courthouse, and we were trotting right out, with several outriders and a police escort ahead of us. **The Attorney-General kept wanting to know if that was as fast as I could go.** He was really getting a bang out of it. "Would you like to go in a gallop?" I asked, "You bet I would," he grinned. "OK, hang on," and I speeded up, crowding in between the outriders and right up against the back of the police car, but I couldn't get around him or get him to speed up much. We were all yelling at him to speed up, but he just wouldn't pay any attention to us.

5/29 MARYSVILLE
layover
Went to hitch up.
Fritz had been busy.
He greased the singletrees, doubletrees hardware, neck chains, everything metal.
Red was MAD.
It was a real mess.

Finally got started. Joe was driving the coach, Tammie was outriding. She dropped off into the "bar pit", and the mares followed her down the ditch. Joe almost lost them, but Tammie turned around quick and helped straighten them out.

Drove to Pony Express barn and took pictures. Mayor and State Attorney General and legislators rode on top of stage to the Courthouse. Ceremony presenting ARBA flag. Then we drove back to Armory. Cooked meat. Went to Seneca to see Doc's horses. He decided to let us take two.

**Mr. Billingsley had been a stagecoach driver on the Overland Trail. He had first driven on the Butterfield Route between Ft. Smith, Arkansas and Sherman, Texas. Later he drove for Ben Holliday on the Central Overland between Atchison, Kansas and Point of Rocks, Wyoming. His wife, Sarah, kept the stage station and fed the passengers when the stage stopped to change horses. A hostler was kept to care for the horses, as Mr. Billingsley, like all the drivers, would be at one end of the division one night, and home the next night. According to most accounts, the drivers usually drove three hitches or changes, averaging about 15 miles each, for a total day's drive of about 45 miles.

Before you know it, even at a trot, a mile slips right by; so we were at the Courthouse. We stayed for the ceremony; then galloped on back to camp to get rested up for our first day of rest, Sunday, which was coming up fast.

After the Marysville parade, Marge had a chance to tell me about one of the passengers inside the coach. **She was Mrs. Minnie Smith, granddaughter of James Billingsley, of Axtell, Kansas,** which is a short distance from Seneca and Marysville.**

Mrs. Smith related stories of her grandparents telling about life in those times. *Stage stations were often alerted by soldiers from Ft. Leavenworth or Ft. Kearney when the Indians were on the war path. "I kept a black dress in my trunk to wear, and we would seek safety in deep ravines for the night",* **Grandmother recalled.** *"Sometimes when they returned, they found the furnishings from the station had been confiscated."*

"Life was never dull or lonesome, but always interesting", Grandmother said. Caravans of wagon trains were often in sight and would camp near the stage stations at night. All would gather around the campfire to exchange the news. Grandfather was a great lover of horses. Even after retirement, he always kept a team. With "Deck and Moll" hitched to the spring wagon, he made weekly trips to Axtell, taking farm produce in and buying supplies. A single driving horse and buggy were kept for Grandmother and her daughter to use to visit neighbors and friends. Company from the East was welcomed to the "Wild West" by a cyclone, one time, which moved Grandfather's house off the foundation. By lantern light, the family made their way to the barn where they spent the rest of the night. My grandparents had a cave almost equal to a refrigerator. It was stocked with bins of garden produce and shelves of home canned jars of fruits and vegetables. There was

The distance varied according to the country; some of the stations out in Wyoming, Utah, and Nevada were 35 miles apart. As the railroad moved west, Mr. Billingsley moved west with the stage line, between various points in Nebraska and Wyoming. "At one time," Grandfather Billingsley said, "I knew every white man between Atchison, Kansas and Denver, Colorado." "I remember, as the railroad moved west, the telegraph wires would sing in the wind, and the Indians (would) stop and look at the wires, afraid to go under them. "

always a huge round cheese, and cured hams, shoulders, and pork bacon in the smoke house. Grand mother set out wonderful meals, and we spent many happy times there. We often stayed there overnight when the weather was bad.

In the 1950's, Mrs. Smith vacationed with relatives, going through Point of Rocks, Wyoming. They were shown where the original stage station was that had been the end of Grandfather Billingsley's division. **This is the station we drove to on Wednesday, July 8th, on our trip.**

We wish to thank Mrs. Smith for her interest in us, and her generosity in giving us this material which had been published in The Advocate and Weekly News of Marysville, Kansas in 1974.

At the time she rode with us in the Marysville parade, Minnie Smith was 80 years "young".

While we were in Seneca, we had visited with the "Doc" and admired his carriages. He wanted to show us his Morgan horses; so I agreed if we got through early enough Saturday, Marge and I would drive back to Seneca so he could take us out to his ranch to see his horses. We liked their looks.

Before the evening was over, we had agreed to take two of his horses along with us to use in the hitch, to try to work them up to lead horses. Doc said he would pick them up in Fort Morgan, Colorado, when we got there.

DAY SIX
MAY 30th

Doc hauled them up to Marysville for us Sunday morning. **Ah Sunday!**
Our first day of rest. I shod six head of horses. Harnessed up Robby, one of the new horses, teamed him up with Roulette, and drove them in a circle from on the ground, for about an hour. Both of the new horses needed shoeing. Robby wasn't much trouble, but when I started in on "Red", he politely told me, "I'm just too nervous to stand for any foolishness like that."

Tammie is on Red

5/30 MARYSVILLE layover day two

Doc brought out the horses. Bought Robby and Red Horse. Robby – registered Morgan; Red horse supposed to be part Morgan. Both had been started by the Amish, but they couldn't handle them.

Red and Joe shod them, Romal, Juliet, and Pete. Muskrat's the only barefoot one left.

Fixed sweet rolls for breakfast, and stew for dinner. Geneva and kids stamped all the mail. Thompsons pulled out. Everyone hated to see them go. We sure enjoyed them. Charlie left too. We're really going to miss our good crew.

"Red Horse", I says, "What you need is a tranquilizer." So I slaps my saddle on him and calls for Tammie to come saddle a good tough horse and come for a ride with me. We were gone for one hour. According to the way the country roads are laid out there on the section lines, we rode ten miles. Anyhow Mr. Red Horse was pretty docile to shoe when we got back; that is, he was docile until he got rested up some about the time I got half way through shoeing him.

At that same time Fritz decided it was time he learned how to shoe a horse. He comes busting up to where I was working, talking and gathering up my shoeing tools as he approached. He spooked old Red and caused him to jerk a foot away from me real hard, almost getting me kicked in the process. I'd been holding my temper in pretty well shoeing Red. He just wasn't the type of horse you fight when you're working on him. When Fritz says it's time he learned how to shoe a horse and he wants to do the work and have me stand there and just tell him exactly what moves to make, it was more than I could stand, "Fritz", I snarls, "I'll tell you what move to make. You just put my tools back down where you found them, turn yourself around, and get the H out of my sight! And we'll both be better off. As Marge put it later, "Shoeing a cranky horse is not conducive to your best frame of mind." I finished the job, but by the time I got to that last foot, the right hind one, I really had to do a hurry up job to keep from getting jerked and kicked to pieces.

Robby is off-swing horse.

DAY SEVEN
MAY 31st

Both Red and Robby were broke to drive. Robby was pretty gentle, but Red saw all kinds of buggers. Every time a big truck went by, he'd about jump out of his tracks. That Sunday, when I rode him, I couldn't get him close to the stagecoach. Most horses are scared of it until they have been around it for a while. I sure like to get them used to it before I hook them up to it. I put Robby right in the hitch Monday morning. Joe was driving, and didn't have a bit of trouble with him in the swing. I rode Red through Marysville and followed the coach out quite a ways before turning around and riding back to the fairgrounds after the truck and horses.

Jack and Charlie and their families, both had to leave us Sunday at Marysville. It was lonesome going on without them. Charlie worked for Farmland Industries out of Kansas City. That's COOP to most people. They handle and mix horse feed as well as a lot of other types of feed. Charlie and Jack had visited several COOP feed stores in the few days they were with us, and had talked them into donating three tons of horse feed to us. When Charlie went back to work, he talked his boss into sending three more ton to us, which Charlie brought to us at Hastings, Nebraska. When we got to Gothenberg, there was another three tons.

Later on in Rawlins, Jack told me that the COOP was furnishing another load of feed, which he'd pick up on his trucks, and drop it off in Rawlins for us. When Charlie met us again when we trucked back to Cheyenne, he said the COOP had another load of feed for us at Ault, Colorado. With what I'd bought before we left, that gave us enough horse

---

5/31 MARYSVILLE to MORROWVILLE

Drove to Washington. Sheriff's posse and saddle club came to meet us. We had four women and three kids from Marysville to Pony Express truck stop. Then at the truck stop, the bank passengers got on. Enjoyed visiting with the ladies.

Don Mosher of the bank is very tall with a bushy brown beard. They took us to Swirly Top Steak House for cafeteria dinner. Had chicken, roast beef, meat pie, delicious gelatin salad, and cherry pie. Picked up more passengers. People of Morrowville got up a quick wienie roast and potluck for us. Pearl made shrimp salad and I fixed jelly sweet rolls. They were quite a hit, and several women asked for the recipe.

grain to run us all the way to California and back to Colorado in the truck. We sure did appreciate it. Those horses did too.

After a week or so on the trail, we got our horses conditioned or worked up to where we were feeding them 17 pounds of grain per horse per day. We also fed them all the hay they wanted. When we left Colorado, we had three tons of grain, two tons of alfalfa pellets, 175 bales of hay, enough harness for 16 horses, our saddles, water trough, portable corral panels enough to make a large horse pen, three dogs, and 15 head of horses, all in that 46' horse van. We also had a 700 gallon water tank up in the top deck which we could fill or use with a garden hose. That water supply sure saved our bacon several times during the summer, from Wyoming on to California.

There is still one of the original Pony Express and stage stations west of Marysville, a few miles north of Highway 36. We had thought about driving up to the station with the stagecoach, but had to change our plans when we picked up the two new horses. There is a truck stop down on 36 called the Pony Express Truck Stop. We had made arrangements for a load of passengers from **Washington, Kansas** to meet us there and ride on into Washington with us. They got quite a kick out of it when we unloaded our colt out of the van, and let him run to his mama for a mid-morning snack, as she was working that morning. I especially enjoyed our noon stop in that town, feeling a very close kinship to the people and country there. My father was born in Washington County, near Barnes, Kansas. That noon while we were there, an elderly couple came up and visited with me for a while, and introduced themselves as Wolvertons. They had lived there all their lives, and were the last of the old tribe still in the area. They were my father's cousins.

We enjoyed a good restaurant meal with officials from the bank and the town along with our passengers. The local Saddle club escorted us out of town. Some of the riders went all the way to **Morrowville,** our last stop in Kansas. A good many times, when different people rode with us, they had trouble with their horses being spooked at the stagecoach. This day, the group was doing pretty good, all except one young man. Every time he'd get up alongside the coach, his horse would really get nervous. We weren't in a real big hurry; so I pulled the horses up enough to let the riders get out ahead of us. Things went along pretty good for quite a while. This one horse had settled down and was traveling along good, until he got to looking back over his shoulder at the coach. Each time he'd look back, he'd slow down a bit, and was working his way from over on the side to right in front of our horses. I'd been keeping a pretty sharp eye on him for quite a while, and was driving with my foot floating on the brake lever. I yelled to the fellow to speed his horse up and get over to the side. I thought he about had his horse back under control. They were about ten feet ahead of us. Then the horse cocked his head around to the side to look back at us again; and he just seemed to freeze.

He sure did stop in a hurry---for a minute, that is. I use a large heavy spreader strap snapped to the inside hames of the lead horses' harness. It's about the right height to catch a horse above his hocks, but low enough down on his butt to pick him up from behind and boost him along. When that horse stopped in front of us, we were much too close to him to swerve to either side. All I had time to do was haul in on the lines, jab the brake lever down as far and hard as I could, and yell, "Whaaoooooo, you sons of guns, Whoooa." I was sure glad we had that heavy spreader strap. A stage coach moving right along is about as hard to stop quickly as a big truck is coming down a steep grade. It'll stop pretty quick but not instantly. We must have boosted that fellow and his horse along for another ten or 15 feet before we got stopped. Even then, he had a hard time getting in motion again, but once he did, he sure kept out from in front of us the rest of the ride.

Morrowville, Kansas was sure a friendly, cordial town, typical of all the Kansas people we met. They provided us with a good small pasture belly deep with lush grass for our horses. They had learned to like their grain, but this was the first real grass they'd had in a long, long time. It had been a cold, late spring in Colorado, and this was the first time we'd had a pasture to run them in at night. The town held a wienie roast and potluck picnic for us for supper. Of all the meals we shared all across the country, no two were alike, and we enjoyed each and every one.

**DAY EIGHT
JUNE 1st**

CHAPTER FIVE

NEBRASKA
DAY EIGHT
JUNE 1ST

6/1
MORROWVILLE
to FAIRBURY NB.

Left Morrowville very late. Had 13 kids and 2 adults ride out of town. Joe drove slow.

Was hot and the kids were complaining. Stopped to rest along the way, and Red came back with orange juice and tuna fish sandwiches and cookies Pearl made.

He drove on into Fairbury and we parked at fairgrounds. Got some groceries. Have air conditioner on. Fixed steaks for supper. Had lots of people come out and look at coach. Lincoln paper had printed it and radio station ran it.

The next morning, with Joe driving, we loaded up the coach with kids, and we all rode out of town, heading for **Fairbury, Nebraska**. I came back to town with one of the carloads of kids to get the horse van.

> We had one built in problem that we started from Colorado with.

That was our Morgan stallion Jackson (his registered name), which we have always called "Fortune".

Fortune on coach - near wheel.

He was such a good faithful, hard-working horse that he was sure worth the extra trouble it took to have a stud along on the trip.

Sometimes the only place we had for him at night, was to tie him to the side of the horse van. He's got about the best disposition that any stallion ever had, but he's still a stud that is concerned for his mares. Usually if he was tied or penned where he could see them close by, he didn't make any fuss. Sometimes he'd get restless and paw the ground or kick at the van. That night, he'd been tied too close to the rear end of the trailer.

The first thing I noticed in the morning when I went to check on him and grain the horses was that he'd clipped a plastic wheel grease cap on one of the axles and it was in pieces. The oil had all run out, and you can't run one of those big trailers very far like that. I had a roll of grey duct tape; so I figured I'd stuff a rag in what was left of the grease cap, pour in some 90 weight oil, then tape it up. It might be messy, but I probably would be able to make it to the closest parts house.

When I got back to the truck, one of the local men was waiting for me. He said he'd noticed a busted grease cap on the trailer, and if I'd run it down by his shop, he was sure he could make a grease cap good enough to last us until we got up the road a ways. He used one of his wife's plastic bowls and some special sealer. Then he wound it with heavy tape. I tried several places enroute to get the new cap. I finally located one in Laramie, Wyoming and put it on while we were camped over the 4th of July weekend in Rawlins. That temporary repair job in Morrowville, Kansas lasted a thousand miles more or less.

While we were working on the trailer that morning, a fellow came by that seemed to be quite interested in what we were doing with the stagecoach. We talked about the trip and our plans for quite a while before I found out he was a reporter for the Lincoln Star. He'd made a special trip out to interview us and get some pictures for his paper.

He said he'd like to get one of us crossing the state line into Nebraska, or as close to that area as possible. We agreed to stop the coach when we caught up with it after getting the trailer fixed. The reporter was pretty cagey in getting his information out of me. He talked about different things and approached what he wanted to know from another direction. That didn't bother me at all. We weren't trying to put anything over on anyone. He talked about several other people that had traced the Overland Trail in the past. He said he guessed what with our truck and trailer and stagecoach trailer, that if we got behind schedule, or when we got out where the towns were further apart, we'd probably load the coach and outfit up and haul it ahead to make up time or get back on schedule. I told him, "No, that isn't our intention. We plan to pull the stagecoach with the horses every inch of the way. If we get behind, we'll just have to drive farther and harder, and use our scheduled "rest" days until we catch up. If something unforeseen happens, we will have driven the coach right up to the very spot where we have to give up the trip." He then told me he was sure glad to hear that; glad we were not going to truck it any. Our pulling it with the horses all the way really made it interesting to him.

We did truck the stagecoach some during the summer, but only to participate in parades on the side, never on the planned trip. Each time we hauled it to a parade, we returned to the exact place where we had loaded it up. We then unloaded it, and proceeded forward from that spot with the horses pulling it. He got some good pictures out on the highway when we caught up with the coach.

I took the truck on into Fairbury and set up camp. Then I returned with the pickup which I traded to Joe for the stagecoach, and I drove the rest of the way into town. The officials of Fairbury were planning to come ride into town with us. They were like lots of others we met along the way; they didn't believe we could make it as soon as I told them we would. None of them were ready when we rolled into town.

We had had some bad luck in Fairbury. The next morning when I went to grain the horses, one of them was hurt. It was Holly Ann, a pretty little blaze-faced sorrel filly with a flaxey mane and tail. She had the hide ripped open and hanging down from one front knee. There was a three cornered tear almost as big as the palm of my hand, right above the knee cap. She had cut it on one of the metal posts in that corral. It had just happened; so I thought the veterinary might want to sew it back in place. I guess he didn't appreciate being routed out of bed at 5:30 AM. He said he'd be there about 8:00 AM when he left home to go to his clinic. By the time he got there, the hide had already started to shriveling up. He decided to cut the flapping piece off instead of sewing it back. I suppose that was just as good. We had Holly Ann back in harness before too long.

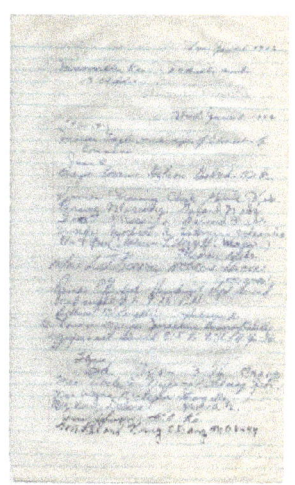

I need to stop here and back up a bit to tell you about Fritz. He was the man who bought the **Santa Fe coach** that I was trying to buy, and we were just slow in coming up with the money. His was the coach we borrowed when ours was not ready to start out on the trip. Marge cooked breakfast for any or all of the crew that wanted to eat, every morning. Fritz came in late, and started giving her a bad time. She finally told him if he had any complaints to come talk to me, she wasn't about to stand and argue with him. He followed me around, still carrying on. I got on to him for coming in late which he'd done several times, and waking up the camp. He insisted he wasn't celebrating, he was just sick. He didn't like to be called down for his actions; so he guessed he'd pull out that morning. **But that isn't all of the story.**

Fritz owned and ran an old West saloon up in Oregon. For a long time he'd been interested in the history of stagecoaching in the West. He'd studied all the owners, drivers, and famous road agents until he felt he was an authority on the subject. Fritz wanted to drive a stagecoach, only he had never even ridden on one, much less learned how to drive one. This didn't bother him though. He figured all he had to do was to get a coach and the rest would come naturally. He was in prime buying condition when the Santa Fe coach was put up for sale. That's how come he beat us to it.

Fritz had big plans. He was going to take the coach to department store lots all over the U.S.A., haul a few passengers, and mainly show people what an authentic coach and six horse hitch looked like. He found a 68 year old man that talked good and had handled horses some, but if he'd ever driven six head on a stagecoach before, he sure must have forgotten a bunch of basic facts. His horses weren't real gentle, docile horses to start with. They hadn't been worked much prior to their initial stagecoach debut.

They hadn't been worked together as a six horse hitch, and most important of all, his driver hadn't been practicing driving six head at home before hooking them up in public. They trucked the stagecoach and horses right up to the busy parking lot of a large city, and proceeded to harness and hook them up. They had an old man holding the lead team. They should have at least tied the lead team up to a truck while they were hooking up to the coach. I guess they must have got the horses all hooked up. When the driver was climbing up to the box, the horses bolted and ran away, running over the old fellow who was holding the leaders. It threw the driver off the front wheel, and the coach ran over him and broke his leg. It must have been a cold November day, as Fritz said they were hooking up the horses when he left to go get some hot coffee. When he returned the spectators were scattered every which way, and the stagecoach and horses were piled into a bunch of parked cars. **Needless to say, that ended Fritz's stagecoaching adventure.**

When Big John delivered the Santa Fe coach to us at Pueblo West, Fritz came along with it. He said he figured if we could use his coach that we could use him also. We sure needed some more help, but mostly we needed the coach. Fritz was OK. He was just a different type of person than what we were. He said he wanted to help, to learn to harness and hitch the horses, and eventually learn to drive, but when we'd come in to a camp at noon or night, he'd stand and gab with anyone that might come around, while the rest of us were doing the work. I didn't mind that so much, as I really didn't expect him to do too much anyhow. What irritated me was that he insisted in telling everyone all about his stagecoaching misfortunes. This was our trip, and I didn't feel it was good publicity for us to have him keep repeating all about his troubles everywhere we went. The first day at St, Joe, he'd embarrassed Marge, who was trying to meet everybody and get things lined up for our departure. While I was busy with the horses, Fritz climbed up on the tongue, and waved his arms, and yelled to the crowd to come over. Marge was talking to three reporters at the same time, when Fritz told everybody he'd tell them all about that coach, and then stood up there giving a speech, while we were trying to hook up. He'd done the same thing several different times. When I politely told him to "Shut up", he got rather irritated, "Well", he said, "Somebody has to talk to the people." I just told him they could enjoy themselves more by looking. The crew got to noticing that every time we'd stop, Fritz would have to make a big play, pretending the coach needed some kind of repairs, and he'd almost always get an audience of some sort. He was always smearing on a dab of grease here or wiping off one he'd put on at the town before. He loved to jack up the coach and take a wheel off, or adjust" the brake.

One morning the week before, we were hooking up the horses. Joe was a little ahead of me, and I sort of noticed he seemed to be watching me out of the corner of his eye, but

I couldn't figure out why. We'd already hooked up the leaders, and had moved back to the swing team. Everything I touched seemed to be greasy. My hands were filthy with grease by the time I got to the tugs of my swing horse. About then, I stopped and looked the outfit over. **There was that old filthy black wagon-axle grease on everything that had a moving part!** The neck chains were greasy. The singletrees were greasy. Where the singletrees hooked to the doubletrees was greasy. The doubletree clevises were greasy. The swing pole ring and hook were greasy. **It was sure one heck of a mess!**

It hadn't dawned on me yet who was responsible for all that grease. **When I let out my breath, a whole chestful of mule skinner's language was expelled at once.** I finished off with, "Who in the Hell put all the damn grease on everything?" There was a loud, "Haw, haw!" from Joe, who was standing right across the doubletrees from me. As I looked up and saw him he was about to split wide open. He was laughing at me and holding his stomach with one hand. When I looked closer, one finger was pointing. I glanced around and followed the line of direction. Sure enough, there stood Fritz, as pleased as a peacock, grinning like the cat that got the canary. He owned right up to it too. He thought he'd really done something good.

"Yeah, well I did it," he says. "What in the world did you do that for?", I quizzed. "John Frizzell told me to be sure and keep everything well greased. Besides, I read in 'Holliday's Handbook for Stagecoach Drivers' that for the comfort and ease to the passengers, to keep all moving parts well greased. I figured if the chains and clevises were greased, there would be less jingling noises to bother everybody." Well, I disagreed with him to the extent that I wouldn't do any more hooking up until Fritz got some rags and wiped a bunch of that grease off, but I don't know if we ever got rid of all of it.

The story about "greasing the singletrees" got around over the country quite a bit. When Big John brought our new coach up to us, we spent a day rigging it out; then hooked it up and drove up town for a test run. Later that evening, we all went down to a restaurant for dinner, and finished up by going over some items concerning the stagecoach. We were about through and ready to head back to camp, when Big John looks towards me with a very sincere look and says, "Something I almost forgot to mention, Red," he goes on. "I had a big bucket of black axle grease set out to bring up to you since Fritz left, and I forgot it!" We all had another good laugh, and I told John, "I'll bet you put Fritz up to the whole thing."

DAY NINE
JUNE 2ND

When we left Fairbury that morning, Joe was driving. We all piled on for the trip through town around the square. **Fritz stayed with us just that far. He yelled at Joe to stop, ran across the street and hailed a police car, and took off. We haven't seen him since.**

I got off then and caught a ride back to the fairgrounds to get the truck. Before I got under way, I was hailed and informed they'd had some sort of a wreck with the coach, and needed some parts out of the truck. You can sure imagine all the worst things that might happen, when you are trying to hurry to get back to your outfit. It seems that after I'd left, Joe went to start out. He yelled, "Hike!" The horses hit the collars, took up the slack and the swing tongue fell to the ground! The iron piece holding it to the wheel tongue had uncurled and flattened out from the force the horses had exerted on it. It sure could have been bad, as it turned the lead and swing teams loose from the wheel team. Of course, Joe still had ahold of the driving lines, but sometimes when something like that breaks, it will cause the leaders to bolt. In this case, with our good gentle horses, Joe just said, "Whoa, whoa.", and they stopped. He was able to pull over to the side of the street, and get out of the traffic. With the outriders holding horses, **Joe borrowed some tools, and applied good old baling wire.** By the time I got there, Joe had chained everything back together so good that we just went ahead and used it that way.

It reminded me of one time in Colorado. I had on six head, and the weather was brisk. The horses were frisky, but handling good. We'd made quite a run and were heading for home with about a mile to go. I was thinking how well the horses were shaping up when all at once, something happened, I never did know just what. But when I saw all six heads come up at the same instant, I knew we were in for it. I immediately jabbed the brake lever on and hauled in on the lines, but in that instant they'd already hit the traces at a full gallop. We had been on a slight down grade; so there was some slack in the

---

6/2 –FAIRBURY KS. to HEBRON NE.
Got up early. Holly Ann (horse) cut on knee from an iron post in the corral. Red got vet out of bed, but he wouldn't come out until 8. He was also the mayor, and not cordial in the least. Charged $25.00 and didn't do a thing Red couldn't have done.

We drove around the town square with Chamber of commerce manager aboard.
While driving down The street, the swing tongue fell off, and we had to make a tie job and pull in a grassy lot behind a station. Couldn't get Red on the CB, so Joe borrowed a crescent wrench and had it fixed by the time Red came along with the truck.

We almost had him surrounded and flanked down, when this calf really exploded. He kicked the one-armed boy and me both clear away from him. I thought the calf had gotten clean away, when I heard someone say, "Here, can I give you a hand?"

I had been kicked clear over backwards; and when I straightened up and looked around, there was "Little Joe", standing and holding that calf up in the air! Its nose wasn't even touching the ground. Joe just stood there, holding that calf by its two hind legs, almost straight-armed, right out in front of him. That calf sure must have known when he was whipped. He wasn't hardly even struggling. I grabbed a front leg, and we laid the old calf out on the ground. Joe told the one-armed boy to rest, that he'd spell him a bit. "Little Joe's" help sure made calf flanking easy for a while.

swing and lead bars. When the horses jumped, that throwed quite a jolt on the equipment, especially since I had jammed on the brake at the same time. When the leaders took up that slack, their doubletrees gave up the ghost right there.

I had a good grip on the lines, but they were really moving when those doubletrees let loose, and those lines went sliding right through my hands. If I'd had about one more foot of line, I'd of held them. As it was, they were almost stopped, when the ends of the lines whipped away from me. "Damn, Damn, Damn!" was all I could think of, as I watched that team of sorrel horses busting down across the prairie. When that team of leaders left the country, the other four wanted to follow right in their tracks. I had all I could do to pull them back and get everything under control again. Keith was with me. He immediately bailed off the coach and ran across the plains, trying to head off the loose team.

Three miles out of Fairbury, Laraine Gibson, our lady mayor, and Vernita Meisinger met us and rode into Gilead. They had lovely blue calico dresses and were so nice.

They had fixed the entire lunch themselves. Had fried chicken, baked beans (5 gallons), potato salad, rolls, and best cherry pie I ever ate.

Afterwards we sat on the steps of the Hall and visited for a couple hours, while the men went back to the school grounds and hitched up. They came into town and picked us up.

They ran out about a half mile, then they circled and headed right back towards us. Keith was afoot out in front of us, and I was beginning to get worried we might have a head-on collision there on that wide open prairie. About then one of the loose horses got tangled up in his flapping harness and fell down. With that heavy spreader strap between them the one standing had to stop also.

Jack was up at the ranch house, watching us come in, when we had the wreck. He saw the loose horses as soon as they got away from me. He yelled at Tammie and they jumped in a pickup and roared up to the tangled team. They got them untangled and up

"Little Joe", *we called him.*
Six feet three or four, 245 pounds, with about half an acre of burr clover hair on his chest. I've seen him stand around outside in the winter with a sleeveless shirt, unbuttoned half way down the front, and no undershirt or coat on. I'd be shivering inside my heavy sheepskin lined corduroy long coat. Joe is a little older than I am. I was about 20, and he was around 34 when we first met. That was way up in eastern Oregon on the ZX Ranch. They had lots of cows, ran a chuck wagon, and usually kept a year round cowboy crew of from 15 to 25 cowboys. We'd been branding calves for quite a while. They always used to heel rope the calves and drag them to the branding fire ahorseback, where two boys flanked 'em and held them while the ground crew gave them the once over, and the roper went back after another. We usually branded 400 head or more a day, for about a month through August and September. That's a lot of long hard days of work. It sure helps if a fellow is young and stout. The fall I met Joe, I'd been teamed up with a one-armed boy. He did his share of the work alright, but sometimes with those big wiry calves, <u>two</u> good arms and hands aren't hardly enough. This particular day, we'd gotten our share of stout calves. It was along in the middle of the afternoon. We were really working up a storm. As quick as we'd turn one calf loose, there'd be another one waiting. About then, some cowboy drug a big calf to us.

and led them back to the corral as I drove the coach up with the other four. We got a new set of lead bars, hooked our lead team back on, and drove for another hour until the six settled down again.

One of our first stops in Nebraska was the big, little town of **<u>Gilead.</u>** Big in heart, little in size. The lady mayor and town clerk met the stage about three miles out and rode in with them. With all the correspondence Marge had had with them, she said it was just like meeting old friends after a long separation. They had fixed a lovely dinner for us, and the whole town had planned on eating with us. We'd lost so much time with the broken tongue piece that we were about an hour late; so the men had already eaten and returned to work, when we got there. I made the most of the situation, eating with the ladies, and I sure got my share of pie.

At Fairbury, that afternoon, Joe was determined to drive the gelding hitch; so Red finally agreed. He started them out, but had no idea they'd move right into a swinging trot.

He almost lost them, but the crew stopped them. Nothing hurt except Joe. He was pulled forward so hard and fast, he broke a blood vessel in his arm. It swelled up and was so sore he couldn't use it.
Red had him drive the truck, and he got stuck.

That afternoon, Joe wanted to drive my hitch of horses. I didn't think it was too good an idea. All six of my horses were pretty frisky, and two of them were just a little more than apt to run if you didn't keep a pretty close eye on them. Joe was a good capable driver, but he hadn't been practicing long enough to handle six head like those six were. I let him start with them anyway. Tammie was riding Max, and Ray was driving the pilot car. I was afoot, and untied the lead horses from the back of the pickup after Joe got on the driver's box and got the lines all straightened out. The horse van was setting at an angle crossways out in front of us a ways. When Ray pulled the pickup out of the way, I stepped back and, by the time Joe called to the horses to start them, they were already in a hard run. I jumped and grabbed the bronc horse in the swing team; at the same time, Tammie bore right in on Max into the lead horse on her side. She crowded the leaders into the side of the horse van. With me hanging onto the bronc on my side, we finally got them quieted down. Joe had hauled right in on the lines to pull the team up when it all started. Instead of stopping the horses, what he did was to pop a blood vessel in the muscle of his right arm. I swung up on the coach with him when we got off to a good start on the second try. By the time we'd traveled up town from the school, a half mile or so, Joe was one-armed.

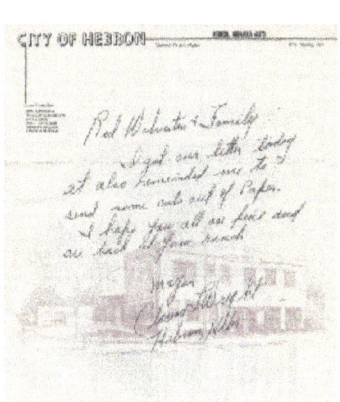

I took the coach on that afternoon, and then drove both hitches for the next week while Joe's arm healed up. I drove the coach on into **Hebron, Nebraska,** that afternoon. **That's a town and a group of people I shall always remember.** We were met out a ways by the town "royalty", all dressed up in black frock coats and stovepipe hats and some pretty fancy long dresses. They boarded the stage, and piloted us into the center of town to the bank where we left our strongbox for the night. Driving up the Main Street was quite a sight. There in the middle of the intersection was a sign announcing "Stagecoach will arrive at 6:30 tonight."

Went on to Hebron. Mayor Clarence Wright and wife rode with us. He was dressed in an old-fashioned starched white shirt, black frock coat, and a derby. His wife had on a beige muslin and lace dress that laced up the front. Kip commented on it. We drove into town, and they had a sign in the center of town, "Stagecoach will arrive at 6 PM."

After the mayor unloaded, we took 4 loads of kids around the block. First load was quiet and polite. Second load, the parents started shoving their kids into the coach. Third load, one woman stood in the door and crammed kids in. I finally told her that was too many. The 4th load wasn't so crowded. We had 12 to 15 kids inside each load, besides Wendy and me. Not one kid or grownup thanked us for the rides.

When we pulled up in front of the bank, there were probably 200 people there to greet us and look over our outfit. As I handed the strongbox down and was waiting for one of my crew members to return, my attention focused on a 9 or 10 year old boy wi**th big blue eyes and red hair. Looking up at me he said, "Do you ever give rides?"** "Sometimes", was my reply. "Would you like to take a ride?" "1 sure would," were his words. It was 6:30 then.

I had been going since about five that morning, but how can you get tired when doing something as interesting as driving a stagecoach?

I guess we hauled a couple hundred kids of all ages around an eight block area before we gave up and headed for our night camp. The mayor and banker and some other officials took all our crew to their private club, and wined and dined us. It was a real enjoyable evening. Before the night was over, I was asked what time we had breakfast, "6 or 6:30", I answered. There was a good truckstop restaurant up on the corner that opened early. We were invited to be the town's guests.

**DAY TEN
JUNE 3rd**

DAY TEN
JUNE 3RD

While eating the next morning, Mr. Koenig from the bank handed me an envelope with a hundred dollar bill in it "to help you on your trip". **I was almost speechless. My wife says that's a new one for me.**

Highway 81 which runs north and south through Hebron is known as the Pan-American Highway. It crosses the old Oregon Trail about three miles north of town.

There's a real nice monument marker there, and the Mayor mentioned he'd like to get some pictures of the coach out by it. We wanted all the pictures like that on our trip that we could get. Mayor

Wright said he'd have a state patrol car there to help with any traffic problems, and he'd meet us out there. There was a county road which we could take, and then we'd have to jog back one mile east. Some of the townspeople were willing to ride out with us to pilot us to the marker. When I first saw the marker, it looked hopeless to me to be able to get the stagecoach anywhere near it. After I studied it, I decided if I pulled across the highway and circled back hard to the left, I might be able to get close enough, but it didn't work out. The marker was down in the barpit on the northeast corner of the intersection.

It was some 6 or 8 feet below the level of the highway. There was plenty of room to get down in the barpit with the coach, but both banks where I'd have to go down and pull back out were real steep. A stagecoach has a stiff tongue, which creates a hazardous situation any time you go over a real sharp embankment or pull out of a steep grade suddenly to level ground. A stiff tongue is one that doesn't hinge up and down where it is

---

6/3 HEBRON to GENEVA
Hebron, Neb. C. of Commerce took crew to breakfast at café. They had steak and eggs. I was too sick to go. Pearl took Joe and me to the doctor. He gave me a shot to settle my stomach. I slept all morning in the camper.

At noon, they came back after the camper, and I got dressed. They all had a lovely potluck at Strang. Mom, Pat and Jess Hoffman, and Mrs. Hoffman were there. I felt lousy, but finally got up and went out.

Mom and I rode in the coach from Strang to Geneva. Pearl laid out supper from the Gilead food. Mom and Hoffmans ate with us and enjoyed it. I felt better. They left after we visited.

fastened to the front axle; so when you go over an embankment like that, and the horses start down a steep grade, the tongue sticks straight out in the air on a horizontal line, with the level of the front and back wheels. The lead horses pull from the end of that stiff tongue; so if they were pulling hard, you could break the tongue off by pulling down too hard from the end.

    The same thing could happen in reverse, when you are going down a steep grade that levels off or even tips back up too sharply. The lead horses pulling up on the end of it could also break it off. **Sometimes one is forced to take chances to accomplish what you set out to do.** I decided we could make it into the barpit and back out again; so I asked the patrolman there if he could hold up traffic while I swung to the far side of the highway, drove a short way the wrong way up the left hand lane; then swung back to the right and went over the bank. It's always a thrill to me to take a coach over a place like that. Your horses drop over the bank and you have to keep off the brake so the coach will roll easy in order to keep the strain off the tongue; then you have to haul in on the horses and ride the brake for all you are worth as the coach starts over the bank. The horses are all way down below you then. When you reach the bottom, and level out, the horses are high and the front of the coach is low. You can reach right out and touch them on the rumps, and sometimes it seems like you are going to be on their rumps before everything gets back in its proper place again. Everything held together, and we got right up beside the marker, and everybody got some good pictures. When I pulled away from it, we just had room to start the horses and swing into a trot before the leaders reached the bank to go up. I yelled at them again and got the leaders and swing team both on the level ground, with the wheel team on the steep climb, before the coach hit the grade and became hard to pull. It was a good pull dragging it up that soft steep bank; and the horses were pulled down pretty slow as the front wheels came over the edge before it topped out and eased up.

> In Geneva, when we got in, the mayor rode with us around the square.
>
> Then they presented us with a beautiful Liberty Bell plaque.
>
> Afterwards Red took five loads of kids around the square.

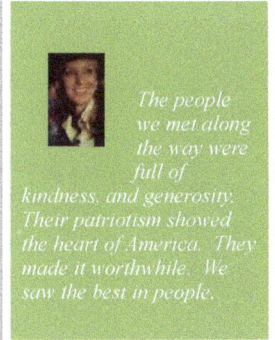

The people we met along the way were full of kindness, and generosity. Their patriotism showed the heart of America. They made it worthwhile. We saw the best in people.

It was quite a thrill to me to stop at that marker denoting where the Oregon and Overland trails had run a century ago. We waved farewell to the wonderful people from Hebron as we crossed the paved highway and headed on down the dirt road towards **Strang, Nebraska**.

It's always enjoyable to get on a good solid dirt road for a run after driving on the pavement for a long ways. Strang is a small country town that sits on a slightly south slope of a gentle rolling country. Its main street is a big, wide dirt or gravel street shaded by a line of leafy trees. At the south end of town, right in the middle of the street is a well with an old time

We unhitched in a lovely park. Then the mayor took us all out for steak dinner at the Legion Club. Loraine and Vermita came up and visited at supper, and brought a lot of their extra food. It was late when we ate, and I wasn't hungry, but had a filet and baked potato, and I ate too much. Woke up about 3:30 sick.

handle pump in it. When we arrived in the town, that pump sure stood out. It was all decorated in red, white, and blue. A pipe ran from the pump to a large water trough, brim full of water, which was also decorated with the colors. The people were really helpful and friendly, and soon ushered us into a large community dinner which they had prepared.

I wanted to stay and spend part of the afternoon visiting with them, and perhaps take them for a stagecoach ride, but I had other things that had to be done. That morning, Marge had gotten up so sick that we all decided she should go see a doctor. Also, Joe's arm was still so sore and bothering him; so his wife, Pearl, volunteered to take the two of them to a doctor. That left our camper and pickup and horse van at Hebron with no drivers. Marge's mother and a former school chum had shown up at Strang that day to visit us on the trip. Of course, they were very disappointed and concerned over Marge. They volunteered to go back to Hebron with me to help get the extra equipment and see how Marge was. She had gotten some medicine and was at the camper, feeling much better when we got there; so we were able to load up and head right back to Strang.

Tammie had things at Strang well under control when we got back. She said everybody in the country had taken a picture of her watering the horses around that colored tank that afternoon.

Here was another place we'd like to have been able to have changed our schedule and stayed over for a night, but we just couldn't. We were due to meet the town officials of **Geneva** at the south edge of town at 5:30 and parade them through town; so we had to hook up and get going. It's only 10 or 12 miles on to Geneva and a level run; so we made it right on time. Charlie and June had caught up with us late the evening before in Hebron and had been invited to join us at the banquet there. Charlie loves a good horseback ride; so he spent all the next day from Hebron to Geneva as a lead outrider.

Somewhere in my stagecoaching escapades, I've learned that an outrider in front of the coach horses can cause as much or occasionally more trouble, as if he wasn't there when you needed him. If there is a rider in front of the horses all the time, the lead team gets to depending on it. If that rider decides to make a sudden sashay left or right, the horses will want to follow. Quite often on a corner or turn, a rider in the lead won't swing out far enough to put the hitch and coach in the right position to make the turn. Occasionally, a lead rider will suddenly get tired of riding in the lead and decide to turn off. Horses that are used to following are sure apt to duck off right after the rider. For this reason, when travelling out in the open country, we keep our outriders off to the sides and at least behind the shoulders of the lead team. When we get in towns or any place that really looks hazardous, we have the outrider ride ahead of us, to watch for cross traffic. That lead team's heads are 36 to 38 feet ahead of the driver; so they are well out in an intersection before the driver can see if the way is clear or not.

An example of those possibilities had happened just a few days earlier. Joe was driving and Tammie was his outrider. Joe preferred to have his outrider lead him all the time. It does make driving easier. They were in that rolling hill country, going down a good grade that was built on a steep high hill. Tammie was quite a ways ahead and in a brisk trot. She thought of something she wanted out of the stagecoach; so she checked back over her shoulder and thought Joe had everything under control. She pulled her horse up and turned down over the side of the embankment to wait for the coach to catch up, while still walking her horse and going in the same direction. Suddenly she heard a change in the sound of the approaching horses. Looking around, she saw the lead team come over the edge of the bank headed right towards her. Needless to say, it scared her into immediate action. She spurred Max back up over the bank and spooked the lead team back up onto the shoulder of the highway, just barely in time to straighten out the coach before it went over the bank too far to come back. Of course, Joe was equally busy gathering in slack and trying to get those leaders back on the road. It could have been a bad wreck.

The same sort of thing happened that day coming into Geneva. We had picked up the town officials and were right in town; so I had motioned to Charlie to take the lead in front of us. We were clipping along down the street at a real good trot, just about 10 or 15 feet behind Charlie's horse, when "Pete" shied at a manhole cover and ran sideways over the curb and way up on the lawn, before Charlie got him straightened out. My leaders didn't shy like Pete did, but they sure followed him. I had my lines up real snug, since we were in town, but I couldn't keep them from following Charlie and Pete up over the curb and across that lawn, before we curved back into the street. Instead of slowing down, we picked up speed as we came off the curb. I was pulling so hard on my leaders that they swerved out around Charlie instead of dropping back behind him.

About that time we came to an intersection, and the police car in front went half way across and then stopped at the side. I thought he was blocking traffic for us so I started straight across the intersection. Then one of the city officials who was on the seat behind me, shouted in my ear that we were supposed to turn right here. So that's just what I did. **A full hard right hand turn with a galloping hitch, right in the middle of that intersection.** Charlie, on Pete, was about even with the swing horse, on the right side, when we started around; and they were in a hard turn before he realized what was happening, and that he'd better move, and fast. Luckily, none of our horses slipped on that pavement, because it sure would have been a pileup. We were right up against Charlie and Pete before we got turned far enough to go on down the street, and we booted them along a few feet. I don't know what our passengers thought, for I just let on like that was regular everyday driving. All the time, during the sashay across the lawn and turning in the intersection, I'd kept yelling out encouragement like, "Come on Charlie, stay with him." We made a turn up around the old folks rest home, then headed on down to the town square. There, at a very nice ceremony, we were presented with a magnificent Liberty Bell plaque, from the local Bicentennial group and town officials. We deposited our strongbox at the bank and then took several loads of local people and kids for a ride around the square in the stagecoach.

When we got out to the fairgrounds where we were to camp that night, we discovered that Joe had turned a corner too sharp coming in with the horse van, and had parked the trailer in a barpit at a very precarious angle. Luckily for us, Charlie had a good heavy winch on his big four-wheel drive truck. We were able to hook it up high over the top of the trailer, and tip it back off the trailer tires enough to drive the outfit on out of the mess it was in. Joe said, "I never claimed to be no truck driver." He just took his turn at driving our big horse van, because we didn't have the money to hire a regular driver for it. So if he got into a jackpot, we looked at the comical side of it and did what we could to straighten things out; and the comical side of it that day was the angle that outfit was parked when we drove up with the stagecoach.

DAY ELEVEN
JUNE 4TH

The next morning things returned back to normal. I had to replace a couple shoes on the morning hitch. Joe's arm was still too sore so I drove a full day again. We finally got underway after swinging back downtown to pick up our strongbox at the bank and then headed west. **All my life it has been a thrill to me to head west**, whether I was in Kansas City, or way out in California. This morning was no different. The air was fresh, and the sun felt good. I guess most of the country was definitely starting to take on a change from the rolling tree studded farm country to the open sand hills and range country that borders the Platte River so far.

I had an odd thing happen that morning, and it wasn't because I was daydreaming and not paying attention to my horses. We were trotting right out along the shoulder of the highway. As usual I had my foot riding lightly on the brake lever, and my lines up snug. Before I could bat an eye, the lead team turned and ducked to the right down a dirt road. The wild grass along the road was thick and belly high on the horses. The barpit was around 6 feet deep and fairly steep, both on the highway and fence sides.

The leaders had a good turn on me before I got the extra slack pulled up and swerved them back towards the highway. By that time, they were far enough down the side road that I would have to swing catty cornered back through the tall grass and across the barpit to reach the road again. Instead of going ahead and turning I pulled the hitch to a stop. Tammie came galloping up, with a smirk on her face. "Where are you going? To sleep, maybe?" I had a hard time convincing her I hadn't, and she still razzes me occasionally. I couldn't see any place to turn on the side road, so Tammie rode ahead through the high grass to check out the barpit and see if we could swing back hard and make it. It was another of those places that is hard on a stagecoach tongue, but we swung around and hit a gallop going down one side and sailed right back up on the highway shoulder to continue on west.

The mayor and sheriff and other town officials and ladies from **Clay Center** met us about five miles from town and rode in with us.

6/4 - GENEVA to HASTINGS

Geneva. Felt much better. Fixed breakfast. Left Geneva and drove to Clay Center. The sheriff rode shotgun and the mayor and ladies rode inside.

We stopped at the ballpark, and had sandwiches for lunch. Drove around the square and down by the swimming pool, and took a load of kids.

Had sort of a mix-up at Hastings. Got into town late; no police escort.

Ray ran out of gas with the Ford Pickup.

Our campers and horse van were waiting for us in the city ball park, but something wasn't quite right. As soon as we stopped the coach, our passengers thanked us and all disappeared. A second small group of people approached us, noticeably unfriendly, and slightly hostile because we'd stopped in the ball park. We didn't know whether we'd gotten in the middle of some political fuss or if the town had some factions that didn't get along with each other; so we had our own private picnic lunch and then hooked up to leave. Some young fellows working there on a project seemed to want to be friendly. I spoke to them, and asked if they'd like to take a short ride downtown with us. They answered, "Yeah, but we have to work." Their boss immediately told them, "Go ahead, it will be all right." We circled downtown and around the courthouse square. I asked one of them, "Where are all the kids in this town? We haven't seen hardly any." "In another hour or so, they'll be swarming all over; right now, they're all down at the swimming pool.", he said. When he went on to mention there were usually a bunch of good looking girls down there, I inquired where it was. **"Now, my dear wife, you know why we made another detour to circle the swimming pool before leaving town that day."**

A short ways north of town out on the highway, we came to a state patrol safety check road block. There were several police cars parked on the left hand shoulder of the road, facing us. Right even with them on the right hand shoulder sat a police motorcycle. One or more of the police cars had an outside PA system turned on, very loud. There were several cars stopped when we pulled up; so we waited until they were through as I wanted to talk to the patrolman to tell him our horse van and campers would be along behind us pretty quick. As we started to leave, the patrolman said, "You'd just as well pull up on the highway and go on your way."

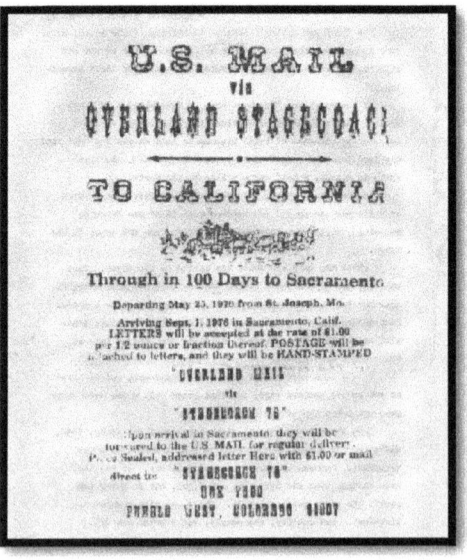

I waved to him and smiled to myself as I looked at that motorcycle up ahead of us with red lights and antennas all over it. It even looked spooky to me, and I'm only half mule. I decided we'd better go on the lower side of it. The barpit here was big and wide, and had a real gentle slope, but right in the middle of it about 20 feet from the motorcycle and even with it, was an old rusty-looking mailbox on a post. I have no idea what it was doing there as I could see no sign of it having ever been used. Anyway, there it sat.

Usually if a place looks bad to me, I'll kick my horses into a trot or gallop to get through it. The horses have less time to get spooked, and it's harder for them to double back on you when they're running. I had them in a good "moving on" trot when I pointed those leaders between that motorcycle monster and that mailbox. I'm sure everything would have been alright even then, although the horses were eyeing that motorcycle awful suspicious, but just at that time, **that blasted PA system on the police car blared out something real loud. I'm not sure what it said, but it was something like, "Watch out ahead, here comes a stagecoach bolting up the right of way!"** And "bolted" is exactly what we did! I just grazed the mailbox with the front wheel of the coach as those horses shot sideways. I was riding the brake real hard and the rear of the coach was skidding sideways enough for the rear wheel to smack it dead center and send it flying! We were a half mile up country before I had time to look around. I didn't see any cops coming after us, so I gave the horses a little slack on the lines and let them move on out. If noone was using that old mail box, they probably wouldn't miss it anyway.

Our motorized crew passed us somewhere along the way that afternoon. Later on Tammie came back in a pickup to see how we were doing. When she met us she said it was 6 PM. We were 10 miles from town, and the Bicentennial people were expecting us in town by 7. "We can make that", I answered, "if you'll quit your jawing and get out of the way." We returned her dirty look with a grin and wave and hit a gallop for **Hastings, Nebraska.**

It had been a hot, still afternoon, and I hadn't driven very hard. Now, in the evening a light breeze came up and cooled the air real nice. At 5 minutes after 7 P.M. we pulled into the fairgrounds where our camp was. We could have been there sooner, but the Bicentennial people were supposed to meet us out at the edge of town to lead us into their park where they wanted us to take part in their Chatauqua. I didn't even know what one was, but I was game. With a name like that, it should be something lively.

Apparently they had checked on us by car at about the same time as Tammie did, and they had decided there wasn't any way we could make it to town before 7:30 so they were in no hurry to meet us. We were waiting there in camp, wondering whether to unhook or what when they drove up all excited, and asked us to drive the stagecoach on over to their "doings". That was my one and only trip to a Chatauqua. I'm sure it was a real good doings, and I enjoyed taking part in it, but I never did get to see any of the rest of it, and I never did figure out just what it was.

Drove to Fairgrounds and got police escort; then drove to Chataqua Park with Bicentennial Committee members. One lady was wife of state senator. Drove into a very tight spot, and waited half an hour to be announced.

Several hundred people crowding around coach made horses and me nervous. To get out, Red had Ray and Tammie lead the leaders forward; then jackknife them back to go between the line of posts, and on a narrow sidewalk. We got the coach through without hitting anything; then went "home".

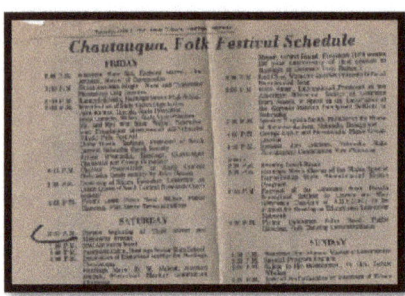

The Chatauqua was held in a large open air pavilion, in the middle of their park. There must have been several hundred people attending it. When we got to the park, I was asked to bring the stagecoach down a narrow winding lane marked out by posts sticking up out of the ground, about two feet high, and four or five feet apart. There was no problem driving down the lane as the police chief climbed up to the shotgun seat to guide me down the lane.

As we started out he looked down to the 30:30 rifle in the scabbard at the left side of the driver's box on the front of the coach. He said, **"I have a feeling this is a real rifle here in this scabbard. "Uh, huh", I grinned. "And I have the feeling it's loaded",** he looked at me sorta quizzical. "You bet", I answered, "I wouldn't have it no other way." He didn't ask if we had any kind of a permit for it or anything.

By that time, we were pulling into the small parking area next to the pavilion. The Chief informed me that in just a few minutes they would be through with the program in progress and they'd dismiss for 15 minutes to let the spectators come inspect the stagecoach outfit. While waiting, I looked around the lot to see about getting out. There was no way out! Nothing, that is, other than the lane we'd come in on, and even if there hadn't been any cars on it, the lot would have been only about half big enough to turn a stagecoach around in. We might have been able to turn around if we could back up, but that's just something else a stagecoach isn't equipped to do. We never use any pole straps or hold-back rigging on any of our horses. On steep grades if I can't hold it back with the brake; then I just plan on outrunning the coach until we hit the bottom.

The parking lot was also surrounded with those two feet posts set in the ground. They were too close together to drive between, all except one place. Up ahead of us where the sidewalk went meandering across the park, the posts were about eight feet apart. Our coach axles are about 7 feet 6 inches long, which meant I'd have to hit that opening pretty straight.

In the meantime, the program ended inside, and we found ourselves surrounded by about 500 interested spectators. I had to watch them so close to keep them out from under the horses that I didn't have time to worry about getting out of the lot. We enjoy showing the coach to a crowd that seems to appreciate seeing it, and this crowd was sure interested; so much so that the horses were getting fidgety from being hemmed in so close by so many people. Marge said inside the coach, she got the feeling she could understand what an old time mob was like; she felt almost suffocated from the tension in the air and the pressure of the crowd as they ringed the coach closer and closer.

The announcer gave us a good introduction over the P.A. system, and everyone within hearing distance of the coach asked questions. Fifteen minutes passed quickly, and the crowd stepped back at a command from the announcer. Some of them went back inside, but many remained out around us. I think they all began to realize what a tight spot we were in and wanted to see if we could get out.

Tammie showed up then, and was I glad. In order to get in line with the sidewalk opening, I had to keep the coach going straight ahead quite a ways after I'd already swung the lead and swing teams back into the opening. This wouldn't have seemed such a hard turn out on the open, but there were also cars parked on both sides of the lane on either side of us, with two more completely blocking off the drive out in front of the leaders. Also, it was now 8:30 P.M. and I'd been up since 5 that morning, tacked on two horse shoes, and driven 55 miles that day. I was a wee bit tired. When I spotted Tammie, my instructions were, "Tammie, you get ahold of Romeo and, Ray, you get hold of Rebel. Go straight ahead as far as you can, then swing back hard to the left, then back to the right through the opening. Keep going unless I call differently." With them handling the lead team, I was able to control the swing team and most important, I was able to keep the wheel team going forward before we turned and swung that coach through that narrow opening.

When we got to the Fairgrounds, Bandera (horse) lay down in the traces. Red jumped down and got her up. She almost pawed Tammie and Red several times before they got her loose. While Red was Trying to get the harness off, she lay down several times. After about ten minutes, she seemed to be OK. They went ahead and unhitched the horses. Went out to cafe for supper. Had shrimp and steak.

I sure hated to ask for help in front of a crowd like that, but I didn't want anyone hurt. With people out in front of the leaders, they could keep the bystanders back and give the horses the room they needed. We made it through the hole without touching a post so I guess that was the wise way to do it. After we got around the curve and ducked under a couple trees and were in the clear, Margie climbed up on the shotgun seat beside me for the trip back to the fairgrounds. Guess she needed a little more air, and we all breathed a sigh of relief.

Our police escort led us back. It was a winding weaving route of a couple miles. With the big red light flashing on top of the police car, we didn't have to stop. What took place going to camp shows how fast those Morgan horses learn. I knew we had to make a right turn up ahead, followed by a left turn in a short half block. I spoke to Marge and said, "Look at my hands and watch the horses for a ways now." After we made the two turns in a perfect maneuver,

Marge answered me, quite tickled. She said, "Why you didn't move your hands or lines at all. Romeo and Rebel were following that red light!" Those darn horses knew for sure that red light was taking them straight to camp.

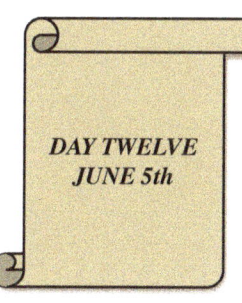

DAY TWELVE
JUNE 5th

CHAPTER SIX
NEBRASKA PARADES
DAY TWELVE
JUNE 5TH

Kearney

ready for parade - Kearney
Charlie Johnson

Kearney parade

Saturday, June 5th, and there were three parades we wanted to take part in, all on the same day. We were quite sure we could make two of them, as one was in the afternoon. We had planned on going to Lexington for the morning parade; then coming back to Kearney for the afternoon parade, but we didn't know that Hastings was also having a morning parade.

6/5 - HASTINGS
Jack got in at daylight.
We got up about 6: AM. Fixed French toast for breakfast. We're in Hastings parade, #3 position behind officials.

Float in front of us was an old time ship with a tall mast. Someone forgot to measure the height of the overhead power lines, and the mast of the ship was higher than they were. As they drove under, the mast hit the lines and started tipping over. It fell to the ground directly in front of our lead horses.

Red had been watching; so had the lines and horses in full control and stopped them immediately.
I don't think the horses were as shook up as I was, watching it fall. People scrambled to fix the situation, while we waited. When everything was OK, the parade started up and we finished it.

After the Chatauqua the night before, they had invited us to be in it. Since Lexington was a 60 mile haul with the truck, and we'd been up so late the night before, we decided to stay and show in the Hastings parade instead. That would give us a little extra time in the morning to polish up the horses and harness, and then we'd drive to Kearney for theirs. We talked the Hastings people into letting us in close to the lead of their parade so we'd have more time to load up for the afternoon.

Jack and his family caught up with us again that morning so we had a full crew that day. When we drove the stagecoach down to the parade make-up area, we also took our horse van and coach trailer. The only thing out of the ordinary during the Hastings parade occurred when the float ahead of us had a small accident.

It represented a large sail boat (one of Columbus' ships I think) with a tall mast. **The mast hooked on a cross wire over the street and toppled over backwards, coming gently right down to the level of our lead horses' heads**. I had Romeo and Rebel in the lead, and when I saw that mast coming down, I got prepared for some action, but I was sure surprised. They just looked at it with an interested look of curiosity, as if to say, "Well, what have we here?", and kept right on walking forward in their usual parade strut. The rest all went smoothly and we rushed around and loaded up and headed to Kearney where we had to sit and wait quite a while for their parade to start.

We unloaded there right beside the railroad tracks. The horses didn't pay any attention to the trains even though they were moving back and forth almost constantly and making lots of noise. Marge almost missed the parade as she was on the opposite side of the train tracks when we got the signal to move up. As she was coming toward us, a train cut her off, and she had to wait until it went by. She was really "sweating it out", wondering if we'd be gone by the time she got across, but she just barely made it. **Kearney had a good parade, but we didn't have a monopoly on stagecoaches.**

Afterwards, we Loaded up the coach and 6 up, and drove to Kearney. Unloaded by railroad tracks. Horses didn't seem to mind the trains. I talked to several other entries. One man had a beautiful team of black Percherons, all polished up, and the fanciest studded harness I think I've ever seen. He was from Iowa, and had shown 2, 4, & 6 head hitches, every weekend during the summers for one sponsor. He was showing the Fort Kearney covered wagon for The Lions Club.

This Parade went off fine. We got lots of applause. There was a 4 pony hitch and real nice stage right behind us in the parade. We loaded up and went back to Hastings.

One of the local ranchers had a 4 horse hitch of Shetland ponies and a half size stagecoach to match their size. Theirs was as interesting to us as ours was to them.

On the way back to Hastings with the truck, we checked out the camp ground at old Fort Kearney. The campground was a mile north of the museum. There was about an 80 acre meadow with lush grass more than knee high. The officials at the fort said we could camp there and turn our horses out in it. The meadow was right along the river bank where the old Platte River crossing had been. It sure looked good to us. We drove on down to Heartwell next to check out our noon stop for the next day. I talked to several people including the mayor, and was informed their celebration was scheduled for the following week. If we wished, we could come to it, but otherwise they didn't have time to fool with us.

DAY THIRTEEN
JUNE 6TH

I drove out of Hastings the next morning. We were traveling right along in a brisk trot as it was fairly cool. Jack and Charlie had passed us a few miles out of town and were waiting for us at a rest area a little further on. For no reason that I could see, the off swing horse, Robby, fell flat on the pavement. He didn't stub a toe, stumble, slip, or anything; just fell flat like he'd been slugged between the eyes. I just happened to be watching him as he was one of the horses we'd gotten in Seneca and I wondered how he was doing. When he fell, it was so sudden that it startled the others. They all spooked and lunged and tried to run. As usual I had my foot on the brake, but they still drug poor Robby 10 to 15 feet before I got them stopped and gave Robby a chance to get up.

He scrambled to his feet without getting tangled up and seemed to be in fairly good shape, so I drove on to the rest area as it wasn't over two hundred yards away. He had the hide burned off his right side, but didn't appear to be hurt seriously. We doctored his wounds and continued west, as this was another of those 50 mile days, and we still had a long ways to go. We said goodby to June and Charlie here as they had to head back home again.

We rolled into **Heartwell,** fed and watered our horses from the big tank we carried in the horse van, and ate lunch in our campers. The few people we saw just stood in their doorways and scowled at us. Noone came over to visit. We changed hitches, hooked up, and left.

Heartwell turned out to have a distinction all its own--- it was the only town on the entire trip that refused to have anything to do with us. They didn't answer our letters before the trip started, and they had nothing to do with us what little time we were there. A short ways west of town, Jack was behind us in his motorhome. Some people in a car waved at him and acted like they wanted to visit so he stopped to talk to them. They lived close by on a farm, and mentioned they sure liked the looks of that stagecoach, and they bet it would be fun to ride in it. Jack immediately told them to follow him and he'd get them a ride in it. Those farm people sent a telephone relay message up the road, and

---

6/6 Sunday –
HASTINGS to FORT KEARNEY
No church this morning. Got up and fixed sweet rolls for breakfast. Only one left out of a cake-pan full. Vacuumed the camper. Geneva did all my laundry.

Have been writing all this in the coach, and it's a little bumpy for writing.

Robbie (horse) fell down while traveling, and cut his knee. We pulled into a rest stop and doctored him. Said goodbye to June and Charlie. They plan to meet us again in Reno.

for the rest of the afternoon, every few miles we changed passengers.

It made us feel lots better. **The town people might not have cared to be friendly with us, but the country people outside of Heartwell sure seemed to enjoy it, and we** enjoyed them**.**

Stopped at Heartwell, Nebraska for dinner about 2:00 PM. A few people stood in the doorways and stared. No smiles. Very unfriendly town. I definitely felt like we were unwanted, and was glad to leave. Only town on the whole trip that refused to have anything to do with us. Some recommendation for a town!

Geneva fixed a lovely meal of pork roast, barbecued beef, baked potatoes, salad and delicious chocolate cake.

After Heartwell we drove to Fort Kearney. Country is changing. More open, rolling grass land, and less row crops and fences. Horizons always hazy. Country is beautiful. Lots of ripe alfalfa; some cut and windrowed, and some already bailed and stacked.

That morning, a short ways after leaving the rest area, we met a fellow on a motorcycle heading east. He went by, waved, then turned around and came back up to us. **He was retracing the Pony Express route via motorcycle**. He'd started in Sacramento and was headed for St. Joe. He was really interested in our outfit, and very pleased when we told him we had started in St. Joe and were retracing the Overland Stage route to Sacramento.

We were to meet him again before our trip was over.

That evening, when I loped those horses and that stagecoach into **Old Fort Kearney**, it was like being in a trance. **It seemed almost as if we were only one of a great line of stagecoaches, freight wagons, and other old time vehicles rumbling in towards that river crossing. I got the feeling of doing something I'd done before, many and many a time.**

It made my whole body tingle when I galloped up through that meadow with that bright red and yellow stagecoach and was a thrill.

Wild flowers are lovely: primroses, some vining blue flowers, deep rose colored ones, and many small kinds.

Got into Fort Kearney for night. Beautiful grassy meadow. Turned horses loose until dark. Geneva made chili for supper. They left afterwards, and we went to bed.

DAY FOURTEEN
JUNE 7TH

The next morning, Joe felt like he could drive again. After shoeing a couple horses and visiting with the owners of the Shetland pony hitch, Joe headed out with the coach, and I took the horse van on to **Elm Creek** and set up camp.

There weren't any corrals so we had to pull our aluminum corral panels off the top of our horse van and set up our own for the night. I went back out with the officials and the local 4H horse club. We met Joe and all rode back into town with him. Joe's arm was bothering him so I took over and hauled several loads of people around before putting the horses up for the night. We'd made arrangements for all of us to have supper in a restaurant across the street as soon as we all got cleaned up a bit. I just happened to be sitting where I could see the back end of the horse van and a corn field behind it. We had just started to eat when a movement in the cornfield caught my eye. It was 18 horses that were laying down and rolling with childish delight in that warm soft black dirt and new corn.

I don't remember what I said, but I know we sure emptied that restaurant in a jiffy. It didn't take us long to gallop "shank's ponies" out into that cornfield and surround that bunch of horses. They were some reluctant to go back into that corral, but we finally persuaded them to go. Apparently, one horse had run another into one of the aluminum panels and caused it to fall down. Of course, those horses didn't need an engraved invitation to leave that small corral and head into the cornfield. We straightened up the panels and backed a pickup to the weak side of the pen. Then we returned to finish our evening meal in peace.

6/7 – FORT KEARNEY to ELM CREEK
Red and Joe shod Bandito and Sammy. Left late, with Joe driving. Red took the truck. I drove the Ford as pilot car.

Can't enjoy the scenery, and the CB talk is irritating. Red met us about 1:00PM, came back to the camper, and fixed sandwiches; then took back to the coach.

Ray took the pilot car. Pearl and I rode in the coach. La Donna Walker and another lady rode into Elm Creek with us, and the local saddle club paraded in front. Enjoyed talking with a woman who raises quarter horses.

After supper we spent the evening visiting with the local people, quite a few of whom were descendants of pioneers, like those we had met in other places.

One of our passengers that afternoon was Roena Mitchell, whose grandparents had moved from Iowa to Nebraska in a covered wagon in 1873. Roena was born in Burwell, which is an old cowboy town. Her folks later moved to Washington State where they took out a timber claim. In 1907, while working in the timber, the team ran away as her father was driving. He fell off the wagon and hit his head on the wheel and was killed. His wife and daughter returned to Nebraska in 1924.
Another old timer we sure liked, whose family helped escort us into Elm Creek, was Roy A. Richards. His father and brother had come from Illinois in 1879 and purchased land from the railroad. They farmed and also raised horses to sell. They were some of the first to have Shorthorn cattle in the area. The Richards' house was built of lumber brought from Illinois. It was of 6 x 6's laid on brick, and sheeting up and down with battens, and lap siding over the outside. Mr. Richards was born in that house and still lives there.

In Elm Creek we were camped just barely more than a city block from the main line railroad track. All night long, every fifteen minutes, two freight trains met and passed on double tracks right across from our camp. Since this was our first night's camp along the tracks, we assumed this was normal rail traffic. We didn't learn until the next day there had been a whale of a derailment up the line which had all rail traffic tied up for several days prior to our arrival. The line had just been opened up that afternoon. In the morning when I asked Joe if he enjoyed the trains last night, he bowed his head and answered me, "I sure decided one thing; I "enjoyed" those trains so much last night, that if I ever get rich and retire, I'm gonna buy me a little white cottage somewheres down by the tracks!"

Got in early, and ate at 5:00. Then picked ticks off the dogs. They were loaded with them around the ears.

Had baked steak and mushroom gravy, potatoes, corn, kole slaw, and hot homemade bread, chocolate cake, apple pie, and ice cream.

Trailer served as inside of corral, and horses broke two windows by Wendy's bed.

DAY FIFTEEN
JUNE 8TH

Joe's arm hadn't healed as much as he'd thought; so I took the coach out again that morning. We hadn't contacted the town of **Overton** as we hadn't planned on stopping there, but when we came up to it, I turned and drove up Main Street. A short ways up the street when we came by the City Hall, there was a woman looking out the window so I pulled to a stop. I asked if the mayor was around. She answered that if we'd wait, she'd get ahold of him.

By the time he arrived, a group of people had gathered around, and we invited them to climb aboard and go for a turn around the block. When we returned, a Bible School class had just let out, and we had a couple more loads to haul around town. Before we were through with that group another church school let out. We were quite popular in Overton that morning. As we started to leave town, another fellow ran up with his little "big-eyed" girl. He wanted to know if we'd haul her to the edge of town on our way out, and then he'd follow in his car to pick her up. I told him we'd be glad just to, but he figured he couldn't get along without her that long.

When we stayed in Hastings for their parade instead of going to the one at Lexington as we had planned, it didn't set well with the **Lexington** officials, as they didn't receive us too warmly. There was a lady reporter from the local newspaper who met us at the edge of town. After visiting a while, she said she'd like to get some pictures. She was a good-looking lady, probably in her thirties. She stepped back off to the side a short ways, raised her camera to her eye, pointed towards me and said, "Smile". At that exact instant a playful puff of wind sneaked up behind her, grabbed the front of her skirt, and pulled it right up to her chin. "Wow!" I thought, "What a unique way for a photographer to attract one's attention." I don't know if she ever got her picture or not, but I sure got a nice one.

6/8 – ELM CREEK to LEXINGTON

Trains woke us up all night. I was up four times during the night. Was awfully tired in the morning. Slept in the stage part of the time.

Red came back to meet us after taking rigs ahead. I went with him in Dodge to get sandwich stuff for lunch, and we came back and stopped the stage alongside the Railroad tracks, and ate lunch. People were taking pictures and visiting.

Went on to Lexington where we parked close to grandstand at fairgrounds. Quite windy, and the dust blew. Who drove the Ford?

DAY SIXTEEN
JUNE 9TH

Joe had an appointment with a doctor the next day so we made arrangements for me to take over the coach after driving the horse van on to **Cozad.** After getting it parked in the shade by the city park, I located the mayor and some other people. We all went out and met the coach and I drove on to town so Joe could keep his appointment. **On the way in, Marge got some of the history of the town from one of our passengers**. *Seems that it was named for John J. Cozad who came from Ohio on the train. He saw the sign "100th meridian", got off the train and walked back, and established the town there. Later on, he was trying to get Cozad proclaimed the county seat. He got into an argument with another man over it, and he shot and killed him. He left town during the night and returned to the East and assumed another name. He was never seen in the West again.*

The mayor invited us to come down to the restaurant and the town provided lunch for us. While we were eating, the mayor mentioned that the City of Cozad also had a stagecoach. I understood it to be one of the Yellowstone Park Abbot-Downing coaches. We all were going to go take a look at it after lunch, but something came up and the mayor had to leave before we got to see their stagecoach.

The Overland Trail took its toll in many ways. Nature's rule, "Survival of the Fittest" was in force. It took a hardy breed to settle our country, and we all owe a great debt to our ancestors who did survive and overcame obstacles and tragedies such as this.

Marge wrote down a couple more stories of local history of the area as we traveled along in the coach.

6/9 – LEXINGTON to COZAD

Joe drove into Cozad. Red drove the truck, and I drove the Dodge. We parked on the street alongside the Park.

Went back and met the stage east of town at a little side park. Rode in with the mayor and some ladies. One of whom knew a great deal of the history of the town. I wrote it down as we went along. When we got to Cozad, the mayor took us to lunch at the café. I had a BLT and cherry pie with ice cream.

One story was about the famous red pump located at the Gilman Ranch between Gothenberg and Brady. This was the only pump on the prairie, and was a well-known stop for everyone who traveled along the Trail between 1858 and 1868. Another incident which probably isn't found in too many history books, concerns Ft. McPherson, which is south of Maxwell and close to Cottonwood Springs, which was also a well known stop for the pioneers. The people at the Fort got scurvy, and a load of them were put in a wagon. It was thought that if they might get out and get some fresh air, perhaps they could get over their illness. Unfortunately, they were attacked by Indians. Trying to escape, they went into Cottonwood Canyon. The driver of the wagon hid in the brush and was overlooked by the Indians, but the sick people were all killed.

We were met by a large group of officials at **Gothenberg** for the long ride through town and clear out to the north side to the rodeo grounds.

We turned and swung down a dirt road for the last quarter of a mile before we drew up to the corrals. My passengers were a joyous group that really seemed to enjoy the stagecoach ride; so I thought I'd give them something to really remember. **I let the horses out into a hard gallop the last quarter mile and rolled up to the rodeo grounds in a cloud of dust.** Charlie caught up with us again that night, and the next morning we picked up another load of that good COOP horse feed.

Joe drove the truck, and I drove the camper to Gothenburg. At edge of town, we stopped, and I told Joe it was awfully hot. Decided it would be OK until we got to the fairgrounds. Someone led us, and it was quite a ways through town, and up a long curving hill.

Dodge boiled over when I stopped. A man came up, said he'd been behind me and the wheels on the camper were putting out blue smoke. Waited awhile for stage and Red came in with a load of people at a full gallop. Drove them through the gate, and into the rodeo grounds. Couldn't turn them loose until after the roping. Rude woman manager of park got mad because I was parked across the exit and told me to move.

DAY SEVENTEEN
JUNE 10TH

Joe took the coach out that morning. They drove down by the <u>Gothenberg Stage station</u> and Pony Express stop, where they posed for pictures. It was a real hot sultry day. By the time I drove the horse van into **Maxwell,** the horses had been on the truck longer than usual, since I'd had to load the feed on after loading the horses that morning. They were pretty thirsty when we unloaded for our noon stop. There was a toe headed 12 year old boy there that pitched right in and was good help taking care of them. After a spell when we were both holding horses while they drank, I looked at the boy and says, "Say Podner, what's your name?" "Debbie Louise" was the reply. "Debbie Louise," I says, "Goodness gracious, I thought you were a boy." "Don't let it worry you," she answered. "Lots of people think I'm a boy."

After we'd all enjoyed a good meal in an air-conditioned building, we hooked up the fresh hitch, and I hauled all the local kids around town. Debbie rode "shotgun" the whole time.

Some members of the crew had a difference of opinion that afternoon, so we ended up leaving the horse van there with the extra horses tied to it. I planned on coming back for it later.

There is a highway scales between Maxwell and North Platte. It was open when we came by with the coach, so we drove in and "axled out" the coach, much to the delight of the scale master. That Santa Fe coach weighed about 3400 pounds that day.

The **North Platte** Bicentennial Chairman met us on the east edge of town and piloted us through the city. Since it was just a short ways out of the way, he suggested we might like to drive by Buffalo Bill's Headquarters Ranch. We stopped by their big barn and posed for pictures; then the

---

Since they charged to stay at the park, we moved camper into rodeo ground. Night was awfully warm. Ray sulked and wouldn't eat supper, because Red told him he'd left the hydraulic brake on the trailer, and that's why the Dodge overheated, and was smoking.

6/10 –
GOTHENBERG to NORTH PLATTE
Next morning Charlie came out. Red and Ray took the truck and loaded up grain that Charlie brought. I drove the Ford as pilot car. Saw a beautiful Palomino mare while driving the Ford. Clean limbed.

We stopped out in front of the Pony Express station, and they took pictures. When they finished loading grain, Red and Ray caught up with us, and I drove the Dodge, and Ray took the Ford. We drove on to Maxwell, and to the ballpark.

manager of the ranch climbed on the stage and rode on out to the fairgrounds to our camp with us. The afternoon had been oppressively hot, with thunderheads building up fast. Along about 5 P.M. the sky started to turn yellow-black. For anyone who's lived in that country, like Marge who grew up near Omaha, you'll know what I mean. She started looking for "twisters".

By the time we pulled out of Buffalo Bill's Ranch, the wind kicked up and the air cooled off, and those clouds started rolling and tumbling. I was sure it wouldn't be long before something really drastic took place. It was about two miles to the fairgrounds and I was determined to beat the storm there. **You bet I shook those lines out. From a swinging trot, we broke into a brisk gallop.** We made that two miles in less than eight minutes. **The wind was starting to blow, and it sure looked bad.** We unhooked from the coach in double time.

Before we were completely unhooked, the quarrel that had started that afternoon was renewed, this time dragging Tammie and me into it. The two men had been snarling at each other like a couple English bulldogs since we'd left St. Joe. I really needed both of them, but the only way I could see to settle the quarrel was to let one of them go. Since one had been my friend for 30 years, I told the other fellow he'd better get his stuff and pull out; I didn't have time to debate the matter. We still had those horses tied to the truck down at Maxwell, and I was worried what might happen if that storm hit down there as bad as it was moving in where we were. Joe said they'd take care of the hitch; so Tammie and I jumped in her pickup and roared off back down to Maxwell.

It was a real scorcher of a day. Potluck at the City Hall and we decided to go ahead and eat because some of the town folks had to go back to work. It was cool in the Hall, and we had another delicious dinner. Visited with several people while waiting for the stage to come.

Red went down to take care of horses while Joe, Tammie. Ray and boys ate. Afterwards I talked to Verna Taylor. She said she tried to get saddle clubs interested in our coming, but they had to do so much for the wagon train, they were rather hostile towards anything else. Also that it was hard to get different factions of Maxwell to work together.

Changed horses and Red drove stage, and took a load of kids through town. Said goodbye to Debbie and went to North Platte.

Right after I left, Marge told me later, Charlie showed up in his truck, and the kids ran down to the fence and told him how to get inside the fairgrounds. Marge and Joe had been unharnessing and tying up the horses, getting ready to water them. Due to the extreme heat of the day, they had sweat marks on them, and with the two mile gallop just before coming into the grounds, this had worked into streaks of salt lather where the harness had been. The horses also were thirsty, as they'd watered last at noon, before being hitched up, and they'd come somewhere between fifteen and sixteen miles in about three hours. It was after six o'clock so Marge went in the camper to start supper. Joe and Charlie led some of the horses over to water at the tank which was a small bathtub, partly filled with water. As they came up, the manager of the grounds turned on the spigot. The tub  was small enough, only three horses could drink at one time, and they emptied it; so he had to turn it on again. About that time, Marge came back out of the camper to help hold horses.

She was just in time to hear Charlie say, "You'd better watch your language." The fairgrounds manager started cussing then and said he'd never seen horses in such condition --- all covered with sweat and so starved for water they'd emptied the tub. Joe came up then and said, "Where I come from, language like that isn't used in front of women." Marge decided it was just complicating the situation with her around; so she handed her horses to the men, and turned around and started walking back to the camper. She figured the two men could take care of things.

As she left, she heard Charlie ask, "Have you got any horses of your own?" Then the lid really blew! Marge said the man got so loud and nasty she could hear him from inside the camper, which was quite a ways from the water tank. He was fast getting on the fighting side of Joe and Charlie. She couldn't imagine anyone not being able to get along

Every stretch brings a little more change in the country. While going to North Platte, the sky started to change color. It turned into a saffron color and became very weird. It looked like tornado weather, and we worried about it. Hoped we could get to town and find shelter before it hit.

Bicentennial man, who was co-owner of a TV station, met us and rode into town. He and another fellow took us out to Buffalo Bill's Scouts Rest Ranch where we posed for pictures; then went on to fairgrounds. When Red took kids for a ride, Joe asked Ray to help him load harness, and Ray told him to do it himself. We ended up leaving harness on the ground and horses tied up. Red and Tam went back to Maxwell.

with Charlie, as he was always laughing and joking and so agreeable; but Charlie was fighting mad inside of five minutes. About that time, the horses finished watering; so the men told this guy to talk to the boss when he got back with the truck, and they turned around and took the horses over to a temporary pen.

In the meantime, Tammie and I got back to Maxwell and loaded up everything and returned to North Platte. The storm had passed over and it looked like things were OK; that is, until we got back out to the fairgrounds. When I pulled into the grounds, Joe met me and said it looked like we could make a good corral if we used those two long buildings for sides, parked the truck in the opening at one end, and put our portable panels across the other end. It looked good to me; so I eased on around the buildings and up into the opening. I noticed some fellow in a pickup following me and watching closely, like he was afraid I didn't know how to drive and might tear the building down, but I never let it bother me. When I got out of the truck, this guy had parked his pickup and was coming across the lot towards me. Joe had already got there, and when he saw the fellow coming, he looked up through his eyebrows sort of sheepishly at me and gently said, "Watch this fella coming here, Red, he's a real kook. We've already had it out with him."

It takes a lot to rile me and especially on this trip it did. We weren't sponsored by anybody so we had no one's image but our own to look out for. We sure wanted people to be glad they'd met us and seen our outfit and want us to come back.

You can't leave that type of image behind you if you're quarreling with everybody down the road. I tried to ignore the warning Joe gave me, and met this guy with a grin, and a "Howdy". He jumped right in my middle, and started telling me he'd never seen a sorrier bunch of horses and a bunch of dudes that knew less about taking care of their horses properly than any he'd ever seen. It soon became hard not to punch him right in his insulting mouth. No matter what I tried to say, he knew more about everything than I could possibly learn in a lifetime.

I went over by horses and got the boys to help. When Red got into Fairgrounds at North Platte, Ray got mad and mouthed off at Tammie; then went back to Red and smirked at him. I walked up, (I'd gotten off coach by the camper) just in time to hear Red tell him he'd better get his stuff and pull out, and hear Joe say he'd had all of him that he could stomach.

Kip and I went back to the camper, and Kip stayed there while Ray loaded his stuff, went to the telephone, and finally walked off carrying his suitcase. Charlie drove in and kids ran to guide him. He and Joe were watering horses when the grounds' manager came over and blew up because they drank so much water; and said he'd never seen such poor starved horses, and that 6 of the 8 should never even be on the road.

By this time, "Fuse Box", as one of the kids had tagged him, was getting hotter and louder. He kept on insulting our "crowbait" horses, and telling me we would have to lay over there at least two or three days to rest these "crowbaits" up, and he threatened to call in the officials. **Finally, I'd had enough.** Instead of doing what I wanted to in the worst way, I merely asked him, "Do you belong to the Humane Society?" "No," he says, "But I can sure get the man out here that does." "Then you just do that, Mister, or anybody else you want; but right now get out of my way so I can get on with my work," I tells him with a cold stare. I guess he must have started to understand me a trifle by then as he stepped back out of my way and didn't bother me anymore.

When I asked Joe what had happened, he told me "Fuse Box" was supposed to be some kind of boss there at the fairgrounds, and that he'd showed up about the time they'd got the hitch horses unharnessed and were fixing to water them. When they drank 10 gallons or so apiece, he'd gotten all shook up to think we'd let them get so thirsty, and then when he looked at the sweat streaks on them he just knew we didn't know the first thing about a horse.

That afternoon had been one of the sultriest of the trip so far, and the hard run trying to beat the storm might have made that hitch look a little tough, especially to guys that have never really worked a horse, and just kept him in a stall and over fed and under-exercised him. Our horses are like athletes in training, and after a couple hours rest and feed, it was hard to pick out which ones had worked that last hitch.

When Charlie asked him if he had any horses, he really got mad and nasty. I walked up, but when the ruckus started, I turned around and left, figuring that Joe and Charlie could handle it. I couldn't imagine anyone not being able to get along with Charlie, but Charlie was fighting mad in less time than 5 minutes.

We herded the horses between barns until Red drove up with the truck, and fixed panels for one end. Horses sneaked out the other end. Kids had to chase them. Tam called Max (her horse), and he led others back in.

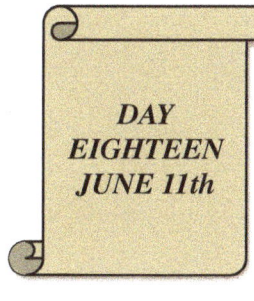

DAY EIGHTEEN
JUNE 11TH

The next morning, we were going about our preparations to get rolling as usual. We fed our horses and had our breakfast at our regular time. We had all the horses tied up in a long line, and had our portable corrals torn down. I was up in the horse van working on a piece of harness when a fellow drove up and got out of his auto. When he saw me, he stepped up and says, "Have you seen Mr ....,?'--- He's supposed to be around here someplace." "I don't know anybody by that name", I answered. "He works here" he says. "Oh him! You mean that man 'old Fuse box'? I haven't seen him this morning." "That's the man. I'm supposed to come look at some horses", was his reply. The newcomer's mouth twitched a little.

I waved my hand and said "There's the horses. Help yourself. But you better tell that fellow something if he's a friend of yours," I cooly states. "Not everybody from out in my part of the West is as even-tempered as I am. The next fellow he insults like he did me, might just up and shoot him." That man from the Humane Society and I looked one another straight on for quite awhile, each thinking our own thoughts, before he finally turns and goes over to our horses.

"Fuse Box", as Eddie named Ray, blew up again when Red got there, and got Tammie in it, and she mouthed off too. Red just told him to get out of his way and go call the Humane Society if he wanted. He did, and Red tells about it in his story.

Had meat pie for supper. Charlie was there. He left late, and we went to bed after an unpleasant evening. "Fuse Box" spoiled the effect of the nice North Platte guys who brought us a pickup load of fresh hay.

6/11 NORTH PLATTE
to SUTHERLAND
We moved everything at once from North Platte. Joe and Eddie on the stage, Kip and Wendy outriding. Tammie drove the pilot car, Red the truck. Pearl driving their rig, and me in the Dodge. Went to Hershey and couldn't find anything. Learned that the potluck was to be in Sutherland.

I just stopped my work and set and watched him. He walked around each horse examining each one thoroughly, before going on to the next one. He picked up several feet to look at the shoes. It took him 15 or 20 minutes before he came back up to where I was. He sure had a sober look about him as he came up to me. I asked, "Well, what do you say'?" "They look pretty good to me. One or two could use a little more flesh, but that bunch of horses sure look like a good healthy bunch of traveling horses to me." **I developed much respect for that Humane Society man right there.** As I let my breath out, I says, "Thanks", I guess we better get in gear so we can get on our way."

With a clean slate and a "Good Luck" from the ASPCA, our stage and horses pulled out, with heads and tails high, and all of us glad to be heading west in the early morning sunshine.

We had a slight mix-up that day at noon. We'd been corresponding with a preacher about a noon meal fixed by the Senior Citizens Club. The preacher lived in Hershey, and originally we had scheduled our noon stop to be there. When I got there with the horse van, I couldn't locate the preacher or where he was or a doggone thing. I was sure I had the day right, so I kept trying and finally located him in the next town west at a church there. They had had to change it to **Sutherland** instead of Hershey, and hadn't been able to contact us while we were traveling.

Drove back and told Joe. Went on to Sutherland, and talked to Reverend Bellas. Since it was late then, we decided to go ahead and eat. Tam came in, and said Fortune (our Morgan stallion) was sick; so Red took Bandito out to replace him. He, Kip, and Wendy came in to eat at 2:30. Stage got there about 3:30; so Joe, Tammie, and Eddie ate while Red took rides around the block.

One elderly lady told me how disappointed she'd been at the Wagon Train because nothing was authentic. She could remember riding in a covered wagon, and her mother cooking over a campfire. The people were so nice and pleasant, and the church was delightfully cool. They had a grand place at their rodeo grounds for us to stay. Water and electricity and pasture with good feed.

That was another six miles which wasn't far, but it was enough to make the coach an hour late for the meal.

    I had to backtrack and tell Joe, who was driving, to come on up to the right town. There was a large group of Senior Citizens there and I suggested they go ahead and eat and I'd eat with them. Then when Joe got in I could take the coach over and give rides while Joe and his crew ate. I'm sure those older people enjoyed riding around town in our stagecoach as much as any bunch of kids along the way. And I know we sure enjoyed that meal, as those ladies really did themselves proud that day.

    One of our passengers there was the wife of another preacher. She was fairly young, but she was totally blind. She said all she needed was for someone to guide her hands and feet. Marge helped her and she climbed in and out, and she thoroughly enjoyed the ride also. One lady asked if I'd mind driving by the Old Folks home up on the other edge of town on the next time around. She said she was sure the folks would enjoy seeing the stagecoach. As I'm a pushover for someone wanting to see our outfit, that's what we did. Quite a group of oldsters came out in the street to get a close look, and after a bit the young nurse there asked me if we could come back and give some of her "kids" there a ride when we finished with what we were doing. "Sure we will". When we got back there, we only had three takers, but we were highly honored to take them for a spin. They were **Blanche Smith, age 95, Allie Knowles, 89, and Edith Welch 88.** They hopped in and out of that coach with ease. **Most of our passengers that day were between 70 and 90 years old, or young.**

> Tam watched some girls run patterns. Red and Joe shod horses.
>
> I baked Kip's birthday cake, and Tam iced it. Got his birthday presents at the drug store in Sutherland. He was 12 years old on that Bicentennial stagecoach trip. Bought ice cream and had Joe and Pearl over for the celebration.

Kip's 12th birthday

    Those old timers really checked out the authenticity of our outfit -- coach, horses, harness, and us. They had grown up with horses and harness. The men were interested in the type of hook-up we used. They were glad to see a "real honest-to-goodness working outfit", and went on to tell me of some of the dude outfits that had passed through the area. The women were all surprised at the red velvet interior of the coach, and were pleased at the long dresses and hair style that Marge wore.

One lady asked if her hair was "real" or a wig. Marge replied, "It's real. You can pull it." Then she pulled one of the long curls out to its full length for her to inspect. *That same lady, who was a 19th century model, told Marge she could remember traveling in a covered wagon with her parents, and still picture in her mind her mother cooking over a campfire.* She had gone to see the wagon train when it came through and was very disappointed at its lack of authenticity.

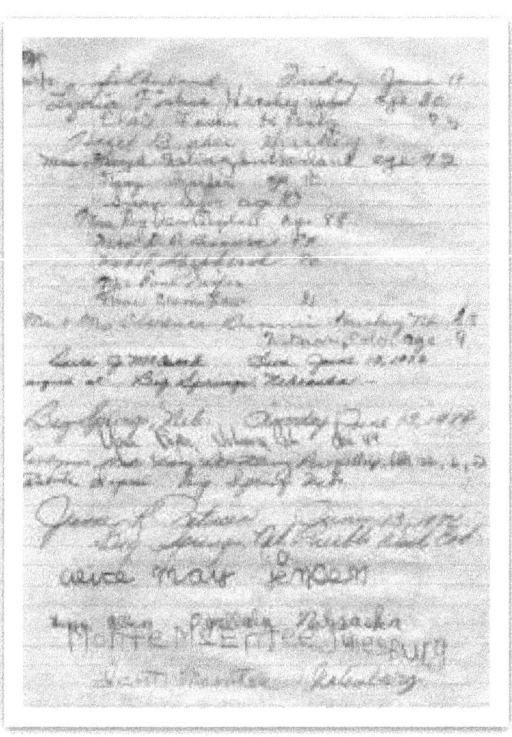

DAY NINETEEN
JUNE 12th

I pulled a boo-boo coming into **Ogallala**. It was a matter of time. The city officials were to ride in with us if they knew what time to expect us. By now, we could guess within a few minutes of how long it would take us. Anyhow, I told the mayor we'd hit town about 3:30. When we got there at that time, there was no one to meet us. Since Ogallala has an Old West Village in the east edge of town, we drove on in to it and stopped. Finally after quite a while, the mayor showed up. He acted surprised we were already there. He said he'd get on the phone and see if he could get the other people out. I noticed him studying his watch a time or two. Finally it dawned on me what was wrong. We'd crossed the time zone back down the road a ways, and I was still running on Central time while Ogallala was running on Mountain time. We were still an hour early.

We waited for the officials and then hauled them downtown where we left our strongbox at the bank. It was a little crowded downtown on a Saturday afternoon, but we did make a couple passes around the area hauling passengers, before going on out to our night's camp. Our plans called for us to lay over in Ogallala Sunday, and then go on to Big Springs Monday, June 14, to take part in their Flag Day celebration.

Late Saturday evening, The Bicentennial Chairwoman from Big Springs came to our camp and told us they had moved their celebration up a day and were having Congressmen and other dignitaries to speak and sure hoped we could come on over.

6/12 SUTHERLAND to OGALLALA

Red drove out on the stage. I was driving pilot car. Tam had the Dodge. They went ahead and stopped at a side rest area in front of a farm. Pearl fixed tuna sandwiches. Joe drove stage, and I drove Ford again in afternoon.
At Ogallala, the others met us and we parked the rigs ,and all rode the stage with the Bicentennial people, to the frontier town, and took pictures.
Took one load of people around town. When the officials came, we went to bank and unloaded the strongbox; then went to the auction yard to stay.

DAY TWENTY
SUNDAY JUNE 13th

Another "rest" day disappeared. Marge and I took the camper and horse van to **Big Springs** and Joe started out with the coach. The President of the rodeo club gave me permission to turn our horses loose in the rodeo club pasture. After I got things lined out, we went out to meet the coach and changed horses at the side of the road. Dick and his family from Pueblo West, where we'd stayed all spring, caught up and spent a couple days with us. After arriving at the park where the celebration was held, I spent most of the afternoon hauling kids around town. It was a real hot day, and we enjoyed homemade ice cream and cake, followed later by a barbecued beef picnic.

Before the ceremony started, I was asked if I'd say a few words about our trip, after the speeches were over. I agreed, and we all sat down on the lawn and curb to listen and watch. The program lengthened out, and the sun was very warm.

With my back resting comfortably against the curb and my hat pulled down over my eyes, I wasn't in any hurry to get up and speak. However, someone goofed, and the program went on uninterrupted to its finish. Now I admit, I did not hear a word that was said, and afterwards several people wanted to know why I hadn't told about the trip; but when the sounds of the general movement following the end of the program caused me to open one eye and peer out from under my hat, it was to behold Marge smirking at me like the cat that ate the canary; the kids crowing with delight; and Pearl triumphantly exhibiting a picture of me ---sound asleep on the curb.

After the evening's social activities were over, we went out to grain and check on our horses. When we got there, the rodeo club was just winding up an evening's roping. Somebody who seemed to be in charge, came prancing up to us and informed us that if those were our horses in their pasture, we'd have to move them or he'd call the sheriff and see what he could get done about it.

6/13 – OGALLALA to BIG SPRINGS
Joe drove coach, Tam drove Ford, Red on the truck, and me on the Dodge. Got to Big Springs and sat and waited while Red went to see where to put horses. McCombs came in with a new crew cab pickup. Finally went back with 2nd hitch, and changed horses at side of road.

Red drove the coach and Tam outrode. I drove the Ford to town. Then we got in coach and rode around town, giving rides.

Kids watched greased pig contest. We went to park and gave more rides. Had homemade ice cream at .25 cup, and cake at .20 a piece. Unhitched, and men took horses to rodeo grounds.

Well, earlier that afternoon a man who lived about a half mile from the rodeo grounds, had invited us to bring our horses over to his ranch for the night; but at the time, we'd already gotten permission to use the grounds so we'd turned them loose and fed them; and they seemed to be enjoying the rest. So we still had a place we probably could move to, but that wasn't the idea. Here it was almost 11 O'clock at night; we'd just put out fresh feed for them, and they were making the most of the relaxation. We thought we had gotten permission to stay where we were from the top dog himself, and here comes along a barking pup.

It took quite a while to convince him that we had contacted the president and the man who owned the land; and we didn't plan on moving at that time of night until we talked to those guys again. Finally, reluctantly, the fellow gave in; and then he became quite friendly. **Thankfully, our horses didn't have to change beds in the middle of the night.**

Had barbecued beef picnic at park. Everyone kind of kept to their own group. Program was afterwards. One ex-Congressman Whitney talked a little long.

Red went to sleep sitting on the curb, and Pearl took a picture of him. Although we were asked to speak, somehow they didn't include us. Afterwards while sitting in the camper, Mrs. Mueller came over, almost in tears, and said Joe had chewed her out because Red wasn't asked to speak. She felt bad about slighting us.

We got it straightened out; also about the caretaker at rodeo grounds who got hostile that night.

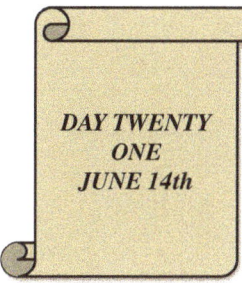

DAY TWENTY ONE JUNE 14th

CHAPTER SEVEN
ON TO COLORADO

DAY TWENTY-ONE
JUNE 14TH

The next morning, while part of the crew went back to Ogallala to retrieve the strongbox which we'd left at the bank Saturday**, the Frizzells showed up at our camp with our new stagecoach on their trailer. It sure was a beautiful sight.**

I guess it should have been for $27,250.00. It was quite different from the Santa Fe. The extra length of the 12 passenger style coach compared to the 9 passenger we'd been using gives the "Shasta" model a longer, more horizontal effect; whereas the smaller coaches have a vertical appearance to the bodies. It took quite a while to get used to the new longer lines of the coach and the difference in the feel of driving it; but we have been very proud to have the only usable "Shasta model Concord coach in the United States today.

6/14 BIG SPRINGS to JULESBERG CO. TV guys met outside of the city limits, and filmed left side of coach; then went around us and filmed the right side from the center of town. It was in the news; but we were too late getting back from supper to see it.

Tam and Pearl went to Ogallala for the strongbox. Then Frizzells came with the new coach. It looks pretty, but not as fancy as Fritz's, and the longer shape is quite different.

Finally got hooked up, and left for Julesberg. Joe driving and Tam outriding. DeLayne Frizzell ahorseback. She traded with Kip. I drove the Ford.

Wind and dust blowing very hard and it was miserable. We made one sashay through town, and on to the rodeo grounds.

NEW COACH DELIVERED JULESBERG, COLO. 6/15/76

Downtown Julesburg, Colo.

A storm was blowing in during the night, and by morning the wind was really whooping it up. Since we had only planned on going to **Julesberg, Colorado**, we fooled around until afternoon. We finally decided the weather wasn't going to improve much right away so we hitched up and headed for Julesberg. Joe drove the stagecoach. I took the horse van, and the Frizzells followed me with the new coach. When we got to Julesburg we were met by the local officials and a TV photographer. He got some good shots of the new coach and met Joe corning in with the other one. When they got into camp, Marge, who'd been driving the pilot car pickup that day, got out to tie up the leaders to the back end of it as we always did. **She doesn't weigh as much as a sack of spuds, and the wind was blowing pretty hard by then.** When she finally got the lead ropes undone, she had to hold them both in one hand and hang on to the tail gate of the pickup with the other hand to keep from being blown away. To top it off, she was wearing one of her long full skirted dresses as usual, and it was billowing out and flapping around those horses' legs. They were eyeing her kind of suspiciously as I came up to help her. I believe if it hadn't been for that pickup, she'd have taken off like a kite in a March wind.

Turned the horses out in a big pasture. Had camper parked close to a building for protection.

Went to a café for supper with Frizzells. Talked about coaches, and history of stagecoaching.

Had quite a night in camper. Wind rocked it like a boat at sea. Boys slept on floor of camper because weather was so bad.

The wind blew so hard that day that neither Joe nor I wanted our women folks bringing our campers over to Julesberg. Later, just before sundown, we drove back to Big Springs and brought them over. Several times, I sure thought I'd lost ours. The gusts would take me clear across the highway before I could get it back under control.

That evening after dinner, Joe and I were discussing, and cussing, the wind. Was it really bad out there, Joe?" I asked. "The damn wind pert near blowed the lines out of my hands several times," he answered. "That cross wind would just grab those lines and yank on them. Then the horses would think I was trying to turn them, and I'd have to pull them back to get back on my side of the road.

I must have drove a couple miles, just zigzagging back and forth across the road."

"I figured you must have had a heck of a time," I sympathized with him. "When I came along in the truck, I noticed several places where your tracks had blowed clean off the highway, over the fence, and were away out in the field, lodged up against a bank! I got a sarcastic look and a loud snort out of that, before we all busted out laughing.

Tarim Depot - Julesburg

**DAY TWENTY TWO
JUNE 15th**

DAY TWENTY-TWO – JUNE 15TH

The next day in Julesberg was quite an event. One stagecoach hitched up is a real sight. We had two. We rigged up the new coach, put six head on it, and circled it around the fairgrounds a few times. Then we hooked up four head to the old coach. With me driving our new one, and Joe driving the old one, all of our crew piled on and we went uptown. To the surprise of the townspeople, we paraded those two coaches around all afternoon, giving people rides and posing for pictures in front of their old train depot which is now a museum. We finally galloped back down the dirt road to the fairgrounds. It was getting late, and we still had to load the old coach on their trailer so Frizzells could head back to Oklahoma City that night.

6/15 JULESBERG LAYOVER

Unloaded our new coach, and hooked everything up. It wasn't as fancy as we expected, and was lacking a lot of things that Fritz's had, such as lamps, elbow straps, rear boot step, velvet on the back seats, curtain on the front boot, etc. Painting on side panel is pretty, but isn't signed.

After breakfast, we hooked up 4 head of mares to Fritz's coach, and 6 geldings to our new coach. Drove through town and down to the depot and took pictures of both coaches face to face in front of the depot. Took several loads of people for rides around town; then went back to fairgrounds and unhitched. Frizzells took us out for supper. Then we loaded up Fritz's coach and they left.

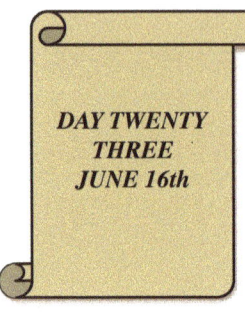

DAY TWENTY THREE JUNE 16th

DAY TWENTY-THREE JUNE 16TH

The next morning it was Joe's turn to drive. I sure hated not being up there on that box on that new coach of ours; but I very reluctantly looked the other way when he pulled out for **Sedgwick.**

Marge and I took the rigs on into Sedgwick. To our dismay, we found that the community had cancelled the buffalo barbecue they'd planned for us because I hadn't contacted them the day before and let them know we were right on schedule. We managed to get the news out around town, and a bunch of us went back out and met the stage and rode back into town with it. Right in the center of town, we got "held up" by some masked bandits, who robbed us of our strongbox. Since it was quite heavy, I had to hold it for the robber so he could get it balanced on his horse. Of course, I was forced at gunpoint to aid these "desperados".

We hauled several loads of people around and were heading for our camp at the rodeo grounds when the townspeople invited us to be their guests for lunch at the local cafe. It sure sounded like a winner to me. As we had to take care of our horses first, most of the town followed us on down to camp. When we got unhitched, someone behind the coach said something didn't look right with the back end of it. On examining it, **we discovered that the rear jack bolster was broken.** It's quite a wood machining job to make a new jack bolster fit, and install it. The only place I knew of that had the proper equipment to do the job was Frizzell's shop in Oklahoma City. That was a long ways off, and we were on a tight schedule. We just couldn't stand three or four days breakdown.

After looking it over, we figured how the bolster could be pulled back together and reinforced with some iron so it would probably hold together, and we could keep right on going until we got a new one from Oklahoma City.

6/16 JULESBURG to CROOK
Joe drove coach, Wendy rode Muskrat, and Tam in the pilot car. Red drove the truck, and I brought the camper to Sedgwick. We set up camp in a pasture at the edge of town. Then got in a pickup with a bunch of townspeople and went out to meet the stage. Several horseback riders had already joined up. We piled in and drove into the center of town and stopped. Opal Hewgley, city clerk, got in and we took three loads of people around the block.

The "bandits" robbed us of our strongbox, and Red had to hold it for the guy to get it balanced on his horse. Went on to pasture and unloaded. Got out and someone said that something was broken. Everyone looked, and the wood crosspiece over the rear axle was splintered and the end pushed up about six inches.

One of the fellas squatted down on his heels and looked up under the coach. He says, "I know a fellow that's got a machine shop that could make that brace and put that back together, and I'm sure he could do it right away." "I'd sure like to meet him," I answers. "You're looking right at him," he grins up at me. It was settled, we'd go eat lunch; then pull the coach over to his shop and see what could be done to get her fixed up.

The next town, **Crook,** had scheduled a big celebration for that evening, with the arrival of our Overland Stagecoach as one of the highlights of their program. I called them, and told the lady in charge we'd had a breakdown, but we'd be there before sundown. We agreed they'd go ahead with everything, and we'd join in when we arrived. The Sedgwick people felt bad about the mixup at noon that day. By the time we got to the machine shop after lunch, a group of them approached me and were having their buffalo barbecue that evening.

They wanted us to stay that night and not leave until morning. I sure hated to tell them that we couldn't, but the bad part about planning a schedule like ours is that you have to maintain it. Their reply was that it would be at least 3:30 before they would finish with the coach, and that it was over 20 miles on to Crook. We couldn't possibly get there until way late in the night. I smiled and answered, "If we get hooked up by 4 o'clock, we can make it in real good shape." Reluctantly, our friends there in Sedgwick said, "Well, if you guys won't stay here with us, then we'll go to Crook with you." And that's just what they did.

Got the coach fixed and took off again about 4:30. Red drove, and I rode in the coach. Townspeople brought the pilot car and our camper. Bob Price and two boys rode with us. Wendy rode Juliet, I think.

We got into Crook just before dark. Took five loads of people for rides around the block. Had 76 on inside, not counting me. Bob and boys robbed the stage 3 times. Almost dropped the box once. Scared one little toddler, and she cried and said, "What are they going to do to me?"

When it got too dark, I went over to eat, and Red took the coach down to unhitch. There were 300 people at the picnic. They had already eaten and had their flag ceremony. The lady in charge made sure we had plenty of food. Rest of the crew finally came to eat. Red made some phone calls. We drove camper down by corrals in a grassy lot with beautiful trees.

With much discussion, and at least a couple cases of beer, we got that bolster fixed, and the coach put back together. **At least half the town had spent the afternoon helping us repair that coach.** At about 4 O'clock, several of them saddled up their horses, and quite a number loaded on the coach and we galloped out of town heading west. **If you've never sat up on top of a swaying stagecoach rolling behind a fiery six horse hitch in a gallop, you just haven't lived.** And gallop we did. I felt kind of sorry for some of our escort riders trying to keep up with us. A saddle horse really has to work hard to keep up with a galloping stagecoach hitch. I really enjoyed myself though, spending that afternoon with those good friends, loping down the highway on a hot summer day.

We rolled into Crook about 6:30 and joined their party by picking up a load of big-eyed kids and circling the city. When we returned down by the park, a group of masked desperados rode out from behind some buildings, to the kid's delight. There seemed to be something really familiar about that group. Their horses matched the ones our escorts were riding that afternoon. Each time we got a new load of kids that evening, we'd get held up again.

"I believe we set some kind of a stagecoach holdup record that night. As far as I know, we are the only stagecoach in history to be held up five times in one day!"

It was way after dark when I got the horses put up and was 11:30 when I got back to the park and got a plate of cold food they'd saved for me, but it sure was good. <u>It had been a long hard day over the coach breakdown with some big disappointments; but so many people had taken part in our trip and seemed to enjoy it that it all seemed to make it worthwhile.</u>

We heard another interesting story that day…

Seems the grandfather of one of the Sedgwick people had been a freighter in the old days, first to Forts McPherson and Laramie, then later to Denver City for Russell, Majors, and Waddel from 1855 to 1861. He ran the first mail stage station, "Camp Cottonwood", in the summer of 1859. This was located about 2 miles south of Ovid and 10 miles east. In his words, "Grandfather always kept his rifle on two pegs over the door. He was down at the barn and he heard shooting at the stage station. Both Slade and Jules were there and they'd gotten into a fight. Jules was unarmed, and Slade shot at him six times with a revolver.

Then he got Grandfather's rifle down from over the door and shot Jules with it. When Grandfather got up to the station, Slade was chasing Jules with the rifle, trying to hit him over the head with it. Grandfather grabbed a neck yoke, let Jules run by, and hit Slade over the head with it. He yelled for some men to bring rope and they tied Slade up. They hoisted a wagon tongue to hang him, but Slade had too many friends around. They finally told him to get out of camp. Old Jules lived. Grandfather always sympathized with Jules. That fall, four or five armed men came into camp looking for Grandfather, but he'd already left. He went back to Nebraska.

DAY TWENTY-FOUR- JUNE 17TH

Joe didn't want to drive the coach the next morning so I took it. One of the local ranchers watching us hitch up sure seemed interested so I told him to come and go for a ride with me. "Next time", he says. **"We only plan on doing this every hundred years," I told him, "so maybe you better go now."** He thought it over a minute, then calls to his wife he's not going to ranch today, he's going to go on the stagecoach, and for her to come pick him up around noon in the next town.

We were out of town moving along when he told me that he'd ranched up in Montana, and they always fed with horses in the winter. He said they usually used four head on their wagons, and he'd driven four a lot but never six. When he mentioned that he'd always wondered what it was like to handle six, I answered him by handing him the lines.

He did real good. We weren't traveling very fast, and there were times he had trouble keeping all his lines even, but he was enjoying himself, even though his hands were getting tired. I let him drive on for about ten miles.

I suddenly realized it was almost noon, and we were due in **Iliff** at noon for a community meal. I took back the lines and we hit a high trot on into town. It looked like it might rain that afternoon so we took all the kids for rides around town before unhooking for lunch. Lucky we did as a good gentle wet soaker was coming down when we came out. I noticed Marge had some mud on the shoulder of her dress when she came in to eat. Since she'd been driving the pickup behind the coach, I wondered how she'd gotten it. When I asked her, she made a wry face.

6/17 CROOK to STERLING
The sun shining through the trees on the horses was so pretty. I tried to get a good picture, but they kept moving around. Finally took one of Pearl and the colt. Red drove the coach. I drove the Ford. It clouded up and started misting.

Two girls rode with us, and a St. Bernard dog came with them. He was weak in the back legs to start with, and by halfway, he was lagging a half mile behind, and the girls went off and left him. I stopped and called him. He finally came, after running in the ditch water several times, trying to drink and cool off. He looked like he was about to collapse; so I put him in the pickup. He was so weak I had to lift his hind end in. I knew I couldn't get him in the back of the pickup, so put him in the seat, mud and all. What a mess!

Seems she'd noticed a dog following our outriders as we came out of town. It was a big St. Bernard, and that type of dog isn't built to follow horses. The further we went, the farther behind he got. He seemed to be following one girl in particular, but she went off and left him. Marge finally stopped the pickup and waited for the dog to catch up. He was so hot and tired, he walked through the ditch water as he came, trying to cool off and drink. When he got up to her, he fell down. He was wheezing and rattling in his chest. Marge said she knew she couldn't get him in the back end of the pickup; so she opened the door to let him in the front. He was too big to fit down on the floorboard and he pawed at the seat, trying to clamber in. He was so weak, she had to lift his hind end in. When she got back in on the driver's side, she said she had to squeeze in. He took up the whole front seat. His head was on her shoulder and his rear against the right door. His feet were in her lap, and he was lying on her white scarf and gloves. Mud and water everywhere. When she started driving, he collapsed on his side and lay there rattling with every breath. She had to open the window because of the wet fur smell. After half an hour, he finally raised his head up, and then he gradually got better.

As they got closer to town, the girl he'd been

following ahorseback, dropped back between the coach and the pickup, as she was getting awfully tired. When the dog saw her, he sat up and started barking. When the pickup came up close by this girl, the dog stood up in the seat, turned around to face her, and got Marge right in the face with his wet, muddy tail! Marge didn't tell me what she thought about then, but she said she let the dog out at the first place she could. When she got to Iliff she found out the dog didn't even belong to the girl.

> He filled it with his head by my back, and his rear against the right door. Muddy feet on my dress, and all over my scarf, white gloves, and purse. He just collapsed on his side, and rattled in his lungs, and slobbered. I had to open the window because of the wet fur smell. After ½ hour or so, he finally raised his head. The younger girl riding was very sore and tired. She kept dropping back behind the coach. Made it hard for me to drive as she'd stop right in front of me.
>
> When we were almost to town, the dog brightened up enough to bark when the girl was close, and finally stood up and turned around; and got me in the face with his wet tail. I let him out a little later.

I went on out to help hook up and Marge stood on the steps and talked to several of the women. One, a Mrs. Garfield, told her of having ridden a stagecoach out of Denver, I believe. She was about seventeen at the time, and was going out to stay at a ranch. She said seeing our coach really brought back the memories.

Joe drove the coach out. I took the horse van on into **Sterling**, rounded up some officials, and we met him and all rode in together. Our Sedgwick friends showed up again and brought along the buffalo bull head that they'd butchered, and we hadn't got to help eat. Our kids talked them out of the head, which created a problem a few days later when the weather warmed up.

A large crowd was waiting at Iliff. Vera Burming and some others rode into town with us. Tam had brought the camper, and Joe, the truck. Parked in the school ground across from the Lions Club Hall.

It was raining; so I got out slickers and my parasol. Had a lovely dinner and sat next to a lady who was very interested in the trip. Red finally got in to eat. Some kids asked me to sign their autograph books.

Joe drove the coach out, and I followed with the pickup. Wendy rode with me. It rained off and on. We went on to Sterling and unloaded horses at the Fairgrounds. County Commissioner and Mr. And Mrs. Corbett rode. Got in at 5:15, and waited for reporters who didn't get there until about 6:30. Still raining, and turning cold. I went in the camper and slept. Rest of them stood out in the rain and talked.

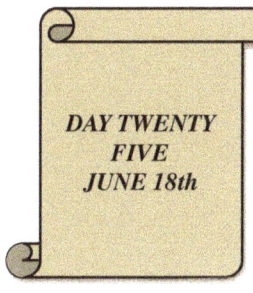

DAY TWENTY-FIVE
JUNE 18TH

I'm not claiming Joe liked to get his picture taken, but the next morning when I told him the Denver Post reporter and photographer were planning on meeting us to do a picture story on us --- well, he was able to drive again even if it was raining. We had a good morning with those two people. They followed us with their car and on the coach for about ten miles and wasted a lot of film.

One of the pictures they used in their paper happened like this: Joe was driving and I was riding shotgun. The camera man had completely disappeared. Joe decided he needed a smoke so he asked me to drive while he rolled himself one. Suddenly, out of nowhere, there was the camera pointing at us again.

Sure enough, when the newspaper came out, in one of the pictures, there I was sitting in the shotgun seat doing the driving.

Bob Price came in and bought one silver and one bronze medallion. Had a big box of fried chicken from Iliff. Put a heavy quilt on the bed because it was so cold.

6/18 – STERLING to BRUSH
Reporter and photographer from Denver Post came out and interviewed us, and took pictures. Joe drove the coach out I rode stage with Pearl and lady reporter.
It was cool so we had windows up most of the way. Went through Merino, since they felt their community was too small to find a place for us to stop at noon.

Stopped by an old stagecoach marker and took pictures. Tried to get Joe to stop for lunch. Red drove by him with the truck and stopped at a narrow crossroads. It was a bad place, but we parked vehicles.

Strange things happen on a trip like this. We had a real hard time getting mail delivered to us in any orderly type of fashion. **Some of our mail was two or three weeks or even a month old before it caught up with us.** We had written the town of Morino requesting that we'd like to stop in their town for our noon break and change of horses. Their answer came back that they were sorry, but they couldn't accommodate us. They didn't have any place we could stop to change horses, and theirs was a farming community and they couldn't take time off at noon at that time of year. Marge wrote back and thanked them and said we'd go on and change outside of town somewhere as we didn't want to be a bother to anyone. Their letter was so definite, we didn't try to get in touch with them again as we came through Colorado.

We picked out a wide place along the highway on up the road a ways, where we had our noon camp and changed horses. Marge said she'd noticed the people in the town looking from the restaurant windows as they passed through town, with a quizzical look as if they were wondering why the stagecoach didn't stop. A couple weeks later our mail was delivered to us again, and in it was a letter from the town of Merino. **Seems they'd worked things out and would like for us to stop in their town for our noon stop -- too late.**

"This was before cell phones, pagers, and the internet.
Our entire communication on this trip was done through CB radios and pouring coins into pay phones.
What is a payphone?"

Joe refused to drive the truck, and insisted on driving the geldings. Red rode with him a little ways, then got off and went back after the truck.

I changed with Tammie when she came up with the camper, and we went on to the Port. Red chewed me out for parking on the wrong side of the road there. Went on to Brush and he didn't have his CB on, so I couldn't give him the directions, and he missed the turn. Had to double around through a farm yard and go back to the right road. Got to the Fairgrounds. Then went back to the coach, and Red took over. Took some passengers and drove down Main, and delivered the strongbox to the bank and took a lot of pictures. Then drove to Fairgrounds, and unhitched. Lots of people visited.

Joe suggested that I take the horse van on into **Brush** that afternoon so he could drive the stagecoach again, even though we'd just hooked up my hitch of geldings. Instead of arguing with him, I agreed that when I rounded up the officials, I'd come back to meet him and would take the coach on into town. We had a good load of city officials with a police escort when we rolled into the edge of town. Shortly after we got past the truck scales, our police escort car had to leave us to answer a call. That caused us some trouble later on.

A few more blocks toward town, we were met by the Black Powder Gang of Brush's mountain men, dressed in full fringed buckskin costumes. They piled

on, and we drove by the bank and left our strongbox, then circled town a few times before heading toward the fairgrounds. While we were still downtown, one of our mountain men wanted to know if they could shoot their musket. Several riders on the coach

Finally went in to eat after dark, at a Drive In. Had a burrito, coffee, and hot fudge sundae.

Tam went to make a phone call, and didn't come back, so we took her supper and went looking. Found her several blocks down the street still on the phone.

Went home and to bed.

instantly answered, "No", for me, but that wasn't what I thought. I said, "Sure, if you tell me when you're ready to let her off. But wait till we get through this main intersection first." I wasn't as worried about the intersection as I was about the pickup just immediately ahead of us.

If the gun was real loud, and the team lunged, we might land right in the back end of that pickup. I used the intersection to maneuver in the clear, then called back to the gunners, "Let her rip!" "Kerboooom!" she roared in a big cloud of blue smoke. I'd gathered in all the slack from the lines and had a good perch on the brake; so what little lunge the horses made didn't amount to much. One of the other mountain men asked, "Can we let off another charge?" "Sure enough, anytime you're ready!" We had a good clear road ahead of us so when the horses perked up after the second explosion, I let them trot right on out to camp.

When we rolled into the fairgrounds, I noticed our former police escort followed us in. I had some trouble getting turned around as I'd driven into a boxed-in area that was almost too small to turn around in. Finally I realized that the city officials that had ridden in with us on the coach were having a heated discussion with the cop.

When we finally got the horses tied up and unhooked, this cop ordered me over to his car and jumped right on me for running a red light down town.

I told him I knew what light he was referring to, but when we'd started through, it had been green. The more the city officials tried to pacify the cop, the more indignant he became.

He then informed me that not only had we run the red light, but furthermore, there had been about 5 kids on bicycles following along behind us. They all had also run the red light, and he felt if we were going to tow a bunch of kids like that around town, we had to look out for them. I didn't know the kids were behind us and furthermore, I didn't feel I had any control over them anyway. When he started in on me again, I finally turned the tide by saying "It looks to me like that if you were so concerned through town you could have controlled the kids." The cop started to stammer an excuse and immediately the city officials realized it was their turn. They pounced right on him, wanting to know, "Yeah, where was our police escort you promised us?"

It was now the cop's turn to get drug over the coals as he tried to claim he'd come to give us an escort, but the city boys hadn't known the cop had been there, and they were really giving him a bad time. I finally came to his rescue, telling them that the cop had been there, but he'd been called to answer an emergency call. The cop was relieved when I sided up with him so he let the red light issue drop. Everything was finally patched up when the cop said if I'd call them in the morning to let them know what time we planned on leaving, they'd escort us out of town.

DAY TWENTY-SIX
JUNE 19TH

They were good for their word, too, as we had two police cars escort us out of town the next morning. We didn't get out of town very early that morning as we were having trouble with a front wheel on our new coach. I had to pull it off and take it downtown to a welding shop and get some repairs done on it.

Jack and his family and Charlie showed up that morning. Also, our friends and neighbors from Wetmore had reserved the ride from Brush to Fort Morgan, so we had a full load going out. In **Fort Morgan**, we parked the coach and horses at an empty service station lot and all had lunch together at the 'Colonial Inn". While we were there, Dr, Berckley's father caught up with us. He had come to pick up the two horses we'd borrowed from Doc in Seneca, Kansas. Instead of giving "Red" and "Robby" back to him, we bought and paid for them right there. After a good lunch, we circled downtown, just in time to fall right in place in their parade, which we'd been invited to quite awhile back. We then went out to our camp for the night.

6/19 – BRUSH, CO. to FORT MORGAN Morrises showed up early and Thompsons. Tam and girls took off to get showers and didn't get back until we were about ready to leave.

Left late, about 11:00 or 11:30 as Red had to work on a wheel. Red drove with Reed Morris on top. Geneva, Jean Morris, and I rode inside. Charlie drove the Ford, and changed off with Jack. Tam rode Max.
Joe and Pearl drove to Fort Morgan and found a place at a saddle club arena to keep the horses. We took the stage into town. Parked stage at a gas station lot across from the Colonial Inn. Loaded up, got police escort to depot for VFW parade. One man rode in parade with us. Crowd seemed to like us. Afterwards we went out to the arena and unhitched.

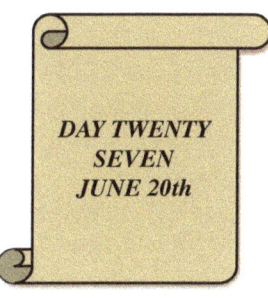

**DAY TWENTY SEVEN
JUNE 20th**

CHAPTER EIGHT

COLORADO HISTORY

DAY TWENTY-SEVEN
JUNE 20TH

Sunday morning, June 20, found us staying around camp for a day's rest. We had a potluck picnic in the park with our Wetmore friends; followed by a church service conducted by Reverend Shotwell, our minister at Wetmore. He spoke about Dr. Harcus Whitman, the first missionary to the Northwest about 150 years ago. *Dr, Whitman and his wife were the first party to take wagons across the Rocky Mountains. Years later, they were massacred by the Indians.* We had a good visit with our friends. We had planned this weekend before we left Wetmore in the spring.   Here it was, June 20th, and we were about 600 miles on our trip, and they'd come up to share a day on the Overland Trail with us.

6/20 – FORT MORGAN (layover)
Everything was very confused. Shotwells and Grays arrived, and no one knew where to eat or hold services. Finally decided on a park north of Freeway.

Got there about noon, and had a nice church service at a picnic pavilion with a roof. Wore my yellow dress. Reverend Shotwell talked about Dr. Marcus Whitman, the first missionary in the Northwest.
Had a potluck afterwards. Herons parked across the road and stayed in their camper.

After dinner, visiting and pictures. The Wetmore People left. Thompsons took kids swimming. We went back to the arena . Did chores and ate late. About ½ hour after we got to bed, John Frizzell came in with the other coach.

When we got back to camp from the picnic, we found a bunch of kids had apparently eaten their lunch in the coach. There was water spilled all over the red velvet back seat, and scraps of hamburgers and food scattered around the inside.   They'd also gotten into a satchel I kept in the front boot, and had turned its contents upside down.

It seems that in the 1930's the sheriff had been out in the Twin Lakes area near Leadville, Colorado on a fishing trip. He spotted a Concord stagecoach very similar to ours, sitting by a ranch house. He stopped to look it over, and a lady came out to visit with him. She told him that she had driven as a stagecoach driver for the government park service up in Yellowstone, and this was the coach she'd driven. When the government had decided to close out their stagecoach sightseeing tourist business, all the equipment had been put up for sale. She had bought that coach. The sheriff tried to buy the coach from her, but she wouldn't part with it. He did leave his name with her, with the promise that if she ever changed her mind, she'd get in touch with him. Several years later, the sheriff said he'd picked up a two month old newspaper one day, to pass the time while waiting on something. In the paper was a story about this lady stagecoach driver. She had died, and her estate, including the stagecoach and harness, and all her other possessions, had been sold at public auction some time ago. The sheriff said he sure was disappointed at having missed being able to get that coach.

When we finally got everything sorted out from the tools and other things I kept there, I was happy to find out nothing was missing.

In the afternoon, one of our stagecoach visitors was a local rancher who had been the sheriff in that area for a number of years. He noticed our hay supply was getting pretty low and mentioned he had about enough on hand to fill our hay storage area on the back of the horse van. I bought the hay at market price, but when I went to pay for it, he gave me a good discount as a donation from him to help on our trip.

I am always a good listener when someone has any kind of a stagecoach story to tell.

We'd had so many problems with our new stagecoach between Julesberg and Brush, that I had called Frizzells. After talking it over, we decided the best thing to do was for them to bring the Santa Fe coach back up to us to use while they took our new coach back to Oklahoma City to make the necessary changes and repairs on it. Big John rolled into Fort Morgan with the other coach Sunday night.

DAY TWENTY EIGHT JUNE 21st

DAY TWENTY-EIGHT
JUNE 21ST

When Monday morning came, I couldn't resist hooking up both coaches for the day's trip to **Wiggins. We had quite a private little parade of our own that day. We had two six horse hitches hooked to two Concord stagecoaches, and five outriders along**. That made 17 of the 18 grown horses that we had along, in use. I thought it was quite a sight.

6/21 - FORT MORGAN to WIGGINS
Red hitched up both coaches. Romeo and Holly Ann, Buddy and Romal, Bandito and Red Horse on ours. Houlihan and Sunny Ann, Roulette and Robbie, Fortune and Suntan on Fritz's coach with Joe driving and Pearl riding shotgun. Tammie rode Max, Kip was on Rebel, Wendy on Muskrat, and Eddie on Bandito.

Police escort through town with his wife and son riding in coach with Dickie and me. Went on Interstate for the first time. Was bad as the traffic whizzed by, and were only interested in where they were going. Mostly they didn't have time to slow down and look. Turned off and cut across Meridian and through ¼ mile of heavy sand. Then went the wrong way down an entrance ramp, and onto another highway towards Wiggins.

We went on the interstate for the first time, and that traffic really whizzed by. I think the people were more spooked by it than the horses though, especially when we got to the Wiggins turn-off and got fouled up somehow. I finally had to cut across the meridian and run down the bar pit through a quarter mile of heavy sand, which was a pretty good pull on the horses. Then we went the wrong way down an entrance ramp, and finally got onto the other highway that led to Wiggins.

Just outside of town, we were met by a 4 pony hitch of Shetlands pulling a steel tired covered wagon. They led us into town with a police escort blowing their siren full blast, and they turned on the fire whistle when we got to the "downtown' part.

Wiggins had scheduled their Bicentennial celebration to coincide with our arrival. They have a community event regularly every year, and ordinarily have 5 to 6 hundred people turn out. The last count I heard at their barbecue that afternoon they had served 890 people, and quite a few filed through after that. I'd planned on taking rides around town after lunch. I was one of the last to eat, and when I got back outside, I found all the horses unharnessed and turned loose. I was a little put out, and embarrassed, as I felt that quite a few people there would have liked to have ridden on the coach that day. We loaded our new coach on Frizzell's trailer to send it back that afternoon. **I sure hated to see it go.**

We drove both coaches to the Community Hall, lined them up side by side for pictures; then face to face, then at a slant side by side; and unhitched.

The barbecue was almost over; so Red wanted to leave the horses harnessed and go eat, and give rides afterwards. When we got back out, Joe had unharnessed everything and turned the horses loose.

DAY TWENTY-NINE
JUNE 22ND

Joe missed the turn the next day going out of Wiggins, and found himself back out on the interstate going west, when he should have been going north. Marge had the maps with her; so they decided they could duck across the bar pit and go up the frontage road to the next crossroad going north, and then pick up the right highway. Later, they talked to a farmer fixing fence along the highway, and verified they were on the right road. Wendy was outriding, and at the junction, a half-grown German Shepherd pup started following her. He was very friendly and looked like he'd been lost for quite awhile. The kids fed him and loaded him in the pickup, with the idea of keeping him. They'd already named him "Scalawag" or "Wag" for short. I had to turn grizzly bear and turn real hard-boiled that night. I reminded them we already had three dogs with us and didn't need anymore. They finally found a local rancher who liked him and said he'd take him to his ranch; **so Wendy tearfully gave him up that night.**

The country through here shows quite a change again. There are trees along the river banks, irrigated hay and corn in the fields, and sandy pastures with clumps of cactus appearing here and there. Starting to climb, with a series of low hills. Even some windmills, and big pastures with cows kegged up under the trees. The morning was hot and sticky. When I got to **Deerfield** with the horse van I decided to wait until Joe showed up with the stage.

As hot as it was, I figured it was a good place to offer the hitch horses a drink, and the coach passengers could probably stand a pop. The station man at Deerfield had the water trough all ready for the horses when Joe rolled in.

6/22 – WIGGINS to GREELEY
Joe drove coach and I rode inside. Tam was in the Dodge. Warm sunny day with a nice breeze. Wendy rode Bandera, and Eddie slept in coach until Masters. Country is changing again. Trees along the river, irrigated hay and corn fields, and sandy pastures with cactus. Cloud banks are hiding the mountains. Starting up a series of low hills. We'll probably be climbing pretty steadily for the next couple weeks. A lovely wide river bottom off to the north. Wide pastures with windmills on the south, and cows under a tree here and there. Red and the campers were stopped at a crossroads, for a change of horses. It was terribly hot when we left. Wind started coming up during the afternoon, and it gradually clouded over. Buddy (horse) was full of vinegar and kept spooking and trying to run off.

Everybody in that small community was as thrilled over the stage stopping there as they must have been 110 years ago when it came through.

I called Greeley and let them know we'd be in on time. Also found out they were sending a photographer out to do a story. We were planning on making our noon camp about 7 or 8 miles up the road at a wide place. Somehow, I missed it. I did see a good private looking gravel road at the top of the next raise. It looked like a good place to stop and change horses; so I took a chance that we wouldn't get into trouble and turned in. We had the relay horses unloaded and watered; and I was shoeing one when a fellow in a pickup drove in. He didn't act real upset, but did want to know what was going on. I apologized for not having contacted him before we arrived there, and said I would have, but just didn't know who to get ahold of. He wanted to know all about what we were doing. After I explained our trip to him, he became quite friendly and assured me we were not hurting anything. He even offered to help us if there was any way he could.

> We got that same hospitable reaction almost the entire trip. Every time, it made us and our rerun of the Overland Trail feel appreciated. We tried not to take advantage of it by imposing on anybody.

Joe wanted to drive my hitch again that afternoon, but I took the lines, and Marge climbed up on the box with me. It was terribly hot, oppressively hot, and the clouds started building up fast. The wind started kicking up, and the pressure was making the horses spooky, You could tell something was brewing; the horses became edgy and hard to hold down. The best medicine I know of at a time like that is to let them get out and travel. Maybe you can tire them out enough so that if something does happen, you have a chance to be able to keep them under control. By late afternoon, we were crossing a small marshy valley on a road fill that was probably about 10 feet high, but real steep on both sides. It was about one-half mile across the fill, and the horses were really up against the bits; so I was letting them out in a pretty high trot.

Photographer from the Greeley paper took pictures and rode part way. He was up ahead, waiting for us at a junction. The wind was blowing in gusts, and we came to a fill on the highway with a deep bar pit. Something scared Buddy, and he lunged and hit Romeo, and scared him. They both bolted and down off the bar pit we went. The coach tipped way over before Red got them turned back up on the highway. They were all running at a full gallop, and only the pull kept the coach from going over. I had to hang onto the railing with both hands to keep from going off. After everything stopped, and we pulled on up to the junction, the photographer said he thought he got some good shots. That was our first runaway! Was still raining and only a few people were there so we unhitched.

I knew I had trouble when the lead team looked off out to the left and commenced snorting towards a great big old fallen bleached out white trunk of a cottonwood tree.

My near swing horse, Buddy, was always looking for a chance to do something, and he found it, right quick. About this time, in the pasture slightly behind us and off to our right, a bunch of loose horses spotted us and came on a hard run to inspect the odd-looking contraption rolling down the highway. The sound of those galloping horses was all Buddy needed. He suddenly lunged and hit the rear end of the leader in front of him. Those leaders hit a hard shying gallop to the right. I was prepared as much as could be. I had my foot on the brake, and I'd worked my left hand down my near lines as far as possible. When they shied, I jabbed the brake full forward and hauled in with all my might, mostly on the near leader. At that, **we ran quite a ways at a hard gallop, barely able to hold the horses and coach on the exact edge.** The fill ended suddenly at the edge of the marsh, into a gentle rolling sandy-looking bar pit, with a slight up-grade. Kip was on his horse up ahead of us. Up to this time, I hadn't yelled to him for any help as I really didn't want anything in my way until I got off that fill.

When we came off, all six horses were in a dead run. It was steep and the coach was really leaning. I had both hands full of lines and Marge had two hands full of railing!

It was a toss-up whether or not we'd tip over, but the horses were pulling so hard forwards, we stayed upright and dropped off into the level. When we hit the sand, I squalled at Kip and he did real good. He dropped right back beside the near leader and crowded the lead team over into the right bank. With the steep bank they were trying to climb, and the sand, they stopped. And I mean stopped! The coach wheels were six inches deep, and these leaders almost fell over backwards.

I almost had a problem holding the swing and wheel teams off the bank as I hurriedly swung the leaders back off to the left and straightened out. The horses had worked off their steam by the time we got through the sand and reached the head of a slight grade.

There I noticed a fellow with a camera flagging us to a stop. It was the Greeley newspaper reporter. He said he'd gotten some good pictures, and he climbed on the coach and rode quite a ways with us. **I got the impression that he never realized he had just witnessed with his camera quite a stagecoach runaway.**

At least none of the runaway pictures ever showed up anywhere.

We proceeded at a more leisurely pace toward town. Those horses settled down as innocent as if they'd never had any other idea in their heads. The weather got steadily worse, so Marge finally got inside the stage.

It looked like the whole landscape was moving. Thunder and lightning soon lit up the sky. She fastened down the side curtains, and I donned my slicker. The cloudburst caught us just as we came into **Greeley**. At first I kept on driving into the rain. Finally it came down so heavy and the wind blowed so hard that I couldn't hold the lead team into it any longer. **Then one of those wonderful big old cottonwood trees, which had almost caused us a disaster earlier, saved us**. Up ahead, and off to the left in an open lot, it stood with its big branches like a giant umbrella. It sure was a relief to both me and the horses to pull under it and sit out the rest of that storm.

The head gal, Christine, had met us just before the rain hit. She climbed in with Marge and told her husband he could drive their car back — she wouldn't miss riding in our stagecoach for anything. While we waited under the cottonwood tree, Christine called the city officials from a nearby phone. They decided it was too wet and rainy to venture out; so as soon as our police escort showed up, we galloped almost all the way across town to the Fairgrounds and our night camp. After sitting hunched up there in that cold freezing rain, it felt good to both me and the horses to get a little high speed action and warm our blood up a bit.

Because of the cold and the rain, we didn't get to meet many of the Greeley people and didn't give any rides that night.

DAY THIRTY
JUNE 23RD

The photographer showed up again the next morning and took some more pictures, and then Joe pulled on out with the coach. **Windsor, Colorado** is another town that took advantage of a deserted train depot. When the railroad mentioned tearing it down, the town talked them out of it, and made it into a museum and community hall. **When we arrived there we got quite a surprise. Full length across the front side of the building was a large sign with red and blue letters on a white background. It read, "WELCOME STAGECOACH 76"!**

It was noon, and they had a good community meal waiting for us; so we unhitched and joined the group inside the hall. The chairman told about the depot and the story behind some of their gifts. When he introduced us from Stagecoach 76, I took the opportunity to present them with one of our commemorative bronze medallions to be placed in their museum. Before we left that afternoon, I had to replace a worn out shoe on one of my horses. Tammie came up with the idea that they might also like one of our old horse shoes in their museum. When she took it in, they were delighted with it. They said they would mount the shoe on a plaque and place it in their museum as a memento of the Overland Trail.

6/23 – GREELEY TO FORT COLLINS
Joe and Pearl were upset. I was trying to get dressed as the photographer wanted a picture of me in a dress and hat by the coach. Also, an old man had jumped all over Kip and Tammie about the water by the trailer. He thought all the mud puddles from the rain were sewage dumping, and was very nasty about it. Guess there's got to be one in every crowd. He jumped all over us again, and threatened to call the Health Department. They came out and didn't seem to think there was any problem. Joe pulled out with the coach and Tammie with the Ford. Then Red drove the truck, and I followed with the camper. Drove on into Windsor, and met the people at the Railroad Depot Museum. Had a big sign, "Welcome Stagecoach 76" over the door, 20' long.

After lunch, we again made a bunch of big-eyed kids happy by giving rides to everyone that wanted one. Not all of those kids were under 30 years old either.

I drove the coach out that afternoon. Just outside of **Ft. Collins,** some more of our Wetmore friends met us and rode on into town with us. They had a pair of long-legged boys that really got a kick out of riding on the seat over the back boot. We were directed on in to the United Bank where a large crowd awaited our arrival. It is always a thrill to be welcomed by such a large group, even though it was kind of tricky getting in and out of the bank's parking lot. After depositing our strongbox, we went on out to camp at one of the college equestrian centers on the west edge of town.

We drove to the edge of town and met the stage. Pearl and I rode in with them. Paraded through town and on out to the Depot. It was windy and rainy; so we went and visited while Joe and Red took rides. Mrs. Hogan welcomed us and gave a speech about the community. Red talked, and donated a medallion to their Museum. Eddie ate too much and got a stomach ache.
Red drove the coach out of Windsor, and I drove the Ford. Joe, Pearl, and Tammie went on to Fort Collins with rigs. At the intersection when the sheriff pulled off, a city cop took over. A driver cut around the cop, and cut me off, and all the cross traffic followed her. I waited for the light, then caught up, and at the next block, the police pulled in behind our caravan which now had several cars.
We unloaded the strongbox at the bank, and went on to the University Arena.

DAY THIRTY-ONE
JUNE 24TH

The next morning when I went to grain the horses, Wendy's little mare was sick. This was Holly Ann, the flaxey-maned sorrel that had gotten the hide knocked off her knee at Fairbury, Nebraska. She was lying on her side and appeared to have a bad case of colic.

I needed to get a vet here anyway to get the Coggins tests for Red and Robby, the two horses we had bought instead of sending home at Fort Morgan; so I called him right away. Sure enough, Holly had colic from getting too much grain, but the vet said he was quite sure he'd doctored her soon enough to prevent her from having any foundering effects from the overeating. We ran all of our horses together, feeding them 17 pounds of grain per horse per day. With the grain distributed in split tires scattered on the ground, it was possible for one greedy horse to get too much.

I had quite a discussion with the vet that morning when I found out he was also a horse feed nutrition expert. He confirmed a point I'd been trying all summer to get across to my crew, to be sure that the horses that had just come in off a long hard run had the opportunity to be on water at least an hour, and preferably two hours, before giving them their grain. If they were grained first, or too soon after taking on a large quantity of water, the two things dumped into their stomach together caused a chemical reaction which gave off large quantities of gas which caused bloat and colic in the animal.

For some reason, every once in awhile, someone would feel sorry for one horse or another and put out extra grain. I know of one day when three sacks (or 300 pounds) more than their regular allowance had been given to them before I got in that night. We followed the vet's instructions the rest of the summer.

6/24 – FORT COLLINS TO VIRGINIA DALE
Steve Thomas came out again, and visited and took pictures. Quite an old fellow. Holly Ann (horse) was real sick so Finally got started. Joe driving the coach to the bank to get the strongbox and passengers. Five people in western clothes; 2 men and 3 women. Very interesting people and a happy bunch. One brought his guitar and played during the trip.

We followed the original Overland Trail out of Fort Collins; a lovely winding road that crossed an old long wooden one lane bridge. River below was beautiful with lots of trees and brush. Tried to get a picture, but couldn't. I was worried all morning. The road had so many curves, and the horses were lunging and rocking the coach. Day was sunny but cool and breezy. Bank crew all said the trip was too short.

The horses were on water for at least an hour before graining them. We never had any more colic problems.

That morning we all piled on the coach for the run up to the bank to retrieve the strongbox and pick up a load of passengers. Joe drove and had to come right

back out close by our camp to reach the Overland Trail heading northwest toward Wyoming; so I dropped off there to get the horse van.

Going out of Ft. Collins, the highway follows the original Trail. It winds and curves as it heads toward the top of the Rockies. It is a pretty steep climb up

the valley and is real beautiful mountain country. It was about twenty miles to our noon stop, and the horses had to pull pretty hard all the way. Joe stopped several times to "blow" them. The higher they went, the crisper and cooler the air got. Everyone was wearing jackets by the time they got to our noon stop, **The Forks.** We had a merry group of passengers aboard that day, including a guitar player, who favored the ladies with songs of the West.

I suspicioned something villainous might take place when we got to the Forks; so I asked them not to shoot while the passengers were unloading, in case our horses took offense and danced around a bit.

At The Forks, we pulled in beside their tourist stagecoach –a simple plywood one. Six Mountain Men with beards and buckskins met us. Then while the men unhitched, a couple guys demonstrated shooting balloons with blanks, and splitting newspapers with a bullwhip. Afterwards we went into an old building for fresh trout dinner, and hot apple pie. Red drove the stage, and I rode with him. Tam took the Ford, and Joe the truck. We left The Forks following the little stage with two gray horses, and took the original old trail out across the hills. Beautiful country, tall grass and rocks. Drove in the old wheel ruts. Forded a creek. Horses hesitated but splashed on across.
Came back out on highway, and headed for Virginia Dale. Wind came up and I had to put on Red's jacket and slicker.

"When the Overland Stage rolled in, it was met by a group of ferocious mountaineers and bad men".

As soon as everyone was out of the coach, and I had the horses in hand, they had a real bang-up shoot-out, much to everyone's delight. It was followed by a display of "blacksnake" dexterity and sharpshooting. We all had a fine dinner of fresh Colorado trout, before bidding goodbye to our morning passengers and heading out again. By the way, the horses hardly even waggled an ear at the latest hold-up.

That afternoon the owner of "The Forks Stageline" hitched up his small coach and led us out for a couple miles through some private pastures and up over a ridge before returning to the highway.

It was rougher than being out on the highway, but what a marvelous feeling.

> *The route he took us on was where the Overland Trail had been over 100 years ago, and we were driving in the original wheel ruts of the old stages and wagons.*

We could almost hear the old coach wheels clucking, the freight wagons rumbling, and the yokes of oxen shuffling along.

One place we came around a curve, dipped down into a draw, and there was a small creek about ten feet wide. The leaders hesitated just an instant, then swept on across. The stones underneath grated on the iron rims of the tires, and the water splashed up. Pulling up out of the water, we left wet tire tracks for a few feet across the sand.

Was a pretty long pull up and down, but trotted the horses real steady. Came past Virginia Dale station, and it was closed. Turned off the highway to go back in hills about three miles to the original stage station. Another lovely winding road through the hills and around curves and rocks. Started down a steep hill, and came around a curve, and saw the truck parked by a bridge with a sign "6 Ton Limit." Red looked at it as we went by, and decided he could get it out. We drove on and saw the buildings. Came across a draw, and up a curve at a full gallop up to the large crowd waiting for us. They all cheered and applauded when we stopped. I got out and one of the ladies took me in and gave me a cup of hot coffee. I was pretty cold and wind-burned. Red took several rides around and then unhitched and put the horses in a corral.

It was a real treat to mix our tracks with those of 100 years ago. Up out of the creek bed, and we were climbing a cliff on the other side. Marge looked back down on that little stream with the slope of the land dropping off behind us. **She said she wished we could have had someone with a movie camera stationed up on that cliff filming the coach as we came across there. It was the only place on the whole trip we forded a stream like they used to do long ago.**

The original old stage station of **Virginia Dale** lies about three miles northwest of the present post office located on the highway. Some time ago, the people in the area purchased the two old log buildings and 18 acres around, to have as a community club house. They had planned a supper and dance that evening in honor of our stagecoach arriving at the old station.

All afternoon we climbed steadily. I kept the horses at a good steady trot as it was cool and breezy. Just before dark we turned off the highway and took the old dirt road leading to the station. It wound around through the hills, up and down, and is a beautiful drive. Finally we topped out on a rise and looked down across a draw on a small clearing. **There stood the two old buildings. One was the stage depot; the other was Jack Slade's cabin. I was alive with excitement, like I was returning to a camp or station that I had been at many times before.**

Virginia Dale Stage Station and Jack Slade's Cabin.

There was a large group of people standing out in front of the old station as we topped that last rise. **Those horses I was driving knew what lay ahead too, and what was expected of them.**

> *The cheer of that crowd was one of the rewards of our trip!*

I didn't have to urge them at all; just give them a little slack and they swung into that ground-eating gallop of theirs. They swept down that hill, across the coulee, and drew to a sliding stop, right in front of that crowd. They seemed to know just how far to run to stop in the exact right spot. One of the old timers told me there were more people there that night than had been to a gathering there in over ten years. One lady was dressed in a beautiful, long, billowing, white- flowered 1890 style dress. She said she wouldn't be satisfied until she got to ride up on the seat beside me. *She had come clear from Steamboat Springs just to see our stagecoach,* and she was thrilled with it.

They had a center table reserved for the stagecoach crew for supper in that historic old depot. We sort of ate in shifts as the women and kids went in while we took care of the horses. Also, there were so many more people than were expected, that all the tables were filled to overflowing. After supper, the band tuned up and all joined in for a good western dance that lasted until after midnight.

I mentioned earlier about the buffalo head the kids had gotten from the Sedgwick people, and how it presented a problem. Well, the problem is that a head with the meat still on it can get pretty ripe in the summer time. This one was no exception. It had finally gotten so bad that I had to put it clear up on the very outside of our horse van, and that still wasn't high enough. I hated to throw it away. I finally asked the man that ranched there at Virginia Dale if we could leave it there at his ranch, and maybe pick it up later on when we were passing by. **Our buffalo head is still up there, I hope.**

Another problem we ran into coming into Virginia Dale was with the horse van. We had to leave it down the road about 3/4 of a mile because of an old rickety bridge. Joe had been driving the truck and luckily, he got boogered at the bridge when he got to it. After stopping and looking it over, he decided it was unsafe for the truck. He had to unload the extra horses and lead them on up the country, and we had to haul our feed up. But the worst problem was there wasn't any place for a mile or so to turn a 40 foot semi-trailer around; so I had to back it out, up that winding steep grade. It must not have been quite as bad as it looked, because I made it.

People inside were all waiting, so Pearl, Wendy and I started the line, and sat down to eat. They had a table reserved for us. There were 2 or 3 times more people than they expected. Some came from east of Greeley, and one from Steamboat Springs. One old man came that hadn't hardly been out for anything for 10 years.

Had a delicious dinner. Kids and men came in one at a time. After-wards they went to another building and started the dance. Tammie wanted to go as there were some young boys; so Red and I went back to Fort Collins after our camper. It was past 11:30 when we got back, and the dance was over. I was quite disappointed. We went in and had coffee and dessert. Then went to bed.

**DAY THIRTY TWO
JUNE 25th**

CHAPTER NINE
WYOMING

DAY THIRTY-TWO
JUNE 25TH

In the morning, we followed the old trail on past the station with the coach. The ranch folk led us through the pastures and fences and up through the rocks. For anyone who appreciated scenery, the Overland Trail must have been beautiful in the 1860's. We sure appreciated the few times, like this, when we were able to leave the highway, and follow it up and down, around the curves, and wind among the rocks and trees.

Joe had gotten a small splinter in his finger. In the morning it was swollen to twice its normal size and throbbing and needed medical attention. That left us pretty short of crew; so I had to put Tammie in the KW with the horse van, and I got to drive the coach on into Laramie. Kip drove the pickup until we reached the highway, where Margie took over. He really liked the job, and couldn't understand why a 12 year old boy wasn't allowed to drive it on the highway. It was a good drive. We left the craggy peaks of Colorado behind.

6/25 – VIRGINIA DALE , CO. to LARAMIE, WY.
Red had to go back to where Joe had left the truck. He backed the truck up the long hill and around the curves about a half mile to get turned around, and then had to take a different road into the old station
Joe's finger was infected, and he went into Laramie to the doctor, so Red drove the coach. I ran out of film and didn't get any pictures of the old station and Jack Slade's house.
We followed the original old trail across the hills again, and through the fences with the ranch folks leading the way. Tammie and the kids and I went out on the highway to get mail and make phone calls; then went back. After loading the truck, Red drove it to the highway and I drove the Ford. Joe drove our camper on into Laramie.

The steep mountains gradually gave way to the smoother, flatter high plains of Wyoming. We stopped once at an old marker which denoted the old boundaries between the Territories of Wyoming and Colorado. Off to the side, we could see places where the stage road had worked its way through the hills. The grass became shorter and drier, and the wind came up pretty steady. We saw the first antelope of the trip just west of Laramie. As much as we enjoyed the eastern half of our trip, it seemed like "coming hone" to be out in big, wide open country, and smell the sagebrush.

We stopped at **Tie Siding** for a "pop stop", but didn't change horses. Shortly thereafter, my big high-spirited Buddy horse went to limping on a front foot. When Tammie went by with the horse van, I signaled her to stop so we could make a change. Tammie wasn't experienced enough to take that size truck on over the mountain into Laramie by herself, so I'd had her run it along slow just a short ways ahead. We swapped Buddy for Houlihan and went on. The **Laramie** officials met us out a ways and rode into the fairgrounds with us.

Afterwards they presented us with tickets to the Shrine Circus which was in town, so we hurried with supper and chores that night and took the kids to the circus.

It was a pretty drive. The steep mountains of Colorado gradually gave way to the smoother, flatter ones of Wyoming. At edge of town, Mayor Ted Gertoch, City Manager, and Chamber of Commerce President Bob Middleton rode the coach. Horses were tired so we came on into the Fairgrounds instead of driving through town. A photographer, also there, took pictures and interviewed Red. Later, the City Manager came and brought tickets to the Shrine Circus. After taking care of the horses, we ate a quick supper and cleaned up, and went. It was real good. During the afternoon, Red talked a little about the coach over the microphone. The Ringmaster got conked by a falling ladder and was taken to the hospital. I liked the bears and camels, and trained horses the best.

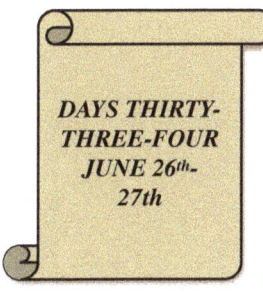

DAYS THIRTY-THREE/ FOUR
JUNE 26 - 27th

We got in Laramie Friday evening, and didn't leave until Monday. This gave us a chance to get all our horses pretty well re-shod. This was just the second set of shoes for several of them since leaving St. Joe.

One of the interesting people we met at Laramie was a lady riding a big white horse around the track at the fairgrounds. Her horse had attracted our attention as he was such a traveler. He sure looked like he could have made the wheels of our coach rattle.

Anyhow after visiting with her, we discovered she already knew all about us. She had received a letter from her mother who enclosed an article about our trip. The article had been taken out of the Chicago Tribune. We were a little surprised at our "notoriety" as we didn't think anyone back "east" had heard about us although we still hoped that if enough people knew about our trip, someone might still be interested in sponsoring us.

No such luck, though.

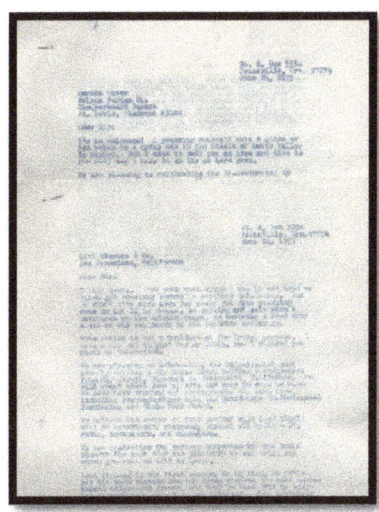

6/26 – LARAMIE LAYOVER

Jack rolled in at daybreak. We slept late. Fixed pancakes. Geneva and I did laundry. Men shod horses. Got groceries. Came home and fixed steak for supper. Afterwards took Wendy to Gibson's and got her new leather shoes and tennis shoes. Tammie had a date.
We went to bed.

6/27
Got up late and fixed jelly rolls and link sausage. Quite a few people came out to see the coach. Geneva fixed pork roast for dinner. Called Dode Saturday night, and Mom on Sunday.
Thompsons left about 4:30. Had leftovers for supper.

Colo - Wyoming border marker

DAY THIRTY-FIVE
JUNE 28TH

Joe had to go back to the doctor Monday about his finger, but his appointment wasn't until close to noon. He started out with the coach, and I was to relieve him later on. I had to fuel up the truck, and try again to get the grease hub cap for that trailer wheel which our stud had kicked off in Morrowville, Kansas. The plastic bowl we'd put on was starting to seep grease, and I was getting worried about it.

After all this time, I finally was able to get what I needed, and we left Laramie to go catch up with the coach. One of the benefits of having a good looking 18 year old daughter is that sometimes they attract some of the boys that like to show they are pretty good hands themselves. That's how we lucked out that morning going out of Laramie. One of Tammie's admirers (*Denny) volunteered to chauffeur the horse van on the rest of the way after we caught up with Joe. He and Tammie went on ahead to **Bosler**. They really "made a hand" that day. When we came in at noon, they had lunch ready and even had the relay horses harnessed up and ready to go.

It was like many other towns in that the town officials met us out a ways and rode in with us. We were led in to the center of town by the sheriff and the local saddle club queens. **When we got there, we were met by another sample of our fellow Americans' whimsical personalities, in the form of a sign which read," No Parking ---Reserved for Stagecoach!"** I'll bet that's the only town in the country that has parking space reserved for a stagecoach.

6/28 – LARAMIE to ROCK RIVER
Joe drove the coach, and I drove the Ford. Police escorted us through town. Left about 8:15. Red finally caught up with us after 10:00 so Joe could go back to the doctor. Denny drove the truck, and Tam the camper. Saw the first antelope today. Wyoming grass is short and dry. Wind is pretty steady. Snowy peaks off in the distance, but road is a gradual climb. Pulled into Bosler, and Tam and Denny had trucks parked at school grounds, and horses all harnessed. I made ham and roast beef sandwiches, and we got away a little after 1:00. They went on ahead to Rock River. Outside of town a bunch of people met us. The Sheriff led us in. Saddle Queens rode ahead. A sign in front said, "No Parking, Reserved for Stagecoach." Red took a bunch of riders around.

Anyway, we made good use of it, using it for our "depot', and hauling the whole town around for rides, before putting our horses up for the night and going in for dinner.

> Rock River isn't a very big town, but it is big in heart, and it sure occupies a big place in our memories.

One of the fellows who'd ridden into town with us had a moving picture camera. I couldn't quite savvy him as he was a little shy about giving out any information. I asked the townspeople who he was, but no one knew. He was here; he was there; he was everywhere we looked, with his camera. It was quite a while before he finally introduced himself as a TV Camera man from Cheyenne. I guess we all have a little "ham" in us too, as we got a kick out of having the TV cameras pointed in our direction, just as much as the next guy. This happened quite frequently throughout the trip. But this wasn't what I meant when I said we enjoyed the town.

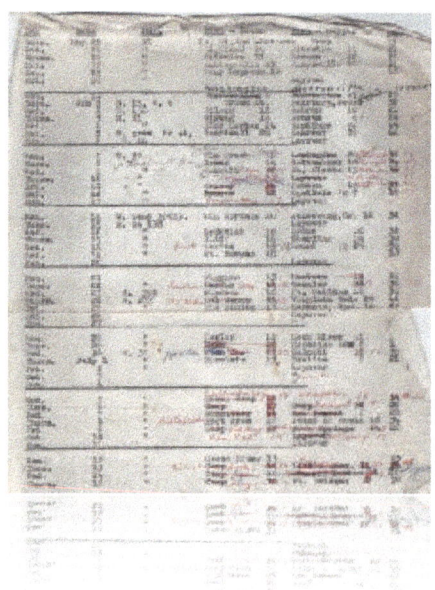

I stood and visited with 3 reporters and several local people. Met the Mullings, whose daughter, Kelly, was Queen and a Mrs. Escobel whose mother was a Wolverton from eastern Kansas. Also a Mrs. Marsh, an old timer who told me about Rock River in 1910 when it was a boomtown.
Went to camper and cleaned up, and went back to Hall and started the line. They had a hind quarter of beef roasted, baked potatoes, and a whole bucket of sour cream. Lots of salads and a scalloped watermelon filled with melon balls; and also a melon and fruit salad. We were seated at a head table with the mayor and his wife. Kids ate outside and fought mosquitos.
At our table was a chocolate cake with a stagecoach drawn with icing, streamers of blue crepe paper ended in little wagons made of Fig Newtons and marsh-mallow tops.

They had quite a feast --a hind quarter of roast beef, baked potatoes and a whole bucket of sour cream. I think Marge got at least a quart of it, and a watermelon full of

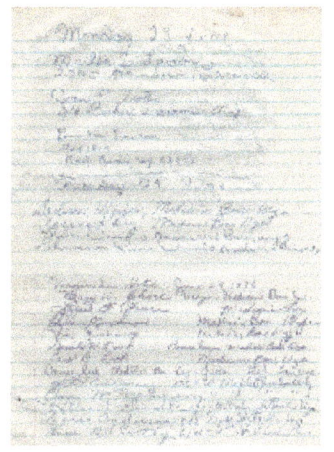

melon balls that was big enough for a bath tub. They topped it off by seating Joe and me and our wives at the head table with the mayor and his wife. In the center was a huge chocolate cake decorated with a stagecoach made of icing. At each place were favors made of fig cookies with marshmallow tops and lifesaver wheels, that looked like covered wagons. I think the kids had a contest to see who could eat the most "wagons".

Twice as many people as were expected showed up and the dining room was filled to overflowing. Quite a number had to move back outside to the sidewalk to find a place to squat down cowboy fashion to eat or climb on the back of a pickup parked nearby. We were all presented with some handmade gifts which we still proudly use to this day.

After supper one of the local rancher musicians brought his guitar into the hall and proceeded to play and sing a few songs. One especially enjoyed was his rendition of "Wolverton Mountain". He changed the words around to fit us and our stagecoach and was greatly applauded for his inventiveness. It wasn't long until, with a little persuasion on our part, that he was joined by a couple or three other members of his cowboy band, and they really made those walls rattle. Of course, by that time, we had the tables all pushed back out of the way, and soon we were all kicking up our heels to the tune of good western swing music. Rock River also had a large "Welcome Stagecoach 76" sign in large red letters on a long strip of heavy white packing paper, which stretched across the entire length of the wall in the community hall. During the evening, I was setting out one dance. I looked up at the sign and realized how good it made us feel when the people did something like that. "That sign would sure make a good souvenir", I thought to myself. When I spotted the lady in charge there, I asked her what they would do with the sign. "Take it down and throw it away before the next doings here, I suppose," she answered. "Would it be alright if we took it with us tonight?" I asked, "It sure would," she replied. My next move was to go over to our guitar picker and ask him to announce that we were going to take the sign along with us, but I'd like for everybody there to dance by it and sign their names on it first, if they would. I wish I had thought of it earlier, as it was pretty late by that time and quite a few of the folks had already gone home. We did get quite a few signatures on it though.

Our horse hay supply was running low again so I inquired around if there was any hay to be bought in that area. Almost everyone we met wanted to have a part in our trip in some way by helping in any way they could.

Rock River only happened one!

Our guitar picker brought us a pickup load of hay and then wouldn't take any money for it. I evened things out the best I could though. He mentioned that his wife had stayed home that night with his three kids who were sick. They sure hated to miss seeing the stagecoach.

The next morning when we learned we would pass right by his ranch heading out, we got him to bring his wife and kids out to the highway where we picked them up and took them for a ride down the "Trail". They really enjoyed it.

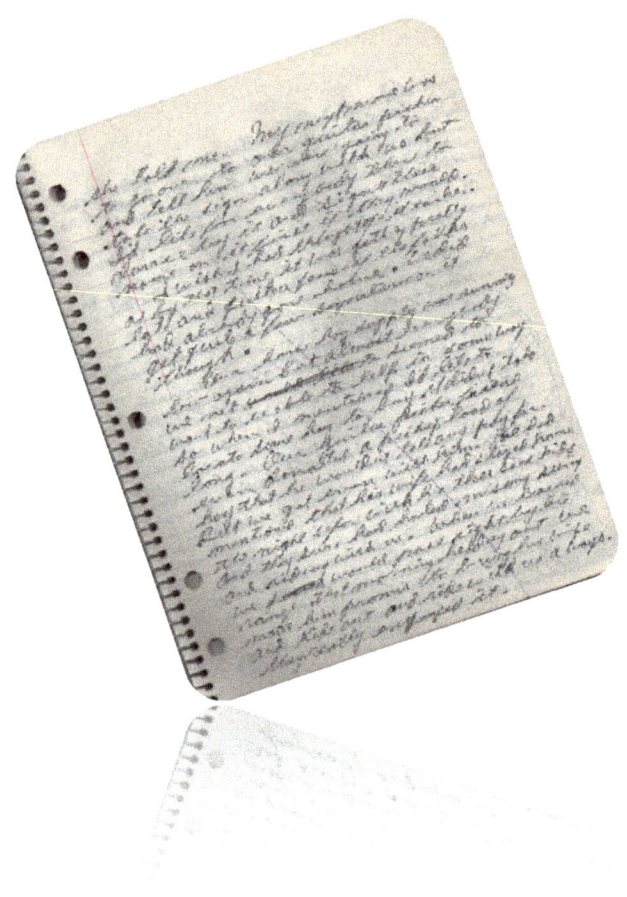

DAY THIRTY-SIX
JUNE 29TH

We left late that morning as we only had a short trip planned to **Medicine Bow**. The country was still climbing, but not steep. I wondered if Owen Wister's ghost was riding along with us that afternoon as we rolled up in front of the **Virginian Hotel**. I kinda have a hunch he was, and that he was perched up on top when we hauled the kids around town. It was history repeating itself as our stagecoach brought to life the old pictures that hung in the lobby and bar of that famous old hotel. **It was another one of those places where the Present was almost blotted out by the Past, with the arrival of the stagecoach reawakening all those old memories**.

That afternoon we were invited down to the "Old West" Cafe for an ice cream social. They had some long tables set up, with old fashioned red gingham napkins at each place. (Marge still has hers.) In the center was a large sheet cake covered with green coconut. A road of mixed nuts wound across the "grass" while "bushes and rocks" of walnut halves were scattered around. Part way along the road was a small metal stagecoach pulled by two horses. Among the group of people we met there were the mayor and his wife and

6/29 – ROCK RIVER to MEDICINE BOW

Slept late as only had one short trip planned. Joe drove the stage, and I drove the Ford. Kip rode. Country still climbing. Pulled in front of Virginian Hotel at Medicine Bow. Pearl and I went through hotel while men took rides out.
Finally unhitched and took horses to the stockyards across the tracks. I rested and read for a couple hours. At 5:00 we went to Old West Café for an Ice Cream Social. Large table with red gingham napkins and huge cake covered with green coconut and a "road" of nuts, and bushes and rocks of walnut halves, and a metal stagecoach and 2 horses. Medicine Bow's queen and attendant were there. Mayor Harry Chase and wife, a red haired photographer. Also Barbara "red head with family" cut the cake.

the queen and attendant of Medicine Bow's rodeo. Marge and I were presented with a small Seth Thomas clock. (They were in business about the same time as Abbott & Downing.) The Queen's brother gave Kip the little metal stagecoach off the cake.

That afternoon we were delighted to be invited to join the mayor and city council members for dinner in the "Owen Wister" room of the Virginian Hotel. It was like living in another time. People who think our red velvet lined stagecoach is much too fancy for the "old days" should see this old hotel, resplendent in all its original furnishings.

Undoubtedly this was the most elegant place we dined in on the entire trip. It had dark red velvet drapes, candle lamps with gold filigree bases, rosy glassware, and fine china and linens. There was an old highly polished sideboard with photographs of famous people long since gone. The comfort and beauty of that room certainly prove my feeling that our forefathers had a taste for fine materials and an appreciation of craftsmanship that have long since been lost in today's modernistic world.

They served cake, ice cream, and choice of drinks. Then the Queen's brother gave Kip the stagecoach off the cake, and they gave us a Seth Thomas clock.

Went back to camper and finished my book. Red took a nap. Went over and took care of horses, came back and cleaned up at 8:00, and went to dinner at The Virginian, in the Owen Wister Room. It was lovely. Dark red velvet drapes, beautiful gold filigree candle lamps on the tables; old sideboard, etc. Had shrimp, and afterwards Mr. Chase gave us each presents: Red -2 bolo ties, me 2 necklaces. One of a hand painted horse and the other of jade cut like a heart. Tam got a jade necklace, and the little kids got polished jade rocks and wooden nickels.

Much to our surprise, we again received some fine handmade gifts. The polished rocks which our nine year old Wendy received were the start of a collection which she added to all the way across country.

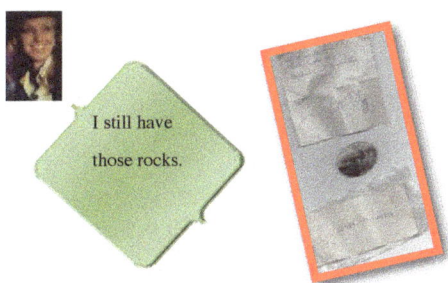

I still have those rocks.

She became a real "rockhound" and would have had all the vehicles loaded down if we hadn't limited her on size and number.

We spent quite an evening there, listening to stories about Medicine Bow's past. It had been one of the largest shipping railroad stock yards for both cattle and sheep in the West. They were trailed into Medicine Bow from all over the west, to be loaded there and shipped east. I would like to have been there when it was at its peak.

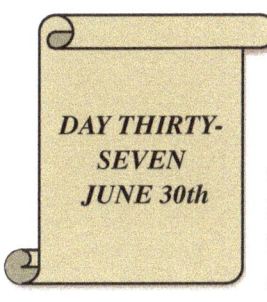

DAY THIRTY-SEVEN
JUNE 30th

DAY THIRTY-SEVEN JUNE 30th

Every town has at least one organization that is interested in promoting the town or helping incoming activities to be successful. Sometimes there will be several different factions in town, and they don't always work together. This was one of the problems we encountered in various places on the trip. If you happen to have an advance man who can go ahead of you soon enough and figure out which organization to contact, you can usually make out fine. However, we weren't able to afford one, and had to rely on the U.S. mail. In some cases you just plain miss or bombed out, and that's what happened to us at **Hanna.**

6/30 – MEDICINE BOW to WALCOTT Jct.

Joe drove the coach and Tam, the ford. Went ahead and checked out a dirt road which Red did not take. He sent me ahead, and he and Pearl waited at the junction. I drove to Hanna exit and turned off and waited at side of road. In the meantime, Red went over the dirt road with someone in a pickup, and they decided they could make it with the coach, and he rode part way down it. We had sandwiches and changed horses. Wendy and Tam watered the horses while the men ate. Red went out with the coach, and I was driving the Ford. Mr. West caught up with us with the hay; so I told him where to catch the truck. I started after the stage and he followed us clear across town. We stopped, and I turned around and told him to follow me. I signaled for a left turn at the underpass so he'd be sure to follow. Instead, he turned right.

We wrote to them, the same as to every other town on our schedule, but were unable to get any response at all. When we drove into Hanna, we found a vacant lot between the railroad tracks and the overpass. We changed horses, had lunch, and moved on out without hardly speaking to anyone, except one crippled fella with a camera. On the edge of town some people came out to the sidewalk and waved, and seemed to be interested in the coach so I pulled over. They wanted to know what we were doing.

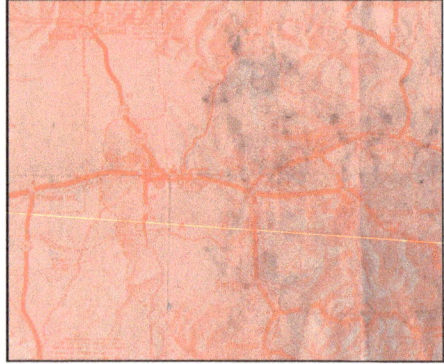

After I told them we were re-running the Overland Trail Stage Route, they asked why we hadn't contacted anybody in their town to tell of our trip. When I explained we had written but could get no response, they became a little aggravated. It seems they were the head of a group whose purpose was to "Preserve and promote the customs of the Old West". They sure felt that stagecoaching came under that category; and that had their city officials informed them of our coming, they certainly wouldn't have let our stagecoach pass through their midst unnoticed. The lady said they would probably have held us up for a full day's festivities, if they'd only known. Well I felt better; and I felt worse. I guess you just can't win them all.

Between Rock River and Medicine Bow I had located a rancher who had some more hay, which he had agreed to bring to us at Hanna. He met Marge in town while I was out with the coach, telling her he'd meet us at the rodeo grounds.

When we got in, she gave us the directions, but we missed the turn somewhere and didn't find it. He caught up with us again as we went out

I had to go a block to turn around, and by then, the truck had already pulled out. Mr. West was not in sight, so I went back through town. I went clear through town and didn't find him; so turned around and followed the campers out. He was back across the underpass, and followed us back out to the stage. Joe told him he'd pull the truck up to a wide spot to load, and I told him to follow the truck. They went by, and Red started out with the stage. Mr. West fell in behind me!
I was so disgusted by then, I went back and got in the Ford and caught up to the stage. We only went a little further and Red pulled the coach off by the truck, and helped load the hay. Finally got started again. It was plenty warm. Country is a steady climb; long uphills and then short levels or slight downhills. Grass is short, dry and brown compared to Kansas and Nebraska.

of town with the coach, and Marge told him where our horse van was located between the railroad tracks and the underpass. He didn't seem to understand and started following the coach; so she took the pickup and led him back to town. At the main intersection where she turned left, he missed her signal and turned right. By the time she got around the block and turned to the right to catch him, he was nowhere in sight.

She followed that road clear out of town, then turned around, and came back out toward the coach. She found him just past the overpass and had him pull in behind her again. They caught up to me on the stage about the same time as Joe did with the horse van. It was not a good place to stop so Joe said he'd pull on up to a wide spot we knew of up ahead, and Marge told him to follow the truck. Joe went by, and I started out again with the stage, followed by Marge in the pickup. Then instead of our pickup load of hay following the horse van, it pulled in behind Marge.

Guess she had neglected to say which truck to follow. Marge stopped again, and got out and explained in her sweetest voice (which is the calm before the storm) that the hay was to go on the big truck. Then she pulled in behind the stage once again. In just a few minutes more, I caught up to Joe and the horse van; so I decided to stop the coach. We tied up the horses and loaded the hay on the horse van. Afterwards when I learned about the "mix-up", I was glad my wife had plenty of time to cool off, driving the pickup behind the coach. From what she said, her Irish temper must have been near as hot as the temperature that day.

It was an agreeable afternoon. The country was changing to long down hill grades and shorter uphill slopes, or vice versa; depending on whether you were riding in the coach behind walking and trotting horses, with a nice breeze; or whether you were driving an old pickup along in first and second gear, and the sun was glaring through the windshield, and only one window would go down so you couldn't get any cross draft. Like I said before, "I'm glad she had time to cool off", while I drove that coach.

> First noticed the smell of sage near Laramie. Beginning to see cactus, much in bloom. Stopped at the little station near Walcott, and the people gave us cold pop. We were all thirsty. A bunch of them rode with us up a long hill. Kip kept riding Rebel way off to the side, and got in a real bad place where the sidehill was too steep to ride back up. Drove out to the old town of Walcott where a sheep and cattle company owned corrals and barns. Mr. Bob Vivian let us stay there. We walked all around and looked. They had two good sheepherder wagons, freight wagons and several bobsleds, and all kinds of wheels, single and double-trees, wagon jack, tools etc. I'd sure like to buy the one good wagon and a good sled.
> Tam cleaned out her pickup to be ready to leave, going back to Pueblo for her rodeo.

Those long down slopes sure made it good for high trotting and galloping.

The people at the Coyote filling station seemed interested in our approach. They were all out in their driveway with their cameras; so we pulled up for a visit. They wound up by supplying us with a whole bunch of pop and by climbing on the coach and riding on down to **Walcott Junction** with us. I'd made arrangements to stay at the Leo Sheep Company's corrals there. It was right on the main line train tracks again, but we did have a good restful night.

DAY THIRTY-EIGHT
JULY 1ST

DAY THIRTY EIGHT
JULY 1ST

Tammie left us at Walcott Junction the next morning. She had to return to Pueblo West to officiate as Queen of the 4th of July rodeo there. She said she'd see if she could round up some help while she was home.

The map indicated we'd have to start using the interstate that morning, but thankfully maps aren't always right. We were even able to cross the Platte on an old road.

From there on to **Sinclair**, I knew how to make it in on a power line dirt road that took us almost all the way to town. Joe was driving. I was riding shotgun. It was a short run so I decided to leave our relay horses there at the corrals as long as possible, and come

7/1 – WALCOTT JUNCTION to RAWLINS
We took the camper to Sinclair after calling in. Del Farris was out hunting us, and we made connections in town. Parked the camper and drove back out with him. Got Joe started with the stage.
I rode in it. Red took the truck. Pulled into town in front of the hotel. We had several passengers.
The Carbon County Queen met us ahorseback outside of town, and rode in with us. Her horse wasn't afraid of the coach at all. Other riders and passengers met us at the gate where we came out of the pasture, and rode in with us. Red and Joe took several rides around the park. Pearl and I went through the hotel with one of the ladies. It is a beautiful building with Spanish tile, a lovely ballroom, high ceilings, and a balcony.

back for them later. It's sure hard to figure how some people think sometimes. We'd come to a hill on our dirt road. Up ahead we could see where it really stood on end for a short ways about of 50 feet or so.

We held a pow wow while approaching the steep pitch and decided the best way to make it over the top was to hit that grade at a hard run which might not be too fast at the best. We were pulling up a fairly good grade and would have to swing into the run just before we started up it. This dirt road was only a short piece from the interstate at this point. As we drew nearer, a car stopped on the highway shoulder. A man got out, crawled through the fence, and walked right over toward us. He stepped out in the edge of our road, just a few steps up the steep part of it. He held up his hand, signaling for us to stop, just as Joe and I were whooping our stagecoach horses into a run for the hill.

He was brave, this tourist. He stood his ground right there in our way, with our horses charging right at him. Joe and I were both yelling, first at the horses; then at him to get out of the way. I don't remember if he finally stepped back or if Joe swerved those horses to get by him. I do remember, he was still standing right close with a hand still in the air as we rushed on by.

{ **I never did know what happened to that tourist.** }

As it was, we just barely made it to the top. We were pulled down almost to a stop before that steep pitch turned loose of the coach wheels and let it break over the crest. I was so relieved to make it over that hill that I completely forgot all about him until just now.

It was easy to forget him and think of other things, because just a short time later, we were met by the Carbon County Rodeo Queen, whose horse was one of the few that had no fear of the coach. We had a full load of passengers going into town again.

For all I know, he might still be standing there beside the trail with his hand in the air, trying to stop a stagecoach coming in a run!

One lady had big brown eyes and beautiful hair, and was so pretty Kip even commented on her. Of course, I didn't notice.

(7/1 – p. 2)
Then went on to a "wild" dinner. Moose, chicken, ham, green beans, rolls, beans, cupcakes and more. Really enjoyed it. Talked for a long time to various people.

Red hitched up by the park, and Bandito was acting up. Had a bunch of people riding out with him, and got off to a jerky start with Holly Ann and Romeo hitting the collar alternately and then stopping. We took lots of pictures before loading up. Drove into town with police escort. Found a large corral for the horses.

It sure sounds repetitious to keep telling about the rides we took and the good community meals we had, but there just isn't any other way of telling it. Many meals were basically the same, but different cooks give the same foods different flavors, and each community meal was unique and special in some way.

> That's what the trip was about. We wanted to share our stagecoach and six horse hitch with people who'd never seen one; and they shared with us the best meals in the country.

In Sinclair, we had a wild game dinner of moose, caribou, and game chickens, along with several others dishes and desserts. Marge and Pearl went through an old hotel there with one of the ladies. She said it was a beautiful building with Spanish tile. It had quite a large ballroom, great high ceilings, and a balcony around it. Just the kind of place she'd love to fix up in the old style and put back in shape for business. Got off to a slightly jerky start that afternoon. I put Holly Ann in the lead with Romeo in Rebel's place, and she didn't pick up the slack too good so first one and then the other hit the collar. Then Bandito decided it was time for him to have one of his rare spells of misbehavior.

After about the third try, we got started, and headed for **Rawlins.**

We were met at the east edge of town by a whole load of people. The fairgrounds were just a short ways from there, but we certainly took the long way to get there. Much to everybody's delight, our police escort led us clear through town to the west edge, then back again, before going to our camp. We arrived in Rawlins Thursday, July 1st and were not scheduled to leave until Monday, the 5th. The Little Britches Rodeo was going full blast that weekend, as well as lots of Bicentennial events.

DAY THIRTY-NINE JULY 2ND

We spent quite a while giving rides around. Also did some coach repairs and some horseshoeing. **One of our passengers there was Verne Wood, a well known photographer and author.** He said when he was about 5 years old, along about 1902, he went by wagon from Iowa to Dakota. There were three wagons moving together. He gave us a book of his western poems, "Desert Dust".

7/2 – RAWLINS LAYOVER
Got up late. Cleaned house some and took a bath. Got boys bathed. Took clothes to Laundromat and then got groceries. Storm came up. Cooked beans all day and made chili for supper. Red worked on coach brakes, and Joe shod a horse. Kids went to the rodeo. We could hear the rodeo dance band close by.
Went to Rawlins Corral Friday night. They sure had lots of clothes at good prices. Would like to have bought an outfit or a pair of pants, but didn't. Got Wendy two pairs of jeans for riding. Then went across the street and got sundaes that we could fix ourselves. I got chocolate, strawberry, and caramel with nuts. Ate all the topping off and got two more helpings of caramel and nuts. It was scrumptious.

**DAY FORTY
JULY 3rd**

CHAPTER TEN

OUR NEW STAGECOACH AND 200 YEARS

DAY FORTY - JULY 3RD

Saturday, the Frizzells arrived with our new coach all repaired and ready to roll again.

Also, Percy Hall, the new owner of Blucher Boot Company, stopped by. He presented me with a new pair of gold-topped boots, on top of the stagecoach out in front of the arena during the rodeo. We were guests at a barbecue that afternoon, as well as at a Bicentennial program on Sunday.

7/3 – RAWLINS LAYOVER
A Policeman came while I was still in bed and delivered a message saying Percy Hall would be there by noon. Had bacon, eggs, and toast for breakfast.
Halls got in early and gave Red a beautiful pair of Blucher boots; black with 14 carat gold scalloped tops and 11 rows of stitching in the "Two Bit" design –circles were made around a quarter. He tried on the boots, and Joe had to try one on; so Pearl took a picture of the two of them with one boot on each man. They hitched up the mares, and we rode over to the arts building. Joe drove and they took about four loads of people around. Then we got in the barbecue line. We drove into the rodeo. In front of the grandstand, Percy presented Red with the boots on top of the coach. Had a good hail storm that made the horses jump and bunch up.

DAY FORTY-ONE
JULY 4TH – 1776/1976

DAY FORTY ONE JULY 4th!

Their celebration also included a parade through Rawlins Sunday morning, which we were honored to lead. We had planned on using both coaches in the parade, and as things turned out, we should have.

The reason we didn't was that some of the Rawlins cowboys had asked me what I thought about them staging a real shoot-out hold-up along the parade route downtown. I had told them it would be OK with me, but knowing Wyoming cowboys to be a little wild at times, I began to get worried they might really get wild. I was afraid of what could happen if we had two six horse hitches on stagecoaches down there when the wild shooting started. I actually only had insurance to cover one stagecoach at a time; so if we did have trouble when we had two coaches out, I might be in hot water. As things turned out, they cancelled their hold-up and left us with a quiet, peaceful parade.

7/4 – RAWLINS BICENTENNIAL DAY! Made coffee cake with caramel frosting for breakfast. Red hitched up for the parade. I think he had Romeo and Holly, Roulette and Robby, Bandito and Rebel. Shag (Kip's dog) got loose and joined us in the parade. There wasn't much of a parade. Us, some kids with a banner, and some saddle clubs. The Carbon County Queen, Sherry Hartzog, wore the long dress and rode sidesaddle. One set of queens had red velvet serapes that were gorgeous. The Little Britches court had carved and dyed leather hat bands, crowns, banners, and serapes. They were outstanding. Got back to the Fairgrounds and unhitched. Loaded Fritz's coach. Had to pay Frizzells another $600.00 for the bearing-up and extras on the coach. The right front wheel is a replacement, and it's very poor.

Then I wished we'd had both coaches hooked up again. Rawlins had a terrific fireworks display that night. We all sure enjoyed it, but our dogs didn't. Every time someone opened the door to the camper, they'd run inside and hide.

JULIET

We are both quite disappointed in the coach, but it does look much better this time than before, with the wider axles and straight set wheels. Frizzells left and we ate cold roast beef sandwiches. Then men went to check on the road to Wamsutter, Pearl and Mildred (Herons' friends) came over for a while. When men got back, we went to Bi-centennial program at the park. Had cake and punch, met several of Rawlins old timers. Halls also left in the afternoon. Joe talked Percy out of a pair of boots, and Red bought a pair for work.
Stopped and got kids some fireworks on way home. They shot them off. Dogs were terribly scared and kept running into the camper. Fireworks display at night was beautiful.
Red thought it was the best we'd seen in years.

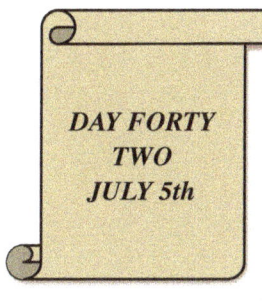

DAY FORTY-TWO
JULY 5th

DAY FORTY TWO JULY 5th

We'd driven on the interstate for about three miles over near Ft. Morgan, Colorado, but this Monday morning was where we really started using it. **We'd be on it almost all the way to Reno, Nevada. Most of the exit and entrance ramps have cattle guards on them. Very few places have gates for livestock and stagecoaches to go through, which presents a slight problem.** Nothing serious though.

That Saturday morning, I'd driven over to a lumber yard and bought two 4 x 8 ft x ¼ inch sheets of plywood, which we carried along in the back of our pilot pickup, following the stagecoach. When we'd come to a cattleguard, we'd lay them down side by side over the rails and drive the hitch right across them. After the first few crossings, the horses never paid any attention to the boards.

Joe drove out of Rawlins that morning. It was hot and dry with the grass getting shorter. The air was sweet with the smell of yellow clover, which was blooming all along the highway, and was belly high on the horses. We were still climbing, but we trotted steadily except on a few of the longer hills. There were gradual slopes with short downgrades or level spaces in between. The horizon was giving way to flat topped mesas and occasional rock formations. Sky was a brilliant deep blue with small fluffy white clouds.

7/5 – RAWLINS TO WAMSUTTER
Got up early and got ready to leave by 8:30. People from Rawlins didn't get there to ride. Joe drove the coach. I drove the Dodge as pilot car. Kip rode Rebel. We went on I 80. Started out driving behind the coach on the shoulder, but after a close shave when a woman veered off into the left lane when she got up even with the coach and caused a "hot rodder" to skid and fishtail before he passed her. Then I started driving in the center lane and forcing traffic to slow down and take single left lane as they went by. Worked better.

Day was hot, and Dodge overheated. I'd been driving in first gear and braking. Changed tactics and drove in automatic and shifted to neutral, and managed to keep it down. Boiled over twice when we stopped, and going up a bridge.

We crossed the **Continental Divide**, which is sort of in the center of a shallow basis. Noone would know it was there unless they saw the marker. We didn't stop, just kept going up one long gradual hill and then down; then back up again.

Across Wyoming, the weather stayed very hot. The kids packed canteens on their saddles; and we had jugs of water and pop in the coach, but almost everyone was dry before we got to the next stop. We ran some pretty long distances between camps. Cracked lips and burn ointment were everyday occurrences. Even with wide-brimmed hats, the wind and sun took their toll. I think Wendy and Joe probably felt it the worst. Wendy because she was so fair-skinned, and Joe because that he was even warm in the winter; he probably felt the heat twice as much as the rest of us.

Kip got stepped on by his horse and couldn't get him off. Was hurting pretty bad, but I got him back on top. Guys with CB's talked all day about the stagecoach. Only one driver complained because it was on the freeway. Most of them waved, tooted, smiled, commented on "The Old West", and really got a kick out of it. We " nooned" by an underpass. Had to get off and back on the Freeway with plywood panels across the cattle guards. Herons refused our offer of lunch and watermelon. Red drove the stage out and I followed with the Dodge. Wendy was riding Juliet, (one of the mares). Joe took the truck, and the women their campers. Red drove most of the time in the bar pit. Country is getting dryer all the time. Wyoming grass is short.

We could sympathize with the pioneers, especially when they had to make dry camps or were unable to reach water.

We always knew we'd have everything we needed at each stop, but while traveling on the coach, we still all learned what it meant to cross the plains in the heat of summer and be truly thirsty. We had our noon camp that day at an exit ramp beside the interstate, what we called our "watermelon" stop. It was about 18 miles out of Rawlins. I'd bought a big cold watermelon before leaving town. It sure tasted good after a hot morning. I picked up a whole load of kids as I was going through **Wamsutter** on our way out to the corrals where we were to camp that night.

The community was holding their Bicentennial celebration at their school the next morning, but for some strange reason they never invited us to attend it. **They were one of the towns that didn't answer our letters.**

Later on I was up town making a phone call and got to visiting with one of the ladies up there. She mentioned that they were very surprised at our appearance and our outfit. They had assumed that anybody that would drive a stagecoach on a trip like that would surely be a scuzzy bunch of bums that they wouldn't care to associate with. Guess some of them changed their minds, because one of the school teachers rode out through town with us the next morning.

Lots of sage brush. Clover along the roadside almost belly high on a horse, and blooming yellow. Really smells sweet. Was bitterly hot. Trotted pretty steady except Red walked them on a few of the longer hills. Still climbing steadily with short downslopes in between. Horizon giving way to flat topped mesas, and some rock formations. Sky. Deep blue with white clouds.

Outside of Wamsutter a young boy met us on a black horse. Rode along a mile or two, and then led us through a gate and an underpass; so we didn't have to cross the cattle guard. As soon as we unhitched, we took the Dodge back to Rawlins after the camper. Red took a bath, and I made all the kids wash up. Went back to Wamsutter. Red and I went over to Herons to visit. Anyway, things all seemed OK.

DAY FORTY-THREE
JULY 6TH

We took our campers on to **Red Desert** that morning; then returned to Wamsutter around noon. I drove to Red Desert with the coach and a full load of passengers and crew. It was a good run as I was able to drive all the way between the two towns on a dirt pipe line road, along close to the interstate. Marge saw her first baby antelope, and we also flushed out a few sage hens. **Part of the time, there was no sign of civilization in view; just wide open prairies and sky, the spicy smell of sagebrush in the air, and long rocky slopes and patches of sand off to the sides.**

Some of the water in the Wamsutter-Red Desert area is almost undrinkable for both man and horse, if they are not used to it. This was where our horses really appreciated that 700 gallon tank in the top of our horse van. Usually that was enough horse water to last two full days. It would have been this time except some of it got wasted. Joe and a friend of his were watering the horses at the same time they were taking on a little liquid refreshment of their own. They forgot the spigot was turned on; consequently quite a puddle of our precious water ran out in the sand.

The next evening at the corrals at the Red Desert, when I went to fill our water trough, there wasn't anything to run out of the hose. I couldn't believe it until I finally climbed up and measured our big tank and confirmed what the hose was telling me; there wasn't any more. The water up at the station hadn't been real bad so I drove the truck back up there and told the station man I guess I'd have to use some of his water after all. That would be fine, he said, but he wanted us to take it out of a different well than what the station was hooked to. I filled the tank in the truck, but doubted if the horses would touch it, for it sure tasted bad to me.

7/6 – WAMSUTTER to RED DESERT
A school teacher and his wife came out, and several other people. After breakfast we loaded the extra horses, and brought all equipment to Red Desert.

Red drove the stage out of Wamsutter. Hot again. I rode in the stage for a change. A gal passenger liked to hunt arrowheads. She really appreciated the historical value of the stagecoach ride.

Wide open prairie and sky. Smell of sage is spicy.

Had supper at Red Desert café; veal cutlets. Kids were hungry, but didn't finish their meals. A beautiful red sunset behind a rocky peak and a flat topped mesa to the north.

It's still warm, but is cooling off. Still light out at 7:30. PM.

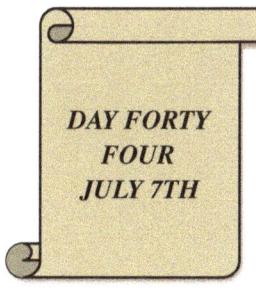

DAY FORTY-FOUR
JULY 7TH

Not a single horse drank that night, and they sure looked drawn up the next morning. I had noticed a slough about a quarter of a mile from our corrals that looked like it had run off water in it; so I walked over and inspected it. The water was milky looking, but when I picked up a cupped handful of it, it appeared to be fairly clear. I tasted and drank some of it. I decided that I could stand it, and if I could, my horses could also get by on it. Luckily for us and them, they drank pretty good when we led them to it.

Joe went out on the morning coach run. I loaded up the relay horses and headed towards the **Bitter Creek** Rest area, about 18 miles up the country. In the spring before we left on our trip, when we were getting ready, we'd come up with the problem that six head of our remuda were mares; and mares do have colts. I was sure a whole bunch of colts was one problem we didn't need. We knew one of our mares had gotten bred early; so would have a fairly early colt. I finally decided we could put up with one colt. One might be fun to have along, but any more than that wouldn't work. We managed to keep our stud away from three of the mares, and had the others preg-checked and aborted by the vet; or so we thought anyway.

The one mare, Juliet, foaled May 2, and we'd had her stud colt along with us all the time. He had become a lovable pet, and we were all very attached to him. In eight years of raising horses, he was only the second colt I'd considered keeping for a stallion as he had excellent conformation and a gentle nature to match. On the days when his mammy worked, he had to stay in the horse van with the other horses, but they all liked him and looked out for our baby.

Our horse van is a converted double deck cattle trailer, with two 20 foot decks in the middle and a full open 10 foot area at each end.

7/7 – RED DESERT to POINT OF ROCKS
Didn't sleep well, Trains didn't bother me, but the highway traffic did.
Joe dove the stage, and I, the pilot car. Had one small incident when two old gray-haired ladies tried to pass a camper on the right as he was crossing to the left lane in front of them. She came up right behind me and had to squeal her tires when she put the brakes on. Truckers' CB comments are interesting: **"There's Miss Kitty going to Dodge". "What a sight." "That's really a beautiful outfit", "Shades of the Old West," "A real live stagecoach!". "You aren't going to believe this, but…" "After this we better start looking for the Indians." "My diesel was broke down for two days. "Hook on to that stagecoach and you'll get there quicker."**

We stored our grain on the top deck and also had our 700 gallon water tank there.

The front nose had hooks for harness, and space for tack, saddles, and equipment. It sounds like lots of room, but it didn't give us quite as much as I figured we needed so I cut the back end out of the van.

I dropped down two feet below the floor level of the rear deck and built a six foot extension, which stuck out behind. This extension would accommodate about 90 to 100 bales of hay, and that's what we used it for most of the time. There was room for 10 head of grown horses and the colt in the bottom deck of the van. When we hauled more than this, we had to put some in the back end compartment, which was just in front of the hay extension; and sometimes put one or more on up in the top deck.

On this morning, when I pulled out from Red Desert, I had 10 head and the colt in the bottom deck and one horse in the back compartment. There was still about a half of a load of hay, or two rows of bales above the floor of the back deck, on the extension. When the ramp lid leading from the rear to the bottom is closed down there is an opening between the bottom of the top deck and the floor of the back deck about 20 inches high and about five feet long. We have a gate for this opening, but never use it hauling horses. It didn't seem necessary.

I'd traveled about half way to our noon stop. I was ahead of the stagecoach quite a ways and in no particular hurry so I was only running about 45MPH. Then a movement in my left hand rear view mirror caught my eye. He was standing on the hay, looking around the back end of the trailer right up at me. I immediately pushed on the brake.

After the campers and horse van passed us, Lloyd rode shotgun with Joe. Then the CB called and told me a colt had jumped out of a horse van at milepost 154. I asked if he was still out, and the guy answered "Yes". I drove up to the coach and told Joe so they could be watching for him. Just the east side of Bitter Creek rest area, Kip came riding along out on Pete, and said it was the colt, and his mouth was messed up, but he was OK. We pulled in and unhitched. Sun was very hot. Went over to the corrals, and Pearl and Mildred had a wet towel over the colt's head. He was standing up and tried to nurse, but his mouth was too bloody and sore. They had given him aspirin, and Red milked out Juliet and poured it down him.

Had I slammed it on hard, I'm sure I could have thrown him off the hay and back into the truck, but just at that instant, he jerked back out of my sight. So, instead of slamming it down hard, I hesitated, pushing it down gentle so as not to slam all the rest of the horses to the front of the trailer. Before I had time to get a second breath, here came his head out again. This time it was moving fast, being pushed by his body, as he leaped from the stack of baled hay.

I'm sure my heart missed a beat when I discovered it was our colt's head sticking around the end of the trailer!

I almost ran off the highway, trying to stop that big rig right there, and watch that poor colt at the same time. When he hit, he just splattered like a big paper bag full of water. There was colt flying and spinning in every direction. He was right in the middle of the passing lane. We'd just dropped over a slight raise in the highway, which really put him in a place dangerous to oncoming traffic. I knew he was beyond all chance of life, but I'd better hurry back there and drag him out of the highway before he caused a serious wreck. I had the maxie brake and trailer emergency brakes set on the truck and was out of it, before it ever quit rolling. I was running back up the highway beside it as my other horses were trying to get back on their feet.

By the time I got to the colt, he was trying to get up. I was sure it was only his nervous energy running out. I grabbed hold of his halter. He was a pretty big colt, being over two months old at the time, and would be a pretty heavy load dead weight; so I figured I'd better take advantage of what help he could give me. By the time we got to the median, I had examined him so thoroughly with my eyes, I was sure he didn't have any serious broken bones. If he just wasn't all busted up inside, was all I could think.

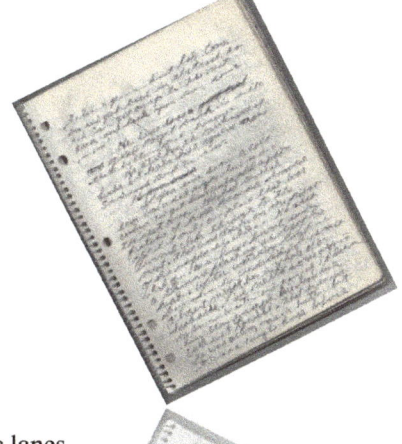

Already several cars had caught up to us and just stopped right in the highway. I had to take my mind clear away from that little colt, and get real hard-boiled with some of the people in order to get them back in their cars and moving out of the traffic lanes.

It was fast building up for a real bad disaster--someone coming over the rise fast in a hot car, or a big loaded truck, and finding the highway full of stopped cars and nowhere to go. The people there thought I was awful cruel when, in answer to their good intentioned suggestions, I told them, "He's just another horse". I can take care of him, now, will you please hurry and get your cars out of the way". This colt was almost like one of my own kids. All the time I was getting the highway cleared, I'd been watching him for signs of bloody, frothy breath. After a few minutes, I nicknamed that guy right there. "Lucky", I says to him, "I don't believe you're hurt bad.

Come on and get back in the truck so we can get on up to the rest area and look you over some more." He sure was glad to get back in the bottom deck with those other horses.

He still has the nickname of Lucky, but his registered name is Sherwood Drifter. **If you ever saw a colt that was a sad sight, he was one when we** got him unloaded up at the rest area. He had several patches of hide knocked off, but only one place that was burned clear through to the meat. That was down on the point of his right shoulder. He also had quite a large bump under a skinned place on the top of his head. After watching him for a few minutes we decided his worst ailment might be a whale of a headache. We melted some aspirin in water, then wrapped his head in a cold wet towel. His mouth was cut up pretty bad, and the teeth were loose. When he'd try to nurse, he couldn't because his mouth was too sore.

With the wet towel on his head, he really looked like he had a hangover, but by evening, he was acting much better. With everyone in the crew doctoring and caring for him, he lost most of his hurting symptoms in a couple days. Other than a small knot on his jaw, he came through the whole episode without any serious injury.

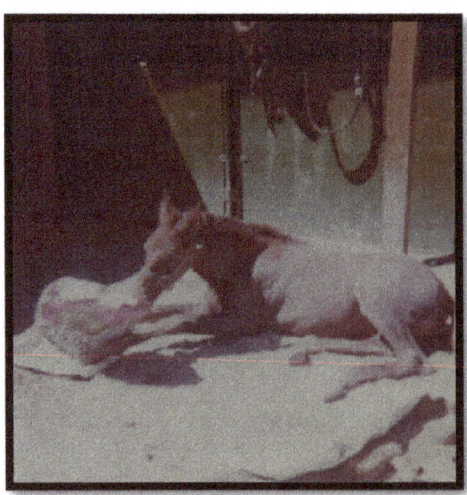

Got back and hitched up and Red drove off with the stage, me in the Dodge, and Kip on Pete. Had two lady passengers. Started going down long easy slopes, country beginning to get hilly. Stopped at an exit for a water break. Had pop for all. When we started up, Juliet's line got caught and the leaders circled hard. Red was yelling "Whoa!". They were going away from me, and over a bank, dropped off another bank and headed straight for the fence. Kip was back behind me. We tried to catch them. Just as they got to the fence, Red turned them and down the fence line they went with the coach scraping and wires screeching. Kip got in front and they stopped. Everyone piled out, and the women weren't scared.

We had three lady passengers sign on at Red Desert. One left us at Bitter Creek, but the other two rode all the way to Point of Rocks with us. Those two gals sure were game. I gave them a wild ride that afternoon quite unintentionally.

I drove the coach out of Bitter Creek. It was another hot day, and after awhile we pulled out on one of those rest areas that is just a blacktopped parking lot along the interstate for sleepy or broken down motorists. We stopped for a "water break", or rather a "pop stop", as those gals had brought pop for all. Just as I started out, my lead horses got in a quarrel. The near leader jumped to get away from the off leader and caused the off lead line to hang up in the harness. I saw it happen and tried to stop the team by jamming the brake on and hauling in on the lines, but they were ready to go and didn't stop.

When I pulled on the lines, it put pressure on the near lead line, but none on the off lead horse. Instead of stopping, it caused them to turn hard to the left. We had stopped close to the edge of the blacktop, and from there the bank sloped down real steep for about 15 or 20 feet before it tapered off to a more gentle grade. When the horses ducked around, they turned so sharp that I guess the backend of the coach more or less blocked them from coming clear around, and the only place they had to go was down the bank. When the stage was pulled around far enough for me to see this, it looked bad. At the bottom of the steep grade was a pretty good rut, but up ahead 50 or 75 feet was the right-of-way fence, a woven wire fence which angled off away from us in the same general direction we were going. In an instant I could see if I threw the slack to that other lead horse, he'd probably curve enough to run parallel with that fence when we got to it.

We backed up the horses by hand, and swung them away from the fence; then Red got off and pushed the coach backwards. He pried on the wire until we got loose. Taking stock of the damage we found the near singletree broken, the front axle bent, the wheel tipped in ,and the "reach" scored by the wheel. Bad, but not nearly as bad as it would have been if the coach had gone over or if they'd gone through the fence.

Red wired up the singletree, and drove them back up on the road. We loaded up and another half mile or so, and stopped again. I held the leaders and Red went to work on the wheels.

Found that the bolts were out of the left front. He spent about 1 ½ hours working. Finally started.

We went off over that bank at a pretty good clip. It was quite a thrill. That old coach was really a bucking and a pitching, but as long as it didn't go to sunfishing when we hit the bottom, I figured I could ride it. You might be wondering where my help was along about now.

Kip was riding Pete and had headed out for the highway when I'd first started up. Marge was in the pickup and had pulled ahead and off to the right to let me go by with the coach. When we hung up, we turned left, away from both of them. The whole thing happened in just about one minute. By the time we came off that bank, both Kip and Marge were already closing in on us, one on either side, Kip ahorseback and Marge afoot. They were just about even with the wheelers when we hit the bottom of the bank. Well, we bounced across the rut, and like I hoped for, that lead team saw that fence and curved enough to keep from piling into it. I went to work then on that set of near lines and pulled them close enough to hook the near wheels in the woven wire. We came to a screeching halt pretty sudden then. I had the gals unload and asked them if they were OK. They answered, "That was a thrill we wouldn't have missed for anything." "The only thing that bothered us was we were afraid we might spill pop on the red velvet inside the coach!"

A breeze and clouds came up, and cooled it down a little. Got to Point of Rocks.. Unloaded the women and piled on a batch of kids that Red hauled around the block.

Then Red drove back to Red Desert for our camper. It was after 11 PM before we got to bed and we were both too nervous to sleep; so talked over the day's events.

Marge untangled the off lead line, and after a bit of wiggling the hitch and coach around, I got unhooked from the fence. With all my lines straight and in working order, we drove up out of there like nothing out of the ordinary had ever happened. When Frizzells had taken our coach back for repairs, they had put bearings in the wheels in place of boxings. They thought sure they had it fixed, and I sure hoped so.

A few miles on down the highway from where we'd had our little turnaround, something got to feeling not right on the coach. It wasn't but a short ways until I noticed one front wheel wobbling a bit, so I stopped to check it. The bearing had come apart. Luckily, I had some heavy lag screws in my tool box and was able to make repairs enough so we could drive on to Point of Rocks.

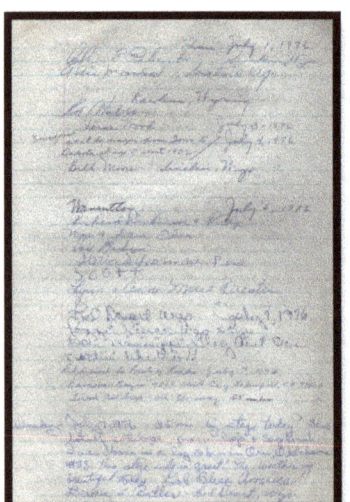

Coach Passengers

The Overland Trail through here ran north of Elk Mountain and through Bridger's Pass. The Cherokee Trail ran south. The Wyoming stations averaged 12½ miles apart. The meals usually served consisted mainly of beans, bacon and coffee. The average speed was about 8 miles per hour. The record, with 12 passengers, the driver and shotgun messenger and ½ ton of mail aboard, was 14 miles in 52 minutes, which works out to just a fraction over 16 miles per hour. The Overland Stage Main Line had 2700 horses and mules and 100 coaches. The annual bill for feed was one million dollars, which included 20,000 tons hay. Virginia Dale, Colorado was the division point, and the stations listed for Wyoming with the mileage to them is listed on the next page.

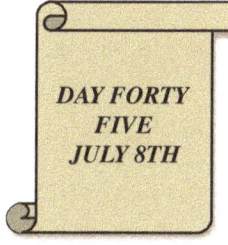

DAY FORTY FIVE JULY 8TH

DAY FORTY-FIVE JULY 8TH

The next day, I had to pull that wheel off and haul it into Rock Springs to a machine shop and get it worked on some more. **Point of Rocks** had been an important stage station in the old main line days. They sported two large rock walled buildings there. Today both buildings are still there. One has been re-roofed and restored, but the roof and much of the walls of the other one have fallen in.

One of the local people loaned Marge a Wyoming Geological Association Guidebook about the state history, from which she copied down some notes.

7/8 – POINT OF ROCKS LAYOVER
Tammie came in during the night. Had two boys that Jack sent up. Just have a five gallon can of water; so no baths, and everyone is dirty. Made the boys wash in the horse trough. We get drinking water from the station. Men took the front axle out from under the coach and worked on it. Then Red and Tammie took a wheel into Rock Springs to get some bolts. After dishes I went with Pearl, Joe, and Eddie in the Thompsons' camper. Pearl got sick from riding backwards. We went over to the original old stage station south of the highway, under the bluffs. One building has been restored, and the other has the walls partially up. A fascinating place. Buildings are of native rock, sort of a sandstone. Mortar was of adobe, grass, and sagebrush.

15	Willow Springs
15	Big Laramie
14	Little Laramie
17	Copper Creek
11	Rock Creek (Arlington)
17	Medicine Box (Elk Mtn.)
8	Elk Mountain (Ft. Halleck)
14	Pass Creek
16	North Platte
14	Sage Creek
10	Pine Grove
9	Bridger Pass
10	Sulphur Springs
11	Washie
13	Duck Lake
12	Dug Springs
15	LaClede
12	Big Pond
14	Black Buttes
14	Point of Rocks
14	Salt Wells
14	Rock Springs
15	Green River
14	Lone Tree
18	Ham's Fork
12	Church Buttes
8	Millersville
14	Ft. Bridger
12	Muddy
10	Quaking Asp
10	Bear River
10	Needle Rock, Utah

I wish it were possible to follow the old trail exactly and drive into each station listed. Anytime we had a chance to do so, like at Point of Rocks, it was a real thrill. After we got the coach back in working order, I harnessed up four head of horses and hooked them up and we headed for the old station. **I felt I could have driven to this one with my eyes shut.** I sure had the feeling that maybe one of those old time drivers was right up there on the box with me. The old station lies up on a slight raise at the base of a rocky point. When we were about a quarter mile away, my horses swung into an easy gallop on their own, like they knew they were coming into a home station. They galloped right up in front of the old buildings and came to a stop without hardly a touch of the lines from me. After the crew explored around and took several pictures, we took a drive on up the road past the station for a mile or so. I just felt like I had to go up that road a ways, like as if to see if it was still the same as it used to be. I really felt at home there. When we came back down the road, those horses of mine galloped right back up to the station again and pulled up on their own accord, once more. It was almost uncanny.

Some of the old timbers are burn blackened. Walls are two feet thick. Inside of building was very cool in spite of heat outside. A fascinating place that would have been a welcome sight to travelers crossing the plains by stage.

We've drunk a gallon of ice water and a gallon of tea already. Hot and dry, but there is a breeze.
Red and Tammie got back from town with the wheel fixed. The men put the coach back together, and then we hooked up Romeo and Rebel, Bandito and Red Horse, and took a load of kids over to the old stage station. We galloped up; stopped for a while; then drove along the old road a ways before turning around and going back. After unhitching we took the kids to the reservoir behind Jim Bridger Power plant and went swimming.

> *I have thought a lot about that day out of Point of Rocks, since then. It kind of makes me wonder about things like reincarnation and such.*

Tammie made it back that day at Point of Rocks. Sure enough, she brought two new crew members with her, John and Dave. They were both good boys, but John only stayed a few days. Dave had enlisted in the Air Force and said he could only stay until we got to Salt Lake City. We hated to see him leave when we got there.

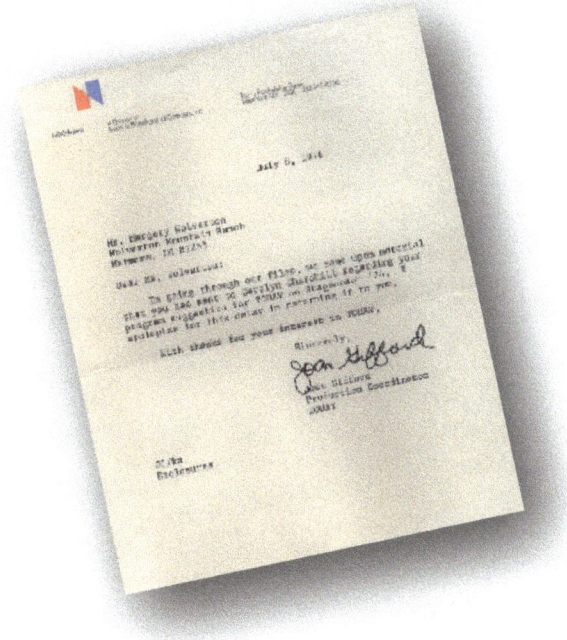

DAY FORTY-SIX
JULY 9TH

Wendy rode her little mare, Holly Ann, out of Point of Rocks. That was not unusual, as she'd ridden her almost as much as we had worked her in harness, but this morning was different. Wendy was trying to stay out in the lead of the hitch, to point the way for Joe, as he preferred. Holly Ann decided this morning that she should be in the hitch. Each time Wendy got out front of the hitch, Holly would stop until the coach horses would catch up.

Wendy is a pretty good little horsewoman, but at nine years old, it is sometimes hard to boss some of those horses around. Finally, when she was out in the lead, Holly Ann stopped and refused to budge until the lead team caught up. The leaders pulled apart and went up as far on each side as their hame spreader strap would let them go. For a few minutes we had three leaders there. Joe had to stop. This time, when they got Holly Ann out from the leaders, Joe decided it would be best for Wendy to ride on the side the rest of the way.

We had our noon camp at **Rim Rock** on the old highway. We had to wait there most of the afternoon, for the clock to unwind. A large group of Rock Springs people planned on meeting us about 5 miles east of town and escorting us on to the fairgrounds ahorseback.

7/9 – POINT OF ROCKS to ROCK SPRINGS
Wendy spent the night with a girl friend. They'd played together all day. The little girl had a mule named Josephine, and they'd ridden and hiked. Got the mares hitched up after breakfast. Joe took the coach, and I got to ride in it. We followed the old Highway 32. The road is quite close to the cliffs here. They are tan, gray, and white with streaks and patches of rust color. Full of holes, and weathered, rounded in places, rugged in others. Not high, maybe 100 feet. Highway must be heading northerly when we started out because the sun was coming in the right hand side. I believe the old stage road must be on the south side of the creek and railroad tracks. We are in the middle with I 80 on the north of us. Weather is delightful; warm with a cool breeze. Sky is clear blue with a few clouds on the horizon.

Even though we waited three hours at Rim Rock before leaving, we were still early for our planned meeting. I drove into **Rock Springs** with a full load of town officials and about eight outriders. A couple of them had quite a time with their horses, as they spooked at the coach. I really got to wondering about the blisters as one fella rode in shorts with bare legs and sandals, and his horse was so full of energy he was taking his rider up and down the hillsides and over the rocks. We spent a couple hours giving rides around the racetrack at the fairgrounds.

DAY FORTY-SEVEN
JULY 10TH

Since we had the weekend scheduled for a layover there, I pulled the other three wheels off the coach and took them to the machine shop to finish the job that hadn't been done right. We had a good weekend, although Marge got a real bad sunburn while standing outside Sunday morning talking to a lady who raised quarterhorses. We rolled our beds outside and enjoyed the cool night air and the freshness of the early dawn.

7/10 – ROCK SPRINGS LAYOVER
Right after breakfast, Red took two wheels down to the machine shop.

I put on a pot of beans to cook; then the three kids and I did the laundry. Only one we could find that looked big enough **charged fifty cents a load.** I told the woman in charge what a gyp I thought it was. I just put 7 loads of clothes in 4 washers to make up for it. Red invited the machine shop people out for rides after supper; so we hooked up and he took them out. Had quite a visit with them. They were appalled at Rock Springs" officials and lack of hospitality. Slept out again. Enjoyed the cool night air.

DAY FORTY EIGHT JULY 11TH

DAY FORTY-EIGHT JULY 11TH

I drove the pickup to Green River Sunday morning, mainly to check out a dirt road that paralleled the interstate. It ran all the way there, but I decided we didn't want to use it as there was a long grade just before reaching town that was too steep to pull the coach over. While I was there, I stopped in at the KUGR Radio station and visited with their DJ. They gave us a good build-up and invited the community to visit us in the next couple days. I also drove by the old Green River stage station, and then went on over to the rodeo grounds while I was there. It was a good thing I located them before arriving with the stagecoach. Their rodeo grounds are about as well hidden as one can be in a small town.

ROCK SPRINGS

7/11 SUNDAY – ROCK SPRINGS LAYOVER
Went back to sleep, and got up late. Red had bought "Texas Rolls" so breakfast was easy to fix. A lady came out to feed the roping steers. I walked over to visit. Had on shorts and a sleeveless top. She was a Quarterhorse breeder. Stood and talked horses until 1:00 PM. It was terribly hot. Got amazed at her telling us what all to do with our horses, and how Tammie should train Max as he wasn't ready for a reining contest, etc. She'd read all the books and recommended we get one written by a professional trainer. I finally went in and fixed stew for dinner. Started turning red on my legs. By evening I had a bad case of sunburn. People came out all day as the radio broadcast the news about us being there. Kip made a cake and Tam frosted it. Had it with ice cream for dessert.

DAY FORTY-NINE
JULY 12TH

I had to get a new tire for the horse truck in Rock Springs; so Monday, when we moved out, Joe took the coach, and I went down to the tire shop, and sent Marge on ahead to **Green River** with the camper to contact the officials. They had expressed a desire to ride into town on the coach. About the time we arrived at the edge of town, a rain also arrived. I had passed the coach just before it got to town, and met Marge after she'd come from talking over the phone to the officials. I guess they figured if we were "rain doctors" they didn't want to have anything to do with us. Anyhow they didn't show up.

I was leading the procession out to the rodeo grounds, with the horse van. To get to the other side of town, we had to negotiate a railroad underpass that was laid out on an S curve. When I came out of the underpass with the horse van, I was crowding the middle of the highway, trying to get the oncoming traffic to slow down some. I must have done too good a job, as a man in a car slammed on his brakes when he saw the stagecoach right behind me. **He stopped dead right in his line of traffic. There was a large semi-dump truck rolling along behind him; he wasn't able to stop quite so quickly.** He tried to pass the car on the right side, but didn't quite make it. It was no place for us to stop; so we drove on to the rodeo grounds.

7/12 –ROCK SPRINGS to GREEN RIVER
Red took other two wheels in to be fixed. I vacuumed the camper and cleaned it. Fixed spaghetti and meatballs and salad for dinner. Hooked up and Joe drove the coach. Tam and Wendy rode Pete and Juliet. Kip and I helped load horses and then Red took the truck to town to get a front tire. I drove the camper on to Green River. Called Dennis Smith and he still hadn't contacted anybody; so I sat and waited at the edge of town. Finished the dish of ice cream. Police were supposed to meet us between 4:00 and 4:30, but the coach arrived at 10 to 4:00. We turned and went through an underpass. When I got through I could see a police car leading. There was an accident just past the underpass, and a truck was run up on the sidewalk.

The police did ask me what had caused the mishap, but didn't feel it was our fault. Although the rain cancelled our giving any rides that afternoon, it sure didn't stop the townspeople from driving by to look the stagecoach over. A good many took pictures regardless of the rain. We had told several people to come by the next morning and we'd give them a ride as we headed out of town.

DAY FIFTY
JULY 13TH

DAY FIFTY
JULY 13th

We had a full coach load to the edge of town as I drove the stage out that morning. We used the old highway since it follows the interstate all the way to Little America. When we crossed the Green River, going out of town, we looked carefully to determine where the old ford had been. It looked like it was just north of the bridge we were on. The steeper banks gave way to a gradual slope down to the water. The shallower water indicated the possibility of a gravel bottom. If there had been some way to get down there, I'd like to have driven the coach down and forded the river in old style. **It's a beautiful stagecoach drive along there with the rippling Green River on the left and towering multi-colored cliffs on the right.** This old road also bypasses the tunnel on the interstate which suited me fine.

We came to a suspicious looking cattle guard on that old road, which shouldn't have caused us any problems, but it did. Dave, who was driving the pilot pickup, circled on ahead of us, crossed the cattleguard, and pulled to the side out of the way. A sheriff drove by about that time. After stopping to visit, he helped Dave lay our plywood panels

We went on to the rodeo grounds next to a large construction site where big machinery was making nerve racking noise. Started raining right after we got there. Unhitched. Fixed chili burgers for supper and potato salad.

7/13 – GREEN RIVER to LYMAN
More people came out to take pictures in the morning. Hitched up Red's team. I rode on the box with him. Wendy too. Kip rode Holly Ann. Joe drove the truck, Tam, the camper, and Dave the pilot car. We let several people ride to the edge of town. When we stopped to unload, one big girl said she was going all the way to Little America. Red said he thought that she'd better get out there, and she said, "Well there was nobody to meet her there, and she'd have to walk back to town."

in place. I started across but something wasn't quite right. When I got the leaders up to the plywood, they hesitated and didn't want to take it. Dave was right close so he caught hold of one of the leaders, and after a bit, persuaded them to follow him across the boards. After Dave got over a ways, he turned loose of the horse and stepped back out of the way. As I drove the coach past him, I realized I had problems. Dave had grabbed the inside check line to use as a lead strap, and had pulled the buckle on the end of it, down through a hame ring. I'd been watching the swing and wheel horses to keep them straight on the boards. When I started to work my lead lines, one of them felt like I was pulling up against something solid. I pulled on both lines, but instead of steadying the lead team the pressure was all on one side. It was on the off lead line, and it took effect just as the lead team walked past Tammie's pickup. I put the brake on and pulled in hard on my other horses, but was unable to stop in time. The right front axle of the coach hooked under the left front fender well of the pickup. Before we got stopped, we drug it sideways four feet! We straightened out the lines, and I swung the horses off a bit. The sheriff held up the singletree out of the way, and Margie backed the pickup away from the coach. It didn't hurt much except it did put a new dent in the pickup fender.

Back in Rawlins, we had met some folks from California with a big fancy horse trailer-camper combination. They were heading for Estes Park, Colorado for a National Morgan Horse Show. All except two or three of our horses are registered Morgans so it was natural for us to get together for a good visit. The morning shortly after the cattle guard episode, I noticed a big shiny black horse van heading up the highway, with arms waving out the windows. Marge was up in the shotgun seat beside me, I pointed and said, "I wonder how they did at Estes?"

About that time, they found a good place to pull their rig over to the side and stop. By the time we'd got there, they'd all crawled through the fence and came over to our road. We swapped news, them telling us about the show and we told them about our trip since Rawlins.

> I wished I'd had the camera going out of Green River. The bluffs would have made a good picture from up on the box with the river winding around. When we crossed the river, we talked about where the old ford was. The sheriff met us later on, just before we had to cross a cattle guard. Rebel ducked off and pulled Juliet. Not long after that, the Morgan people we'd met in Rawlins passed us on the freeway. We changed horses at the Church Buttes exit. Red sent me on ahead with the Dodge because it had boiled over with Tam, and blown out a seal. He whittled down a piece of wood and plugged up the hole. I got about 10 miles down the road, and had to stop because the awning was becoming unrolled in the front and tearing. I tried for 10 minutes to roll it up and couldn't. Red came along and fixed it and we went on.

They claimed to be in a hurry, but it didn't take much persuasion to get the parents to let the kids get on and ride with us for a few miles.

Our horse van was waiting for us a short ways east of **Little America**; so when the Davidsons came to it, they stopped and waited for us. When we left Green River that morning, I wasn't sure how far we'd go that day. I figured if it was hot and sultry, we'd probably noon at Little America, then go on to the Church Buttes rest area for a night camp.

The morning had been cool, and my horses weren't even settled down good yet; so I decided I'd take my hitch on to Church Buttes. Joe could run his hitch on to Lyman that afternoon. You can spend a much more restful night at a small town's rodeo grounds than in a rest area alongside the interstate.

It was 33 miles from the rodeo grounds in Green River to the Church Buttes rest area. The last mile or so is a fairly good up hill grade. That hitch I was driving was still trotting right up against the bits without being urged, when we topped that raise and spotted the rest area turnoff ahead. Our horses were all in pretty good shape and condition along about then. I'm sure I could have jogged my hitch on that 18 miles to Lyman in 2½ hours without bothering them.

When we laid out our original schedule, we hadn't planned on stopping in Lyman, but the day before, when I contacted their mayor and other officials, they said they'd be delighted to have us come through their town. The mayor met us and rode through town to the rodeo grounds.

After taking the Lyman exit, the valley started getting green, with pretty trees and meadows in contrast to sand, shale, rocks, and sagebrush. There was fresh hay stacked in the fields.
We stopped at the edge of town, and Red went to see Grant Walker and the mayor who owned the Polar King.
It was awfully hot, and we got ice cream cones free. Went back to the highway, got the truck and took the horses to the rodeo grounds.

Unhitched and Tam herded the horses in the grass. The mayor invited us to the Polar King for supper.

It was pretty late and we had had a long hard day. We weren't planning on moving on until the middle of the next afternoon; so we decided not to give any rides that evening. We promised to hook up early the next day and give rides to everyone who wanted one. The mayor owned and ran the hamburger hut in Lyman. We really appreciated it when he invited us there for supper.

54 ABOARD - OUR RECORD - LYMAN, WY

DAY FIFTY ONE JULY 14th

DAY FIFTY –ONE
JULY 14TH

We were running low on hay again, but I found hay in two places to buy there, so I was out early the next morning rebuilding our hay pile. We had an early lunch; then hitched up and hauled kids around 1:00 to 3:30. We've hauled a good many loads of kids that we'd counted from 33 to 38 at one time. This day in Lyman, it sure looked to me like we had a whale of a load; so I asked one of the bystanders to count them as they unloaded. **Fifty-four kids climbed off that coach!** No wonder my horses had to get down and scratch to start that coach moving there on the soft ground.

The Ladies Mounted Drill Team from Lyman decided to saddle up and escort us over to **Fort Bridger** that afternoon. Something like that always pleased us. About half way there, we were met by a lady riding a big classy mare under a side-saddle. She was dressed in a beautiful blue 1890 style sidesaddle costume.

The first chance I got, I asked her if her mare was a Morgan. Sure enough, she was a registered Morgan. The lady, Anne, and her husband, lived a short ways west of Ft. Bridger on a little place. They had a couple other Morgans and invited us out to see them, and have coffee, ice cream, and cake with them.

7/14 – LYMAN to FORT BRIDGER

Got up late and fixed breakfast. Another dry camp so no baths. Cooked stew meat and added it to spaghetti for dinner at 1:00 PM. Red hooked up and took several rides out. One man told his kids, he guessed they could ride to Fort Bridger. I said it would cost $5.00, and they backed off. We left about 3:00. Tam and Eddie rode Pete and Muskrat. Wendy and I rode in the coach. She wore a dress too. Joe loaded up things after we left, but didn't drive the truck. He caught up with us with his pickup and rode in. It was a lovely trip across the valley, green and pretty. Had a good breeze and I had to hold my hat on. Several people rode from Lyman to Bridger with us. Just east, a lady in costume riding sidesaddle came to meet us; name of Anne Poshak.

Several of the original buildings built from stone are still standing, and have been restored to excellent condition. We were given a good pasture for our horses, and a nice grassy lot for our campers. We unhooked the coach over by the museum.

The arrival of the stage was as intriguing to the local people and tourists there, as the old fort was to us. All the local people connected with the fort itself dress in appropriate costume. It was quite a sight to be met by soldiers in cavalry blue and women and kids in long dresses and high button shoes. Each evening they shoot off the old cannon and play "Taps" as part of their flag-lowering ceremony.

We managed to get unhooked and free of chores in time to observe this American tradition. The evening we arrived, they were presenting a melodrama, portraying some happenings concerning the fort in the old days.

The melodrama was for the benefit of the Wyoming State Historical Society people who were there on an inspection tour. We just happened to arrive at the right time, and were invited to attend the activities. We certainly enjoyed it. Sometimes amateur actors are better than professionals. This play was about an episode between the local Indian Chief and the Major of the fort. Of course, the West being what it was, the plot was spiced up somewhat by some scarlet ladies and a culprit or two.

After the melodrama, we all were conducted on a moonlight tour of the fort.

All of the rooms in the museum that were fixed up with 1860 furniture and trappings were occupied by people dressed in proper attire from that period.

She was riding a good looking Morgan mare. Reminded all of us of Fortune.

We got into town and picked up a load of kids, only to find out they were the same ones who'd ridden about 3 times in Lyman, and expected to ride to Bridger free. We drove in a small gate to the Fort, and stopped north of the museum, and unhitched. Were met by several people in long dresses, and Union Army uniforms. About 5:00 the army crew played Reveille and fired off the canon, and took down the flag. Came back at 8:00 and watched their melodrama about Jim Bridger, and the early days of the Fort. It was very enjoyable. Then we went to the cafe and got hamburgers. Went back to the museum at 10:30 for the moonlight tour of the Fort. Scenes were acted out in all the buildings. It was good. Finally got to bed at midnight.

Fort Bridger was one of the really important forts back in the old days of mounted Cavalry, Indians, and freighters.

As we passed each room, a light came on in it, and the people acted out an episode of life from that time. The same occurred at all the buildings as we were escorted through them. It certainly was a well presented program and very enjoyable. Besides the flag ceremony each day, they also have an outside PA system that plays different bugle calls and gives commands all through each day. It is quite a place.

> *I think the kids all absorbed more history in that tour than they'd ordinarily get in a month of school books.*

Sunday School Enjoyed Trip To Fort Bridger

The course nine Sunday School class motored to Fort Bridger Thursday. This is an annual event and helps highlight the lessons on the Mormon Pioneers. The group enjoyed a guided tour that included instruction in the Indian art of making arrow heads, fish hooks and other weapons and implements from rock and bone. The beautiful stage coach traveling from St. Louis to California was in Fort Bridger and the children had the privilege of climbing aboard and inspecting the coach.

I do feel like perhaps I have lived the west that most people only read about.

DAY FIFTY TWO
JULY 15th

DAY FIFTY-TWO
JULY 15TH

We had a pleasant surprise Thursday, when Dick and his family dropped in on us. They planned to stay with us on into Salt Lake.

West By Stage Coach

7/15 – FORT BRIDGER -LAYOVER Slept in again. After breakfast Tam moved the camper under the trees because it was hot. Had the horses turned out in the pasture by the camper. Good water and grass. Turned Fortune out part of the time. Wendy and I walked over to the museum about noon and went through it. The display was excellent. Civil War uniforms, guns, pioneer artifacts, and history of the fort and region. Red and Dave went after a load of hay. McCombs drove up in a new camper. I went back to the museum with them. Red finally finished and went through the fort too. Got some high priced groceries, and went to the camper. Poshaks came over and looked at our horses. Anne brought spice cake and fruit Jello. Slept inside as the mosquitoes were bad.

DAY FIFTY THREE JULY 16th

**DAY FIFTY-THREE
JULY 16TH**

Friday morning, July 16, saw us heading west again. We hated to leave that pretty valley, but it was time to move on. Noon brought Joe and the coach into **Kemmerer Junction.** It isn't very far from Bridger to **Evanston**, but there are several pretty good hills. A couple of the city fathers drove out from town and rode into Evanston on the coach with me that afternoon.

The local radio station announcer saw us go by; so he grabbed his tape recorder, ran across the street, crawled through the fairgrounds fence, and climbed up on the coach beside me. Looking at his wristwatch, he said he would have to hurry in order to get back to his station in time to make his 5 o'clock news report, and he'd like to play the recorded interview on it. He got the interview, checked his recorder to make sure it had worked properly, hurriedly climbed off the coach.

The last I saw of him was as he cleared the fence heading back for his station.

7/16 – FORT BRIDGER to EVANSTON

Fixed breakfast in shifts, and had to hurry to get dressed to ride in the coach. Grabbed the comb and brush and did my hair. Darla, Dottie, Edie, and Anne Poshak rode too. Wendy and Betty Jo were on Juliet and Bandera. Later Dottie rode Bandera a little, then Edie and Eddie. We stopped for noon (about 3:30) at the Kemmerer, Wy. Junction. After eating Red left with the coach, and Tam was riding. Darla, Eddie, and the girls all went with me in the Dodge. We drove onto Evanston and did laundry. Got back to the rodeo grounds just as Red finished up and they were starting to unhitch. We fixed a potluck for supper. I bought shoulder blade chuck steaks for 99 cents a pound. Served outside. The steaks were good and big, and everyone enjoyed the meal.

We hauled several people for a ride around the fairgrounds. About that time, a young fellow and two gals rode in on horses, leading one pack horse. They had started out from Kimball, Utah, and were heading up toward Idaho or Washington. Margie had found a good bargain on some steaks and we'd planned an outdoor steak fry for the crew that night. We invited these kids to have supper with us. We had quite a feast with the extra potluck dishes the other crew members brought, and then sat around the fire and visited.

DAY FIFTY-FOUR
JULY 17TH

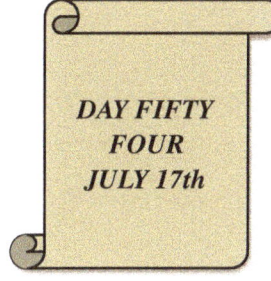

DAY FIFTY FOUR JULY 17th

Joe drove out of Wyoming the next morning and went through the Utah port. Jack's boy, Eddie, who was outriding, commented he'd ridden into Wyoming, and now he was riding out of it. I brought the horse van. The port officials gave us free passage for the truck since our outfit was a non-profit Bicentennial project. Joe drove to the **Castle Rock** exit, where I'd set up our noon camp on the shoulder by the exit ramp. A fellow showed up there just after we'd unhitched Joe's horses. He said he was a reporter from Echo Canyon, Utah, and he had hoped to get some pictures. He was terribly disappointed that we'd already unhooked. He was quite relieved when I told him we'd be hitching up again as soon as we were finished with lunch, and that he was welcome to take the pictures. Also, if he had the time, I'd like to have him come ride down the canyon with me.

He was a third generation Echo Canyonite. His grandfather had been one of the original founders of the community.

7/17 – EVANSTON to COALVILLE

Flint, Wendy's dog, barked at the horses running loose, and woke us up several times during the night. Joe drove the coach out. Had to hurry. I was upset. Kids took turns riding Muskrat. First Eddie, then Edie, then Darla. I felt lousy so finally lay down in the coach and slept awhile. Felt better afterward. Went through the ports at the state line. Country was leveling out then gradually giving way to rocky bluffs and eroded chimneys and caves. Streaks of red dirt showing. We stopped for dinner at Castle Rock. Parked in the meridian to change horses and eat. I heated up leftover spaghetti and salad for lunch. Red drove out with the stage, with Tam outriding. Joe drove the truck.

The Summit County Bee

THURSDAY, JULY 15, 1976 — NUMBER TWENTY-NINE — Volume XXXVIII — Coalville, Utah 84017

Traffic on state 80 ... while Ivo... hitched... his stage... to conti... excursion... vehicles... crease... nology... Echo C... fare over...

The Wolverton caravan is following the old Overland Trail from St. Joseph, Mo., to Sacramento, Calif. This is the first time a stagecoach has traveled completely the historic route since the 1890's, Wolverton said as he drove his $27,500 rig down the canyon.

While riding on road not yet freeway, the nineteenth century vehicle slowed westbound traffic. The travelers didn't seem to mind, as many stuck their cameras out their windows to take pictures of the coach. Truck drivers, east and westbound, beeped their horns and waved. "We've become a familiar sight to many truckers," Wolverton said as he waved back. "We've been on the road since May 15. We plan to be in Sacramento by Sept. 4."

"Roads and fence lines do not allow us to follow the original 1,913 mile route," Wolverton said. The route is now 1,749 miles." The Utah trek extends from the Wyoming state line to Echo, Coalville, Parley's Summit, Salt Lake City, Wendover.

All along their trip the family has given free rides to people. Riding down Echo Canyon was Mrs. Lenora Toone, Sonora, Calif., granddaughter of James E. Bromley, builder of the stage station in Echo, main stop between Ft. Bridger and Salt Lake City.

Planned Echo

"We planned to stay in Echo," said Wolverton, "but we received no response to our correspondence; therefore, we phoned the county sheriff the other day and made arrangements to stay

and was infuriated because no one told her of our coming," he said.

Unincorporated, Echo has no town council. Still many Echo residents expr... disappointment at not... ing farther in advan... prepare something f... arrival of the stage. basis for Echo was the... coach," said Mike Ri... "bringing its first re... and business."

A few people met in... to greet the stagecoa... waving hands and... pictures. One greete... Belva Nowling, Hene... former Echo resident... lost her vision a numb... years ago. With the h... her hands and her so... daughter-in-law, she... ioned the Concord... stagecoach with its tra... al colors of red and y... its brass trim and red... upholstery. The stage... built in Oklahoma Ci... the plans of Buffalo Bill's personal model.

On to Coalville

Additional people sa... state in Coalville. Wolv... gave rides to Coa... residents Sunday at... fairgrounds. Wolverto... tall red-head from Wet... Colo., would sit tall in... driver's seat as he drov... 12 passengers around.

"I've been working... horses since I was a kid... said, clad in western a... "Me and my family de... this trip would be a grea... to celebrate America's... birthday."

His wife, Margery,... "Driving a stage has a... been one of Red's drea... another reason for...

in their semi-trailer to continue their jaunt. They left Tuesday, planning to reach Salt Lake City on Wednesday.

Station Served as Major Stop on Stagecoach Trail

ECHO—

Six Morgan horses will be pulling a Concord stagecoach into Echo on Saturday, July 17, as the 12-passenger "Cadillac" of the stagecoaches approaches the two-thirds mark on its overland excursion.

The Bicentennial dream of a Colorado family to retrace the Overland Trail, began three years ago when he bid the monument on a $27,500 stagecoach. The 1,749-mile trail, extending from St. Joseph, Mo., to Sacramento, Calif., had not been followed since the 1890's. The Ivan "Red" Wolverton family started from St. Joe on May 15 of this road to follow the original routes on near as roads and fence lines would allow. They plan to be in Sacramento by Sept. 1.

Echo's affiliation with the stage began in 1854 when James E. Bromley, town founder, built a station for the line. His Echo station served as one of the major stops between Missouri and California.

Echo's stage station no longer stands, but the Wolverton family still is stopping here to give free rides to those desiring. Riding on the coach will be Mrs. Wolverton, who will relate to passengers her in-depth research of the history of the Overland Trail.

The family is financing its trip "Stagecoach '76" through the sale of medallions, carrying mail and donations. The stage is carrying a Wells-Fargo type strongbox. In the stopbox are medallions, both silver and bronze, which commemorate the centennial efforts of Custer County, Colorado's only centennial county.

operator of Pueblo West, Colo., and his family were riding through Utah with the Wolvertons, too.

Wolverton, a college grad-

The stage is also carrying a mail sack of letters. The charge for sending letters to Sacramento is $1, the same rate charged a century ago. At forementu the letters will be hand-stamped with a special "Overland Mail '76 Stagecoach '76" stamp, and sent by regular mail to their destination.

Construction of the stagecoach took place in Oklahoma City. It was built with specifications from the original horse-drawing plans. This is a scale model of the Concord-type stagecoaches carried dignitaries of the 1800's across the West to "luxury," red velvet cushions.

Members of this family are Red and his wife Margery plus three children: Tammy, 15; Kip, 13; and Wendy, 5. Their permanent residence is Westmore, Colo.

Stagecoach Visits County on Bicentennial Tour

One I especially liked was Calamity, also a third generation grandchild. Her grandfather, James Bromley, had worked for the stagecoach companies and had helped lay out the route across much of Wyoming and Utah. He had driven a stage into and out of the town of Echo Canyon for a good many years. Calamity's father had apparently been quite a character also, as she pointed out to me all the different canyons that he had operated whiskey stills in.

One of the men on the coach with me came from a long line of lawmen. First his grandfather, then his father represented the law in the area. Apparently, the grandfathers of my two passengers were more or less friends, although they were often at odds. The same must have been true with the second generation. The way they told it to me that day was that every so often, a federal man would show up with a report there was a Still being operated in the area; so the sheriff would have to take him out to hunt for it. Somehow, they always found the place shortly after the Still had been hastily torn down and moved.

We had several other passengers that afternoon.

It was quite an afternoon, driving down that canyon on the old road and having that couple tell their stories and point out the landmarks. **Echo Canyon** had been an original stage station, and we had looked forward to spending an overnight stop there.

It started sprinkling just as the stage pulled out. It was quite a series of hills, starting down Echo Canyon. A beautiful drive. Joe had a little trouble with the truck on the hills. I got behind once because the pickup wouldn't go over 25 mph pulling the camper. We got into Coalville and came out to the rodeo grounds. It rained off and on, and was really pouring when the stage got in. They were all soaked. The men unhitched and took care of the horses. Tam was cold and wet so she changed clothes. I fixed hot tea for supper with hamburgers and salad, cake and ice cream.

We wrote the town and got no response. Likewise when I tried to call there, I couldn't make any connections. After several futile attempts, I finally contacted the police department in **Coalville**, a town 7 or 8 miles farther on. They told us we could use the fairgrounds or the railroad corrals, which sounded good to me. We drove on down through the town, and made a circle up around the church which was one of the original buildings of Echo Canyon.

Quite a few people gathered to take pictures and look over the coach before we headed on up the side canyon to Coalville. After starting up the canyon, the road climbs up the left hand side of the wall at an angle to pass over the top of a dam that holds back a large beautiful lake. The road is quite narrow, and we were nearing the top when suddenly a train came rumbling over the crest of the dam, seemingly right in the sagebrush and rocks just barely to the left and up above us. I don't know which was the most startled -- the horses or me.

    I didn't have an idea in the world that there was a train track there above us. After the horses got me quieted down, we pulled on over the dam and headed on up the country. A cold driving rain came up that I think must have followed that train down the valley. Those cold rains sure make a good excuse to let the stagecoach horses out into a good run. There were a great many people camping, swimming and fishing along the lake. They seemed to get quite a kick out of seeing our coach go galloping by, as much as I enjoyed driving it that way. We were a pretty wet bunch of stagecoachers when we pulled into camp that night.

CHAPTER ELEVEN
UTAH

We had planned for over a year to participate in the Days of 47 parade in Salt Lake City. At first we didn't think we would be able to make the all horse parade on the 19th, but when we got in Saturday night in Coalville, I decided maybe we could.

DAY FIFTY FIVE
JULY 18th

DAY FIFTY-FIVE
JULY 18TH

We spent Sunday in Salt Lake making some repairs on vehicles and checking out the downtown area for the parade area.

7/18 – SUNDAY COALVILLE LAYOVER

Fixed sweet rolls for breakfast, late. Weather was warm and sticky.

Red and I went with Dick and Darla to Salt Lake City. They needed to get their camper fixed as Darla broke a fitting on their holding tank, the day before when she turned around in a gravelly place on her way back out to meet the stage.

We went to make phone calls. Neither of us had any success as the repair shops weren't open, and Red couldn't get ahold of anybody.

Got home about 6:00 PM, and Darla fixed chicken. I cooked mashed potatoes and gravy, made salad, and we had cake and ice cream. Afterwards, we all went over to their camper and watched an old John Wayne movie on TV.

DAY FIFTY-SIX
JULY 19TH

DAY FIFTY SIX JULY 19th

The parade was to be at 6 PM and we would have to truck the outfit in. That meant unloading the hay off the rear extension so we could load the coach on the back. Also, the horses would have to be scrubbed and the harness polished. About 4PM we headed for Salt Lake.

It's about 40 miles to where the traffic and red lights get thick. All the lights seem to be red when you're late and in a hurry. We drove right up to the area reserved for parade assembly, only to decide we needed a dock to unload the stagecoach. I knew where there was one two blocks away, and told everybody to follow me there.

7/19 – COALVILLE LAYOVER
SLC parade

Dick and Darla left early to get their camper into the shop by 9:00.

After dishes, I started scrubbing harness. Eddie, Rowdy, and Wendy helped scrub. Dave oiled some and we finished it up. Then I washed Romeo, Rebel, and Bandito. Tammie, Wendy, and Betty Jo were washing some too. Red shod Rebel that morning, and they also had to unload the hay off the truck. Then he spent an hour talking to a newsman. Had a bad time loading the coach on the back of the truck. The dirt bank was uneven, and it threw the wheels lopsided. Scraped the coach. Took an hour and a half.

Joe decided to go further down the street to look for a better one, and got lost. We had the coach unloaded and the horses almost ready to go when he finally found his way back to us. Then we had to wait on someone to change his shirt. We finally hit a trot up the street, only to have to pull up to a walk to pass a bunch of startled saddle horses.

It was 6:20 when we made it back up to the assembly area. We had been assigned the number 65. As we drove up, the numbers going by were in the 80s. All we could do then was to sit and wait and fall in at the end of the line. We didn't have to take the last place after all.

The parade officials in their open convertible motioned for us to pull in ahead of them. It was a good lengthy parade, with lots of spectators. We decided it was well worth it, even with all the hustle and bustle it had taken to make it. It was quite late that night when we got back to Coalville so we didn't bother to unload the coach. We just took care of our horses and hit the sack.

The 3 boys took baths; then Tam, then me. Girls washed and cleaned up. We got clothes for them as I wasn't about to let them go to a parade in dirty clothes.

Red finally finished with the coach, loaded the horses, and came in. He changed clothes and took a plate of food out in the truck and ate it on the way.

Tammie, Dave, and the boys rode in the Dodge. The girls and I rode in the truck with Red. Truck is missing badly, but we got there.

The parade went well, and we seemed to draw lots of applause. Tam led our procession wearing her gold checkered outfit. It showed up very well against all the red, white, and blue outfits of the other groups. Wendy carried our flag on Holly Ann, and Betty Jo rode Bandera.

DAY FIFTY-SEVEN
JULY 20th

We hadn't really gotten underway very far the next morning when a car drove up with two men and a woman in it. It was the TV crew from Salt Lake. They wanted to film us on the road, and I had told them previously we'd be coming from Coalville to Salt Lake on the 19th. I figured for sure they'd say, "Sorry", and leave, when I told them there wasn't any way we could be ready to pull out before noon. Instead of dropping us they said that would be fine, it would give them a chance to eat and relax a bit,

At times like that, when we had a TV crew after us, we'd leave all our vehicles parked and all pile on the coach, so long as we continued to hear the camera shutters clicking. This was for two reasons -- one being the stagecoach is so big, it doesn't look its best unless it has a load on it. The other reason being none of us are the least bit camera shy.

It was Joe's turn to drive. I really hated not to be the one doing the honors; as a matter of fact, I hated to ever relinquish the driving to anyone. Not that I felt someone else wasn't capable, but simply because I don't know of any other job or hobby in the world I'd rather be doing. I think Joe felt the same, because he sure hated to give up the lines to me. The camera crew followed us out on the interstate and started their filming. They shot us from every direction.

They filmed us from ahead, from both sides, with the camera stationary and following in their car. They took shots from an overpass, and more from down over a bank looking up at us. Finally they motioned us to stop and said they'd like to take a few shots from

7/20 – COALVILLE to SALT LAKE CITY
Planned to leave early but it didn't turn out that way. After breakfast I cleaned the camper.

Red unloaded the coach, and then he and Dave reloaded the hay. KSL TV man from Salt Lake came out and talked to them. He decided we'd all ride out on the coach.

We left at 5 minutes after noon with Joe driving. The TV guys filmed from several different places ---in front, beside, and behind the coach, at the horses, the wheels. Then Red got down on the tongue and climbed on Fortune backwards. Afterwards the reporter did the same, and took pictures looking up at Joe. Pearl took a picture of him doing it. Later, the two got inside the coach and took pictures of us riding in it.

inside. Next they decided to ride on top. After a ways, the camera man asked if he could get down on that pole there between the horses to get a shot looking back up towards the coach. Joe didn't think it would work, but it sounded OK to me; so I said I'd climb down on the tongue and check it out to see how it would work. We were trotting right along at a pretty good clip as I climbed down between the wheel horses and worked my way out to the end of the tongue.

The horses didn't mind me being out there between them, but the tongue was so limber and wiggly, I couldn't see how the camera man could manage to stay on it and operate his camera. I stood there on the tongue riding backwards for a ways, wondering what to do to get that camera man down there safely, when I got an idea. I ducked under the lines and swung my leg over Fortune's back. He's our stud horse, and is the near wheeler in the hitch Joe drives.   I mounted him backwards, and looking up at the cameraman I asked, "How'd this be?" "It looks good to me", he answered, "but you better stop for me to get down there." After I got the camera man mounted backwards on Fortune and got his camera back in his hands, I climbed back up to the shotgun seat. Turning to Joe, and grinning, I says, "I sure hope he knows how to ride a horse!"

Joe grinned back and kicked his horses into a gentle trot. The photographer was doing OK riding backwards and holding that heavy camera which weighed about 25 or 30 pounds. But he could not hold it where he wanted it, and look through the eye piece at the same time. He tried several times to lean over into the lines between the horses and aim the camera, but he just couldn't keep his balance leaning over that far, and still aim the camera all at the same time. I'll say one thing for him, he was sure determined to get the shot he wanted. Finally he sat up straight on Fortune, got the camera in his left hand with the trigger under his finger. He ducked under the lines, reached out, and pointed it up our way and turned it on. I guess he decided that was enough. After a few minutes of filming, we stopped and he got off.

The TV crew loaded back in their car, waved goodbye, and sped off down the highway, leaving us behind, wondering if they got anything good enough to show. That turned out to be one of the few times we ever got to see the coach on film. I saw the whole sequence on TV a couple times.

The valley is beautiful and green with a meandering stream. Trees growing along the banks, neat farms and small pastures with cattle grazing in them. The hills rise sharply on both sides as the valley isn't wide. It's a beautiful day but getting hot. Dick and Darla came back from Salt Lake City about 2:30, and took us back to Coalville. We broke camp and ate sandwiches and punch for a late lunch and left. Red and the boys were in the truck. I drove the Dodge with Wendy. On the hill, the Pickup overheated so I passed Red. It boiled over twice, but I made it on to the top. Caught up to the coach, and when they stopped, I gave them the lunch box I'd fixed with sandwiches, beans, and koolaid. It was about 3:30 and I figured they'd all be starved. We went on to the exit past Park City, about 21 miles from Coalville.

All of it was good, but that last shot was really interesting, with all those six lines a dancing and swinging, and seeming to come right out of the camera. The TV station re-ran that episode several times with their Days of 47 Parade promotion.

Dick had taken his motorhome back to the city to be worked on some more that morning so he'd missed all the excitement. Lucky for us, he showed up right after the TV crew left, and took me and the other extra crew members back to Coalville to retrieve the vehicles. I took the horse van on past the coach, and pulled off the road a short ways above **Kimberly Junction** at 4:30 that afternoon and got the relay horses harnessed and ready to go. It was 24 miles from that junction to our night camp at the fair grounds at **Murray**, on the south side of **Salt Lake City**.

It's been in TV, and the movies since then, including "Tombstone".

At 5 O'Clock I pulled my hitch out on the highway, with Dick's daughter, Edie, on the shotgun seat beside me. At 8 o'clock that evening, we galloped into the Murray fairgrounds. It was a good run, nothing out of the ordinary, but I did manage to grab several hands full of ripe cherries from overhanging limbs, on our way through the edge of town.

We invited a lot of people to ride with us or take part in our project in any way they wished. Some never answered, some declined, and many accepted.

We were greatly honored when Governor Rampton of Utah said he would come out on the steps of the capitol to say hello to us, if we cared to drive the coach up there.

Stopped off the edge of the road, and changed horses. Red drove off with the coach, with Wendy on Holly Ann. Left the truck there with Kip and Rowdy to watch it. Tam drove the Dodge, Joe and Pearl their camper, and Dick leading in his. It was 5:00 PM when Red left. We got almost down the big hill, and all pulled over to the side. Got in Dick's camper and watched TV. First time we'd seen the coach, and we all thought it was great. We went on into Salt Lake and set up camp at the county fairgrounds in Murray. Some people came by to look at the coach and talk about the trip. Man's name was Bryce Wolverton, and his folks live in Grantsville. Red came in with the coach about 8:30. Made pretty good time. Several horseback riders came around to visit. One had a half Morgan-half Quarterhorse that was a perfect match for Bandito.

DAY FIFTY-EIGHT
JULY 21st

That was all we needed to roll out extra early Wednesday morning.

We all dressed up in our "Sunday best" and piled on the coach and headed up State Street. The TV camera crew happened to be driving up the street that morning and spotted us. They took several shots, and then came over and rode a ways through town with us. Dick got razzed a lot for being right in the middle of things that morning, and making up for what he'd missed out on the day before.

I had never been all the way up State Street to the Capitol before. If I had, I don't know if I would have been willing to drive that stagecoach up there or not. When we got there, there was no turning back. It was nearing the time for us to meet the Governor, and I wasn't about to chance missing that. The street is already on the up grade when you cross that last red light and head straight up towards the Capitol, and I do mean up.

The light was about to change and I didn't want to have to wait; so I'd let the horses out to a good trot as I came to the intersection and crossed it. We'd actually started up the grade before I realized how long and steep it really was. As we started onto the climb, I could see it was by far too long to trot up; so I was pulling the horses back down to a walk. I don't know what everybody else on the coach thought, but I had a bunch of back seat drivers that all started to yell at the horses to keep them in a trot. I about had them in a walk when I stated rather gruffly, "If you guys'll shut up, I'll do the driving." I guess I got my message across as it grew very quiet there on the coach for awhile.

The horses were all ready in a hard pull, and it was taking every one of them to keep us moving. I felt sure they could do it, if nothing slipped. At each step that every horse made, I could hear their slick steel shoes giving a little; slipping a trifle on the black top.

7/21 – SALT LAKE CITY (MURRAY) Fixed breakfast and then got ready. Wore my lavender dress. Red hooked up Romeo and Rebel, Roulette and Robby, Bandito and Red Horse. After I got in the coach, Darla and the kids got in. She had an open can of Pepsi, and Betty Jo and Dottie dumped it right down the front of my dress. I was awfully mad and disgusted.
Went down State Street. Tam rode Max and wore her brown outfit. Wendy wore her Easter dress, and Betty Jo wore Wendy's blue dress and bonnet. Drove up to the Capitol just at 10:30. The four block hill to it was real steep, and the horses were pulling so hard, their feet slipped on the paving. Joe and the boys got off and walked up.
Governor Rampton of Utah came out and shook hands with the men. Red presented him with a silver medallion.

I pulled them down harder, to a slower gait; I'd say about two miles per hour. They were all working together, perfectly, like a good piece of machinery.

It takes a lot of stagecoaching to learn to concentrate on all six horses simultaneously. Sometimes after I've been in a particularly tight spot, where what each horse does makes the difference of whether you make it or not, someone will mention something else that happened close by. I might have noticed it, but my horses blot out everything else.

That's the way it was going up that hill that day. We made it because I was watching all six horses so closely, I was able to pull one in a fraction or let one out a hair whenever it was needed, to hold all six of them in a slow, even pull, where each horse was putting out his maximum pulling ability.

I could see the muscles of every horse straining, and forcing their hooves back, all in a rhythm that was breathtaking to watch.

We went back to the fairgrounds. Unhitched and ate lunch. Red took the truck down to be fixed, and I followed with the Dodge.

It was hot and we slept awhile. Kip and Rowdy each spent a dollar on candy, pop, and gum.
They got the truck fixed, and we went back to camp. The dirty dishes were still on the table, so I had to wash them.

Then we went out to Salt Lake and went swimming. Red, Tam, and Joe went to Grantsville and Wendover to make arrangements ahead of us.
Went home and rolled out the bedroll, and slept outside. The bed was wet clear through from the rains. I didn't sleep well at all.

{ *That last six blocks is nothing but Just Plain Steep.* }

When we were half way up the hill, it leveled off for a very short ways at a cross street. I thought we could get started here again so pulled up for a rest. We had a full load of passengers on the coach; so Joe, Dick, and a couple of the bigger kids climbed off and walked the rest of the way up the steep grade. We had to circle around to the back side of the capitol to get on the drive that comes back up in front to the steps. We pulled up and stopped right in the center of the front of the Capitol. In a few minutes a well-dressed, very impressive looking man came out and walked up to us, holding out his hand.

"Welcome to the Capitol, I'm Governor Calvin Rampton." We had quite a visit with him as he looked inside the coach and discussed our trip. He signed our stagecoach passenger book before bidding us goodbye, as we headed out. **We felt greatly honored that the Governor of Utah had taken time away from his duties to come meet us.**

We drove down Main Street going away from the Capitol. It's a wider street and not quite as steep as State Street, but it's still steep enough to give a loaded stagecoach problems going down it. Even though I don't use any pole straps or hold-back quarter straps on the wheel harness, the horses can still hold back some even if their harness is pulled forward a little. If we'd been out in the open, I wouldn't have been so concerned about bringing the coach off that hill. In the city with cross streets and traffic, it sure pays to be careful, and I really took it slow and easy.

I drove the coach about a foot and a half from the curb. When it would get to pushing too hard on the horses, I'd increase the brake pressure enough to lock up the rear wheels. This would cause the rear end of the coach to skid sideways, rubbing the wheel against the curb, and would help slow us down a little more. Tammie was riding Max; so I had her stay right close in front of my lead team which also helped me hold the horses down to a slow walk. It sure was a relief to get back to relatively level ground again and let the hitch jog out some.

We got back to Murray shortly after noon, with nothing to do but get ready for the big parade coming up on Saturday morning. We found a pasture to rent near Grantsville and turned out about half of our horses as we wouldn't need them for over a week.

DAYS Fifty-Nine/Sixty
JULY 22-23

DAYS FIFTY-NINE/ SIXTY- JULY 22nd / JULY 23rd

In the next couple days, we all enjoyed some rest and a swim in Salt Lake. Dick and his family had to leave, all except Rowdy, their son who was Kip's age. He and Kip were pretty good friends; so when they approached us about staying, we agreed on one condition: Rowdy would get his shoulder length hair cut. I think everybody thought we were kidding. Rowdy fought like a young mule at roaching time, when Marge went after him with the scissors. He put up such a struggle, that he wound up with a short butch, to get it anywhere near even.

7/22 – SLC LAYOVER

Cut Rowdy's hair right after breakfast. He lost his curls.

Red, Joe, and Tammie went to Grantsville to see about the set up there. Pearl, Wendy, and I went to a Laundromat. My can of spot remover had the nozzle broken, so I walked to the store for another. Ended up going five blocks down and back. The muscles in the calves of my legs were knotting up. Finished the laundry about 1:00.

Went home and fixed cheese sandwiches for lunch. Then Dave, Wendy, and I went to the store. Bought groceries. Came home. Cleaned and vacuumed the camper. Fixed supper. It was terribly hot all day. Red got home about 7:00.
Another day gone.

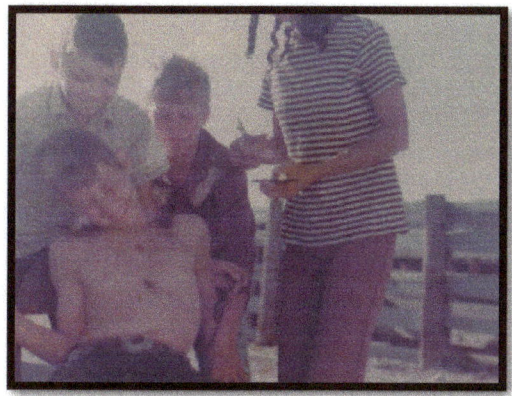

Jack and Charlie were planning on catching up with us again Friday night so as to be able to go with us in Saturday's parade. They knew where to come, but when they got in late, they stopped at the first set of corrals they came to at the fairgrounds.

Since they didn't see us, they figured we must have pulled out the evening before and moved closer up town to where the parade would start.

7/23 – SLC LAYOVER

Got up and started breakfast, but felt pretty bad. Had to lie down, and Red finished cooking. I slept almost all morning.
Red, Tam, and Joe took the horses to pasture at Grantsville. The kids went over to the park to play, so it was quiet.

Wendy came back in and lay down under the table, and was there when I woke up. She fell off the airplane at the park and hurt her back. Toward noon, it got hot, and I woke up. I felt better and ate a little lunch. Didn't do too much in the afternoon; just a little mending. It was too hot to do anything except try to find a cool place. Fried steaks for supper. Right afterward, Red and I took Dave to the bus depot. He left for Arizona. Tam washed all the horses by herself.

DAY SIXTY-ONE
JULY 24TH

We were supposed to be up town in position by 8:30 so we had to roll out early that morning and get with it.

It was over 5 miles up to the parade lineup area from where we were staying. I was very disappointed that morning when I got up and Jack's motorhome wasn't anywhere in sight. We sure could have used their help in getting ready. I didn't want to have to drive the horses hard going up to the parade. Tammie had put in lots of hard work the evening before, washing and grooming them, and I didn't want to get them all sweated up; so we were all dressed and hitched up by 7:05 that morning, ready to go.

We heard a vehicle start up and pull out around the corrals down at the other end of the arena. There was Jack. He'd decided to go up town and see if he could locate us, and he'd had to pull ahead far enough to turn around, and here we were. His crew wasn't dressed and hadn't had any breakfast yet. After a quick powwow we decided he should drive his motorhome up town as far as he could before parking it. That would give them a chance to dress and get ready without us having to wait.

The parade on the 18th had come down State Street. I assumed this parade would be the same, as it was being assembled in the same general area. We drove up Main Street to find it blocked off as the parade route. The policeman there wouldn't let us through and said we'd have to find another route to get up to the assembly area, but he didn't make any suggestion of what route to try. I had a hard time getting the coach backed up enough to be able to turn it around there, but finally got headed back down the block. When we got back to the first cross street, I decided to head west to see if we could make it up that street. I think I should have gone east and tried State Street.

7/24 – SLC – 2nd parade and Cheyenne

Jack showed up early. Had slept just outside of the fairgrounds. Finally got started and moved out. Charlie drove the pickup, and Jack drove his camper part way in to town, as the women weren't dressed yet. We picked them up, and Geneva and June both wore long dresses. June wore a lovely nosegay print with lace trim. We went down Main to where it was blocked off. We had to turn sharp and go through a gas station, to turn around; then go north through traffic. The cop was going to stop us, but she said it was OK so Red loped them up, and we went through. From then on we galloped the wrong way up the parade route to the surprise of the crowd. Tam found out she wasn't going to be announced so she got mad; took off her banner, crown, hat, and jacket.

We no sooner got turned back north on the street paralleling Main than we were hopelessly surrounded by automobile traffic. It was four lanes deep and bumper to bumper. I could see we'd never be able to travel a mile or more of that kind of traffic and make it on time. It was already past 8 o'clock. Tammie was riding Fortune in the lead; so I shouted to her and told her to turn to the right on the first cross street that wasn't full of parked cars. The second intersection we came to had an opening down it so we took it. We kicked into a good trot and headed down that way. I could see on up a couple blocks to State Street and it looked like it was also full of traffic. When the policeman who was guarding that cross street saw us coming in a high trot, he immediately cleared an opening through the line of spectators for us, which put us back on Main Street again --the parade route. The crosswalk on the east side of the street was full of people; so our only choice was to turn and head up Main. Tammie looked back to me as she rode onto Main, and saw my thumb pointing to the left; so she knew just what to do.

As we circled onto Main in a high trot, I called to her let's go, and immediately shook the slack out in my lines to my horses. I wasn't going to take a chance on some other cop running out to try to head us over to some side street again. By this time we were in a good high gallop, heading right on up Main. The sidewalks and curbs were already lined with thousands of spectators and they started cheering us on.

We had traveled about a block when I heard a siren and here came a motorcycle cop up alongside us. I figured if he was going to try to stop us or turn us out of

Finally got started in the parade. People on both sides 6 to 10 deep. An announcer about every 4th block. It was about the best parade we'd ever seen. We had Red Horse in the hitch, and he got his bridle hooked once, and went to fighting. We had to stop and fix it during the parade.

Tammie rode Fortune, and Wendy was on Holly Ann. We got continual applause all along the entire parade route. The announcer who'd seen us go the wrong way, got a real kick out of it when we came by. The TV guys covered us from start to finish as we went by.

The route was long and hot. I got worried about Wendy, but she made it all right. We finally got to the park where the parade disbanded. Then went straight back through town to the fairgrounds, and left the pickup.

the parade route, I'd make him get with it, and I shook a little more slack to the horses. By this time, we were moving along at a good hard gallop. The cop didn't try to stop or turn us. He just pulled on out in front with his siren going full blast and crowded the pedestrians back. Almost immediately he was joined by a second motorcycle cop that took the other side of the street up ahead of us. We galloped on.

That was quite a moment ---galloping up Main Street almost as hard as six head of horses could go, for over a mile. We did manage to get up past the starting point in plenty of time to get in our position, without causing any problems up there.

When we came back down the route during the parade, we got some kidding from the announcers on the PA system about our "charge" up Main Street. One announced, "And here comes the "Clown" entry that was the first entry of the parade this morning, only they were going the wrong way!" Charlie wanted to go punch him in the mouth, and we were having a hard time holding him back, when the announcer came back again, saying, "They might have been going the wrong direction, but we all sure enjoyed the show they put on!"; and Charlie grinned along with the rest of us. We really lucked out again with the live TV coverage that day. The same station and crew was covering the parade as had filmed us coming in from Coalville. I saw them up ahead and was wondering what kind of coverage we'd get. I noticed their camera swing towards us when we were barely in range. I didn't look right in the lens and- grinning as we went by, but I did manage several glances back their way to check if they were still following us. The last time I looked, I could see the camera out of the corner of my eye; they were still following us. We didn't get to see the parade replay that evening, but some people we knew did. They said the camera had followed us on the way up the street with their MC giving us a good buildup all the time. Apparently we were on the screen about 1 minute and 45 seconds, which is a long coverage for one entry in a parade.

We had some special guests on the stage that day, officials of the parade and bicentennial commission. They boarded the coach at the assembly area and then rode all the way back to Murray with us. That Days of 47 Parade was quite an event as far as all of us were concerned. The parade route was about 2½ miles long with an estimated 250,000 spectators watching it. There were lots of horse-drawn vehicles and at least one other stagecoach, and one or more six horse hitches on wagons; but we seemed to draw lots of applause and appreciation as we rolled on down the street. Of course, a lot of the people felt they knew us after having seen our coach on the TV several times in the past week.

> Then we loaded up and headed for Cheyenne. Joe and Pearl decided to stay in Salt Lake, so we left Tam's pickup with them. Tam drove the Dodge with the camper. I rode in the truck with Red. Jack had a lot of trouble with his fuel pump, and Tam ran hot in the Dodge. We stayed at the fairgrounds in Evanston that night.

We are quite proud of a certificate of appreciation we received from The Days of 47 Parade Committee, thanking us for exhibiting in their parade. The parade was just the start of the day. As soon as we fed the animals, we retrieved Jack's motorhome and ate. We packed up, loaded the stagecoach on the coach trailer which Jack had brought, loaded the horses and headed for Cheyenne and the Frontier Days. When we got to Evanston , Wyoming fairgrounds that night and found the gate unlocked, we made ourselves at home. The horses sure enjoyed being turned loose in that 80 acre pasture after being corralled for so long.

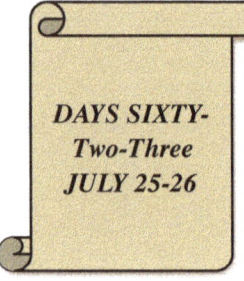

DAYS SIXTY-TWO/THREE
JULY 25TH-26TH
(Travel days – back to Cheyenne)

      The next evening we made it to Laramie and used their corrals again for a rest. Monday morning, we had driven about half way to Cheyenne, when a red Ford pickup passed us. There, grinning out the open window, with arms waving in every direction, was our oldest daughter, Holly, and our granddaughter, Lisa. Her husband Wallace was driving, and the new baby, Cody, was in the middle. Wallace had broken his arm in a truck wreck in the winter.

    It was a bad break and healed slow. He'd just gotten the cast removed, but it was so weak he was afraid to go back to work for awhile. They had wanted to come with us from the start, but hadn't been able to because of his arm. Now that they'd caught up with us, we hoped they were planning to finish the trip with us to California.

DAY SIXTY-FOUR
JULY 27th
Cheyenne Frontier Days Parade

      Almost all of the horse drawn vehicles in the several parades held in Cheyenne during Frontier Days, belong to the Rodeo Committee. A local rancher furnishes the horses and harness to pull the vehicles. This last summer, he had 109 harnessed horses pulling vehicles in the parades. We were given a good spot to park our horse van and campers, and we all got to attend the rodeo a couple times while we were there. We planned on staying three days, showing in one parade, and it had its own personality. Everybody hitched up at the rodeo grounds and then drove down-town to assigned spots where we could assemble.

7/25-26 – GOING BACK TO CHEYENNE PARADE
Going back east through Wyoming, it was almost impossible to believe we've crossed all that land with the coach. No wonder everyone on the highway is so surprised to see us, and no one can believe that we've run it the entire distance with the horses, and not trucked them. It's hard to believe it ourselves. Just a little ways out of Laramie, Red said," There's Holly." We all stopped on the highway. I was so glad to see them.
7/27 – CHEYENNE PARADE
We all got up early to get ready for the parade. We were ready and hitched up at 9:00, half an hour before the others. The buffalo wagon and one other were also ready; so we followed them down to the parade starting point.

It was a grand sight that morning seeing that many horses hitched up to that many 19th century vehicles, all at the same time. We waited around as long as we dared, but still had to wait over half an hour after getting down to the assembly area, for the outfits that were to be in front of us to get in line.

There were a number of marching band units in the parade, and one of them filed in right behind us. I don't know what was the matter, but they couldn't keep up, and the parade didn't seem to be moving that fast either. Anyhow, we kept getting instructions from the parade marshals enroute to slow down and try to stay half way between the unit ahead of us and the band behind. I kept slowing up, and by the time we were half way through the parade, we were two blocks behind the unit in front of us, and the band behind us was at least that far back of us. We had quite a unique position in that parade --it was a one unit parade within a large one. At least we had the spectators undivided attention when we came along. I held the horses down slow until I saw the route end ahead; then let them out into a good jog trot. It wasn't long before we caught up with the units ahead of us.

Like in the old days, we didn't care to fool along at freight wagon speed driving a stagecoach and six horse hitch; so started easing by them. Most of those ranch horses didn't pay much attention to us, but when we caught up with Budweisers, I could see we might cause them a problem. I pulled down to a gait just barely fast enough to pass. As I drew near, their horses started getting a little nervous; so I slowed down some more and drove right along side of them for a ways, visiting with their drivers.

> Holly wore my gingham dress and really filled it out. Lisa enjoyed the parade and waved at everyone. Kip rode shotgun, Charlie & Tam were outriders. She didn't wear her outfit again. Miss Rodeo America was there, and Wendy noticed she didn't have a serape. In spite of all the vehicles, the parade didn't compare at all to Salt Lake. On the way back we trotted out and passed up the Budweiser Hitch. They stopped to let us pass by.

They finally pulled their hitch to a stop to let us by. As soon as we were in the clear, I shook my lines out, and we moved right on towards the rodeo grounds in true stagecoach style. We were back out to the grounds and unhitched almost an hour before the rest of them got in. Well, we'd come to Cheyenne and enjoyed showing in one of their Frontier Days parades. Now it was time to pack up and head back for Salt Lake City to continue our journey west.

DAYS SIXTY-FIVE/SIX
JULY 28/29th

TRAVEL BACK TO MURRAY, UTAH

DAYS SIXTY-FIVE/ SIX
JULY 28th / 29th

Charlie returned to Salt Lake with us, but Jack had to go home to take care of some business before he could re-join us out at Grantsville. We had driven into the fairgrounds at Murray with the coach, when we interrupted our westward journey to go parading, so when we left Cheyenne, we headed back to Murray.

We unloaded the coach in the exact same spot where we had loaded it up to head to Cheyenne.

7/28 – BACK TO SALT LAKE
(2travel days)
We started back to Salt Lake. We went on until late. Stopped at a rest area and made a corral of the vehicles, and unloaded the horses. Rolled out and went to bed.
7/29
I rode with Tammie for awhile. Just after going through the tunnel, Red stopped to tell us about a radio ad he wanted to see about. Tam pulled over to the center line as a Jaguar was passing. A cop gave her a warning ticket. Then he had to check out all the horses and Red's truck papers. I got after Tam for her driving when she crossed the center line, and almost got hit again. She got mad and didn't want me to ride with her so I got in the truck. Got back to the fairgrounds at Salt Lake. Looked like rain so Red put the bedroll under the camper. Didn't have too good a night.

DAY SIXTY SEVEN JULY 30th

AND THE TRIP CONTINUES…

DAY SIXTY-SEVEN JULY 30th

Joe and Pearl had stayed in Utah to take care of our extra horses we'd put out on pasture, and to rest up, instead of going with us to Cheyenne. They weren't anywhere around the next morning when we hitched up at Murray; so I drove the coach out of town. It sure was a relief to be heading west at a good clip again. We found ourselves right in the middle of the crowded bumper to bumper morning traffic going out of Salt Lake that morning. Where there was a heavy traffic flow, the on ramp into our lane would be a continuous stream emptying into our highway. That would put us in a center lane with traffic on all sides, until I got a chance to work over to the right again. It didn't seem to bother our Morgans though. More than once when we were galloping, we were keeping up with the traffic that had us surrounded. I got quite a kick out of it. Marge, in the pilot pickup behind the coach, did have a few problems though.

She started signaling a block ahead for us to make a left turn. I'd already swung the horses as I had a momentary clear shot, and she was right behind me. Then an old man in a pickup camper came up from behind and passed her on the left. When he saw the stage and horses crossing in front of him he had to stop suddenly. Marge had to swing back out to the other lane to avoid hitting him with the horse trailer which she was towing behind the pickup. When he got stopped, and she had clearance, she pulled on across and caught up with the coach. She also had another problem motorist. Two women in a sedan thought they were in more of a hurry than what the horses were going. I was in the right hand lane, with Marge behind me. Traffic was heavy behind us and on the inside lane. The women decided to pass us on the right, just as we came almost even with a service

---

7/30– SALT LAKE to GRANTSVILLE Started out for Grantsville. Red drove the stage, with Charlie on Mojo and Wendy on Poco. I drove the Dodge for pilot car with the horse trailer on behind. Tam drove Charlie's truck, Holly drove the PU, and Wallace the truck. While going out State Street, I heard Tam on the CB. She couldn't get the truck started and everyone had left. I stopped the stage and Charlie got on the CB and told her how to get it running. By then, Holly had come back for her. We turned west on 21st and the traffic was terrific. Part of the time it was whizzing by on both sides. One old man in a PU camper kept going when we started to turn left, and I almost ran into him with the horse trailer, but straightened out in time. Later 2 gals in a sedan tried to pass us on the right in a real tight place.

station with some cars parked along the highway. Marge honked and yelled and signaled at them to pull back. They didn't like it a bit, but they stopped. Their front fender wasn't over a foot from the axle of the coach. I doubt if they ever knew how close they came to getting their nice car creased. It wouldn't have hurt the coach at all.

We finally got out of town, and found an old road right beside the highway which I pulled over to drive on. Something had needed adjustment but it wasn't important enough for me to stop on the highway. When we hit the dirt road, I decided to fix it. When I looked around, a state patrolman had stopped behind Marge and was talking to her. He told her they'd been advised of our slow traveling outfit on the highway, and for her to drive the pickup directly behind the coach, leaving both traffic lanes open. She said she'd be glad to do whatever the Patrol advised, but if he was interested in knowing, she'd tell him what she'd learned about it so far. He said, "go ahead, shoot." Marge told him she'd tried several different ways, and found that when both lanes of traffic were open, people would generally disregard the warning lights. On top of the pickup were two revolving amber lights, and on the back end was a large yellow sign, reading "Caution - Horses", emblazoned with a red arrow. With two lanes of traffic running fast, they'd roar on by the pickup and get even with the coach and horses, before they suddenly realized they were there. Then they didn't know what to do. Some stared open-mouthed, some grabbed their cameras, and some panicked. The latter either slammed on their brakes or veered away from the horses into the left hand lane. Either reaction was hazardous. As we felt the traffic situation was our problem, we had to avoid bad situations.

Marge found that if she drove the pickup in the right hand traffic lane while the coach was over in the emergency lane, and had all the lights and blinkers on, all the traffic behind slowed down a quarter mile back and passed carefully in single file on the inside lane. They were already looking for the cause of the warning signals---something out of the ordinary; so they weren't as

---

Further on some TV guys picked us up and rode awhile. When Red pulled over to stop, and I followed, a patrol car pulled in behind. He came over and told me to stay in the lane directly behind the coach. After talking quite awhile, and telling him what we'd discovered about driving on the freeway, and forcing traffic into the left lane, he finally said to do whatever we thought was best. Went on past the factories and around the lake. Just before the Grantsville turn off, we met Joe and Pearl coming in. At the intersection, Joe had brought the Ford so we swapped vehicles. Charlie loaded his horse in the trailer and took it on in with Joe. Eddie rode Poco a little ways and then Wendy rode again. 10 miles out of Grantsville, Wallace brought the truck up, and we changed horse. The town officials rode in with us.

totally unprepared at the unexpected sight of a stagecoach and six horse hitch. This also left an empty lane between them and the coach, and no one got scared as happened when someone suddenly found himself within three feet of a bunch of horses. This empty lane in front of the pickup also served another purpose. Many of the people going by wanted to get pictures; so they pulled off to the emergency lane up ahead of the coach and waited for it. Frequently there would be a steep bank or ditch preventing easy passage for the coach over into the barpit; so when the coach arrived at the stopped vehicle, it had to go around. The only place to go was in the empty traffic lane in front of the pickup. After Marge finished explaining this to the patrolman, he said, "With all the experience you've had on this, and as far as you've come, I'm sure you know better than I how to handle the situation; so just go ahead and do it however you see fit. Looks like you're doing fine."

Just after we pulled off the interstate heading for Grantsville, we met Joe driving up the highway. He helped us get across the cattle guard then headed for Grantsville to try to find Wallace in the horse van and bring us a change of horses. We were within about five miles of town when they got back to us with our relay string. You would have thought we were somebody important the way Grantsville escorted us into town: with a police car and a firetruck and both sirens howling away full blast. After spending a couple hours giving rides around town, we were treated to a Dutch oven supper prepared over the coals at the fairgrounds.

It was topped off with watermelon for dessert. We were serenaded during supper by two local musicians playing a guitar and fiddle, which we all appreciated. About bedtime that night a most welcome rainstorm blowed in to cool the desert off. It also ran us under the cover of one of the show barns with our bedrolls. Jack drove in at dark, and we all sacked out, to the accompaniment of a tremendous electrical storm.

We were escorted into town with a fire engine and a police car blowing sirens, and the sheriff's car behind, followed by a string of cars. Unloaded in the center of town, and Red took several rides. Sent Kip for candy bars, and he only got 4 for a dollar. Holly and I went on out to the rodeo grounds and cleaned up. Coach got in about an hour later. The townsfolk fixed us a Dutch oven supper on a barbecue pit. Had stew, fried potatoes, vegetables, tossed salad, rolls, watermelon, and pop. Was delicious. Two fellows played guitar and a fiddle while we ate. Western music, and they were <u>Good</u>! Joe and Pearl danced. After supper, it looked like rain, so we moved some of the rigs in the shed. Jack got in just before dark with his new camper. We rolled our beds out between the picnic tables. There was a tremendous electrical storm followed by a drenching rain. Glad we were under cover.

We wanted to make one long run on the trip to more or less compete with the old time stagecoach records. They quite often ran 100 miles in 24 hours. They had a larger horse herd to draw from than we did. Most of the time they changed horses about every 13-15 miles. There were a few of their desert stations around 35 miles apart, due to the lack of water. In those areas they didn't make such good time.

DAY SIXTY-EIGHT
JULY 31st

We had a good full crew to make our run across Utah's desert and salt flats the next day. It's about 93-95 miles from Grantsville to Wendover. Twelve of our 15 head of stagecoach horses were in real good travelling shape when we got to Grantsville. I decided we'd change horses every 15 or 16 miles, and since it's fairly flat country, we'd use four horse hitches instead of sixes, which meant that all the horses would pull two 15 mile hitches with from 4 to 6 hours rest in the horse van in between runs.

I figured we could make the 95 miles in somewhere between 12 and 24 hours, depending on the weather conditions. Everybody had been warning me all along about the summer heat to be expected on the salt flats. I didn't tell them how many times I'd been across there. I just said, I'd already put in my order for a rain.

7/31 -GRANTSVILLE to WENDOVER STRAIGHT THROUGH – 20 hour STAGECOACH RUN

Joe drove the coach out. Just had 4 head on the coach. Jack's daughter, Debbie, and grand-daughter, Tara, and 2 nieces rode in the coach with me. I had Holly's Lisa, also Eddie. Tam was outriding. Joe stopped at the edge of town, and talked to the guitar player for quite awhile. Red went in Jack's camper and when they passed us, we were only 3 miles out of town. Seemed like Joe was slower than usual, and the closer we got to our noon stop, the slower he went. When I told Tara she couldn't get on top of the coach with Dickie, she went to bawling. Enjoyed the ride. The weather was cool after the rain, though it heated up by noon. Could hardly see the lake, but the islands stood up tall and blue.

Well, our rain had come, and it was nice and cool when we hitched up the next morning at Grantsville. The evening before, some fellows from the Teddy Bear Truck Stop about 16 miles out, stopped and asked if we'd stop at their place and take part in their C.B. benefit rally for disabled children. I didn't have the heart to tell them we were planning a timed run across there and wouldn't have time; so I said OK. We did stop there and hauled everyone there around for a short ride, with all the money donated to their fund.

We got away from Grantsville at 8:30 that morning. With the 1½ to 2 hours spent at the benefit at the truck stop, it was around 1 PM before we got going again with our second leg of the trip. Joe drove the first leg. I drove the second 15 or 16 miles in about an hour and a half. Then Joe took over again. I was riding shotgun. The morning had turned hot and sultry, but suddenly the desert changed to extreme cold and wind in one of its typical "about face" moods. I guess I must have put in a double order on that rain by mistake. The rain came. Again. Not in buckets, but in waves and sheets, and blasts, head on into us. There was no place to pull up and stop. I think the horses must have known it, for they just bowed their necks, dropped their heads, and kept pounding on into it. Finally our horse van and camper

---

Got in to the Teddy Bear Truck Stop. They were having a charity benefit. Red sold rides and donated about $50.00. We were breakfast for our dinner. It was good.

Red drove the stage out. Used the second hitch of 4. I went on the stage. The weather was warm but there was a breeze, and it was pleasant riding. After awhile it got chilly, and by the time we changed horses, it looked like rain, and was dark and cloudy. We changed at an exit on the side of a hill. Red put Romeo and Rebel, Bandito, & Red Horse on, and let Joe drive for the 3rd hitch. Wendy was ahorseback. I rode inside. We just got a little ways when the storm moved in, and it really poured. Had the windows rolled down and fastened, but the wind blew the rain in on the south side; and it got the velvet wet.

trailer caught up with us. They stopped on the edge of the highway, and we pulled up beside them and tied up to set the storm out. Marge had the windows of the coach rolled down and fastened, but she still got wet. Joe and I on the box, and Wendy, who was outriding, were soaked to the skin, in spite of slickers, coats, and chaps. We all put on fresh dry clothes, but I don't think I had thoroughly dried out by the time we hit another rain storm out in Nevada a week or so later.

When we started out again in an hour or two, Joe took the frontage road up ahead that I knew followed the interstate all the rest of the way to Knools, our next stop. What I hadn't thought of was that there had

been enough rain to make that road muddy. For 6 or 8 miles, that coach bogged down six inches or more, most of the time. Joe kept the horses going slow and steady; so I crawled down inside the coach, hunkered down between the seats and slept the afternoon away. Every time Joe would have to stop to blow the horses, it would wake me up. As the coach weights over 4,000 pounds empty, the horses really had to get down and pull. It sure seemed like a long pull across that mud flat.

They were a wet mud-spattered, lathered up hitch when we stopped next. We changed horses the 4th time up on the overpass just east of Knolls, just as the sun broke out from under the clouds and did its gandydance on the salt flats before dropping down behind the Nevada mountains.

When my dress and white sweater were against it, the red ran on them. Rain, hail, and wind were so strong that when the truck and camper went by, we stopped and waited it out. Red and Wendy got dry clothes. When it lessened, we took the frontage road, and soon were running 4 to 6 inches deep in gumbo. It was real hard pulling for the next 2 hours, awfully hard on the horses. Got in to our next stop just as the sun was going down, peeping through the clouds and reflecting on the salt flats. I took a picture as we came in. Geneva had a hot supper ready, and it was sure appreciated. Red drove out with Joe's first team. Holly rode on top with her dad, and I baby sat on the inside. Rowdy slept on the floor, Wendy on one seat, and Kip on the other. I slept for a little while. The moon came out, and it was a beautiful night.

I took the next leg of the trip and Joe said he believed he'd ride in his pickup with his wife a ways to see if he might get thawed out a little. It sure is tough to freeze to death in the middle of the desert in the middle of the summer. Jack said he'd come ride with me as soon as he got his camper under way. He'd handled a team a lot, and four head some, when he was younger. When he got situated beside me, I handed him the ribbons. He drove about 17 miles under that cool clear starlit desert. He had his problems with the lines. He hadn't driven four much, and that had been a long time ago; so he was somewhat out of practice. Once along in the night, after a while, when the horses hadn't been handling very good for him, Jack says to me, "Red, what in the dickens do you do with the other two lines when you drive six-up?" A chuckle was about my only answer. I could appreciate the problems he was having. Joe was going to drive the next hitch, but since Jack had driven most of that one, I decided to go on driving. Somehow I got my mile posts mixed up, to thinking we only had 18 or 20 miles more to go; so I told Wallace to take the horse van on to Wendover, and I'd run that hitch all the way in. It wound up to be about 30 miles or more yet, and when the near lead horse started limping I decided I'd made a mistake.

Charlie had his four horse trailer with him, and his wife was driving it along. Charlie had loaded his horse and hauled him a ways; then he decided to stop and wait for us, and ride ahorseback on into Wendover with us. I was sure glad to catch up with his outfit, but when I checked over what horses he had, they were all saddle horses. I had driven one of the mares he had in there a few times so decided to use her the rest of the way in. The wheel would have been the best place to have put her, but that meant switching more horses around; so I decided since we were only using four to put her in the lead. She worked out OK --- that is, I was able to drive her enough to keep her in the road, but we had some fun. When I'd call "Get up", she wouldn't start until her singletree bumped her in the rear; then she'd lunge and take off, and it would take a ways to get her settled down. About every mile, the rest of the way in, we'd be going along in a jog trot road gait when she'd suddenly stop. Before I could pull the other horses up, the single tree would bump her and away we'd go again. **We finally jogged into Wendover at 4:25 A.M.**

> Red drove the last change too. I had to drive the pilot car, as the girls were tired. Jack rode shotgun and slept. Charlie rode Mojo, and Tam rode Max. Had to change 2 horses in the hitch to make it on in. Got to Wendover at 4:30 A.M.
> Rolled out our bed just as dawn was breaking. Red got in the coach with his slicker on, and fell asleep on the floor. I crawled in to a sopping wet bed, but slept awhile anyway.

> *We figured 95 miles in 20 hours wasn't too bad with all the interruptions and natural elements we'd encountered and withstood.*

We drove up to the corrals where we were camped, put the horses up, and then as daylight was fast flooding the mountain side, we rolled into our wet, soggy bedroll on the ground. It had been on top of the stagecoach during the storm. As wet as it was, it really felt good.

DAY SIXTY-NINE
AUGUST 1st

When I had driven over to Wendover to check things out for our stay there, the first person I'd run into was 'Hoot Gibson'. Not the movie star, but just as interesting a character--one of Wendover's old timers and a 'father of the town'. He pitched right in and got the ladies club to set out an excellent Sunday meal for us. He also escorted us into town at 4:25 AM that morning and led us to our corrals. Before and after dinner that afternoon, we took everyone for a ride that wanted one. Hoot had told me he had an old friend that especially wanted to ride in the coach.

This friend had cancer real bad, and from what I was told that afternoon, he'd stayed away from the hospital for the past couple weeks living on his nerve, waiting for our coach to come to town.
He wanted to be sure to get his ride on it before he gave in.

It had been trying to rain all afternoon, and about the time Hoot and his friend climbed on top of the coach, it started to coming down pretty good. I asked them if they wanted to hold up awhile to see if it would blow over in a little while.

The answer I got sent us trotting down the street. Those two old friends weren't going to let a little desert shower interfere with their stagecoach ride. We only drove part way around town with our other passengers, but on this run, we circled the whole town. Those two old friends sure seemed to enjoy that ride. The next morning, as we pulled out of town, I noticed Hoot's old friend sitting on a rock up by our camp, watching us pull out with a far away, wistful look to him.

8/1 – WENDOVER LAYOVER

Got up and made sweet rolls for breakfast. Jack was planning on leaving early, but they all came over and ate. June and Charlie had some when they came out from their motel. After dishes, I got the crew started taking baths. Red hitched up the coach and went down about noon to give rides. Tam, Wendy, and I came later as we had to wait to clean up. Almost missed the dinner as just a few were eating ice cream when we got there. It was sprinkling, and Joe took out a couple rides. We went in and ate. Had homemade noodles, tomatoes, rolls, chocolate cake, and ice cream. Afterwards we went back to the camper, and Holly and I took the clothes to the Laundromat. We all went to bed early.

{ **It was rather a lonesome sight.** }

Charlie left us at Wendover. He'd planned on going on with us for a few more days. Then one of the local cowboys mentioned within Charlie's hearing that he was going to take his horse out on the desert and look over the mustang herds, and he'd sure like to have some company. That was more than Charlie could stand. All summer, all you had to do to get Charlie's attention was to mention the word "mustang". That had been one of Charlie's lifelong dreams --to get out on the desert somewhere on a good horse and ride up on a mustang herd. With present day government interfering into the mustanging laws, I don't know for sure what happened that day. I suspicion one old truck driving cowboy got a thrill of a lifetime. The last time I talked to Charlie he told me he had a new horse. Said he was a mate to our "Muskrat" horse. **I caught Muskrat out of a wild bunch 21 years ago.**

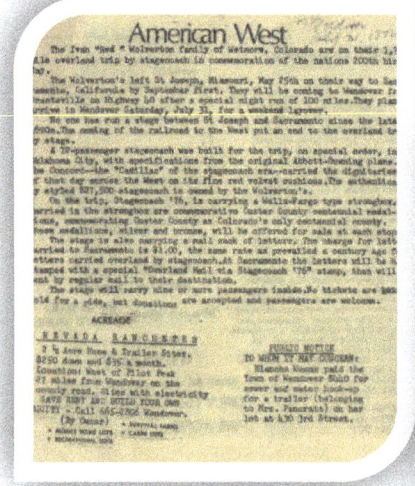

**DAY SEVENTY
AUGUST 2nd**

CHAPTER 12
NEVADA

DAY SEVENTY
AUGUST 2nd

Monday morning, August 2nd, found us heading into Nevada. Joe was able to drive all morning on an old road that paralleled the highway. I think he had a sore arm by moon from waving at passing tourists. He liked that part of stagecoaching as well as any of us. Having Holly and Wallace along sure made a big difference to Marge and me. Wallace drove the horse van, leaving me to be with the coach most of the time. Holly helped Marge with the housekeeping chores which didn't get left at home. I had to make some phone calls that first morning after crossing the state line into Nevada. I guess I might have stopped at any pay phone, but that sounded like a good excuse to stroll through the gambling casino.

I didn't waste much money but a couple dollars in a two bit slot that had stagecoaches to line up instead of cherries and oranges. It gulped my money down as fast as my own coach had, without a thank you or burp; so I quit. Down near the phone booths stood a slot machine bigger than an old-time upright piano. It took big money to play it too - silver dollars. Ah, but it was quite a machine. When a dollar was dropped in it, and that handle as big as a hickory cane was pulled, that machine started to humming and rumbling and vibrating like it was just about to bust wide open and pour silver dollars out knee deep on the floor. I think it was alive and had a mind of its own. Up along its top it showed how many dollars had been put in since its last pay off, and there was a big sign saying they guaranteed to refund your money if the machine never made a pay off after ten silver dollars had been put in it.

Two women had been playing it, or it was playing them, I'm not sure which. They'd get several dollars in it; then it would reluctantly give back a couple dollars.

8/2 –WENDOVER to OASIS

Charlie went wild horse chasing. Joe drove the coach out. Tam drove the pilot car. I rode in the coach. Wendy and Rowdy rode ahorseback. Red stayed in Wendover to phone, and came out with Pearl. At noon, we found out he'd gotten Holly new Levis, and both her and Kip new lined jackets, and a new shirt and jacket for Wallace.
We ate lunch at the side of the road. Holly cooked it and had it ready. Red didn't eat, so I fixed him a can of potatoes, hamburger and onions, and biscuits and honey to take along. Changed horses, and I had to drive the pilot car. Stopped to talk to a van load of people— 14 of them. They were foreign students on a tour through the U.S. They rode the stage for several miles. Pulled into Oasis late afternoon.

Of course, if you should hit the right combination, you could win more silver than you could carry. Mostly I think, it was programmed for 2 dollar payoffs. These gals finally quit playing, with six dollars in the slot since its last pay off. I studied the situation and figured out if I put 4 dollars in it, and it didn't pay off, I'd get 10 bucks back (on their guarantee). If it paid on ten, with the usual $2, pay off, I would only lose 2 dollars. If it paid at 9, I'd only lose one dollar, and if it paid on 8, I'd break even. I felt like a big time gambler; so decided to give it a whirl.

When I dipped my hand in my pocket, I didn't come up with enough silver dollars-- the four I'd need to run it out; so I stepped over to a cashier's window to change a $5 bill to silver. Wouldn't you know it? A man stepped up right in front of me and crammed a dollar in old money bucket. It wheezed and whirled and clanked; then swallowed the buck and opened its mouth for more. On his second try, which made 8 in a row on the scoreboard, the silver mine grudgingly coughed up its usual 2 dollar pay off. He broke even and left. I stood there looking at that beautiful money machine for another minute, shrugged my shoulders, dropped my silver back in my pocket and left. Guess I just wasn't cut out to be a gambler!

At noon, when we stopped for our change of horses alongside the highway, Holly had fixed a good cowboy dinner of fried meat, taters, salad, and hot biscuits and honey. I took some extra biscuits along in the coach. That afternoon, we were on a long downhill slope. The horses were feeling good so I'd let them out into a good ground-covering rocking gallop. There's nothing that will make your blood circulate and wake you up like a good gallop.

One of those large panel type vans stopped on the highway on the east bound side, and a whole herd of people swarmed out of it and came running across the highway. I really had to pull in on the lines and get after the brake in order to get stopped before passing them, but I made it. These were young people around 25 years old; there were 14 of them in all. They were a young business people's group from England, Europe, New Zealand, Australia, and where else, I don't know. They were real excited over meeting our stagecoach. They said they had toured all over the U.S. and Canada, and that stagecoach of ours had been the most exciting thing they'd seen. I couldn't resist inviting them to climb on and go for a ride. They asked how far they could ride, and I told them as far as they wanted, but they would have to worry about getting back to their bus, as our stagecoach only went one way. They all wanted to ride so decided to go with us a couple miles and then they would walk back. They felt the *ride would be worth the walk back. We sure enjoyed hauling such an enthused group.*

Outside of Oasis, Nevada, we were met and piloted into "town" by a fellow that lived at the state highway maintenance shop there. Several car loads of tourists followed us into the station. It was surprising how many people we gave rides to there in Oasis. The town only has two buildings in it, but I drove around about there for the better part of two hours. This fellow and Wallace got to visiting, and before I knew what was coming off, I was loaded into a pickup with them to go look at a couple of palomino mares.

Wallace liked their looks, and bought them; so after supper and chores, he and I got our saddles and returned to where the mares were and rode them to our camp in the moonlight. One mare was a present for Holly, which she didn't discover until the next morning. We had a hard time getting Holly off her so we could move camp.

Holly + Wallace + girls

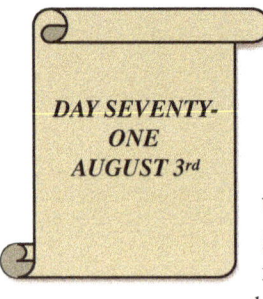

DAY SEVENTY-ONE - AUGUST 3rd

DAY SEVENTY-ONE AUGUST 3rd

Wendy and I rode the two mares that morning going out of Oasis. Those mares were fat and pretty, but hadn't been ridden regular so were pretty soft. I found out one thing that morning.

It sure takes a pretty good saddle horse to be able to keep up with a stagecoach for a half day. It seemed we continuously had to swing into a gallop to keep up with the coach horses in a trot.

Nevada isn't as crowded as some of the states further east are. Many of the towns are a good day's gallop apart. Some of them are one long look, or about two days run apart. We had another dry noon camp on the highway shoulder; then I took the coach on into Wells. We were met by a group of mounted cowboys out a ways, and escorted into town. One of the cowboys was the Wells Chief of Police. The local Bicentennial committee had arranged a potluck evening meal in the park for us. We had arrived in town fairly early in the afternoon; so we drove to our camp at the fairgrounds and cleaned up a bit before driving the coach back over to the potluck. After that good supper, we gave rides until full dark.

8/3– OASIS to WELLS, NV
Wallace bought two palomino mares. Joe drove the coach out. Tammie, the pilot car. Red and Wendy rode the mares. Holly and I washed and curled our hair, then left later with the Dodge. We went ahead of Wallace, and stopped at the bottom of the hill. We fixed lunch, and helped unload horses. Almost lost Max as he'd gotten tied with a slip knot which tightened up. Changed horses, and Red drove out. I had to drive the pilot car. Pretty country between Oasis and Wells. Hills, junipers, like Central Oregon. Took the old road part way in to town. Chief of Police came out ahorseback, and rode in with us. Had 4 police cars escort us to the bank where we unloaded the strongbox. Then we went to the fairgrounds. The people had a potluck supper for us. It really seemed especially good after cooking so many meals.

DAY SEVENTY-TWO
AUGUST 4TH

DAY SEVENTY TWO AUGUST 4th

The next morning when I went out to feed, Joe had company. His daughter and son-in-law from Oregon had come down. We had a day's layover planned so they decided to take advantage of it to go visit the Bonnieville Salt Flats. Right after they left, my brother, Tom and his wife Beverly, also from Oregon, showed up. In the afternoon we hooked up the coach to take them for a ride. We'd just started out when Joe and his family returned. It hadn't been a very pleasant day on the salt flats so they didn't stay too long. They all climbed on, and we made the $20.00 tour of Wells, going down Railroad Street full length and returning up the main drag.

8/4 – WELLS – LAYOVER

Shirley, Don, and Kim McCullough came in to Herins last night. After breakfast Holly and I went to do laundry. When we got back, Tom and Bev were at camp. Herins and McCulloughs drove to Salt Lake. We had sandwiches for lunch in Tom's camper. Then we hooked up and started out for town, just as the Herins drove in; so we all loaded up and drove through town. Went back to camp and had a potluck supper. Had a good time visiting.

Beverly and Dawn

When we returned from town, the big empty arena by our camp beckoned to me; so I turned into it and limbered the hitch up a bit. When you spend days and weeks of mostly straight away driving, like on the highways all the time, the horses sort of lose their ability to maneuver in a figure 8 pattern smoothly. Whenever I have time and can find an empty arena, I usually take advantage of it by working the horses in there for awhile. Everybody accused me of driving through the turns so hard that I was slinging the rear end of the coach around just to give them an extra thrill. I was driving hard, but what they didn't know was that the ground was so soft and worked up, that the front wheels of the coach were making a rut from 4 to 6 inches to hold the rear wheels in the same deep groove, which was enough when turning in a good run. I never heard anybody asking to get out so I thank they all liked it.

DAY SEVENTY THREE AUGUST 5th

DAY SEVENTY-THREE
AUGUST 5th

The next day, we had been invited to an outdoor steak fry at a guest ranch at Starr Valley. It was only about 18 miles; so we left Wells late and made it with one hitch. Joe drove. The steak fry was great and so were the people. Marge made biscuits and gravy for breakfast the next morning which we ate outside on a picnic table by the creek, with the owner of the place.

8/5 – WELLS to STARR VALLEY
Bev and I both fixed breakfast so we put it together and all ate outside. McCulloughs left before we hitched up. Red and Wallace rode the palominos. Joe drove. Holly, Bev, and I rode in the stage. We stopped at the bank and picked up the strongbox; and headed west out of town. Wallace lost his billfold. He rode back a long ways, but didn't find it. Red drove into the ranch. It was a lovely place with lots of trees and grass, and a rushing creek. Mrs. Gerber invited us in. They had a very nice old farm house which had been remodeled. It was cool and comfortable. They had a thick rug we put Cody down on, and she almost crawled. Gerbers were fixing a barbecue for about 40 realtors. They had large T-bone steaks. One announcer gave us a big build-up and boosted the price of the kids' buttons to $1.50. I think we'd have done better if less had been said.

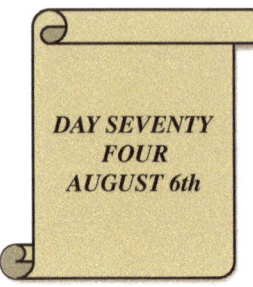

DAY SEVENTY–FOUR
AUGUST 6th

DAY SEVENTY FOUR AUGUST 6th

Joe drove out that morning, taking the back roads through Starr Valley, on down by Deeth. Since it was a dirt road with little traffic, Tammie decided to let the dogs run for a change. Ordinarily they rode in the horse van with the extra horses. Marge was driving the pickup behind.

Unaccustomed to the exercise, the dogs got hot and tired as the morning heated up. Marge stopped and Tammie loaded the dogs in the back of the pickup. One of them, Flint, went to jump out. He slipped and fell, running his front leg between the racks and the tail gate of the pickup.

The force of his jump flipped his body right on over, and there he hung by one front leg. Marge ran to hold up his body, while Tammie had to unhook the caution sign, and open the latch on the racks. About five minutes later, they finally got Flint free. To everyone's surprise, he wasn't hurt; just scraped up a bit. That was the first of his escapades. He got into more trouble later.

We had our noon camp at the old Fort Halleck site. No one would know there had once been an important army post there if it weren't for the sign. I took our camper on to Elko that morning; then checked out the frontage roads on my way back to noon camp.

8/6 – STARR VALLEY to ELKO
Woke up to the sound of the creek. Fixed biscuits and gravy for breakfast. Tom and Bev had juice and milk so we all ate at a picnic table outside. Joe drove the stage out; Tam and Wendy outriding. I drove the Ford. We took the old road which wound around. Mr. Gerber went ahead and opened gates for us. On the first one, Joe drove right up to the fence; then had to make a sharp turn down the bar pit and straight to the other fence; then swing the leaders and go through the gate. He made it, but they were in a gallop when they got through, and they galloped all the way up the first hill, down and almost to the top of the second hill; then trotted on over and down, and finally pulled up to a walk on the third.

When I took over the coach that afternoon, Marge and Wendy climbed on with me. Kip was outriding on Muskrat.

The first few miles of it were on a power line road, with several steep crossings and sharp curves on it. The horses acted like they were glad to get away from the pavement and on a good dirt road for a change. They were sure willing to step right out. We ran out in the sagebrush, climbed up ridges, dodged around rocks, and ducked off across washes and coulees.

With each hill, the downslopes got a little steeper and the drops at the bottom a little deeper. We swooped down one, with the horses hitting a gallop before we hit bottom, and then dropped off a two foot bank, and had to scramble to get out and up the otherside. We decided our road had given out, and figured we'd better be finding another one. We picked up another set of ruts across the sagebrush and followed it until it came out on a frontage road.

Tam had the dogs along and they got hot and tired; so we put them up on the pickup. Flint jumped off so Tam made him run until we got to the highway. Then put him in the back. He slipped and fell, hanging by one front leg. I thought he'd broken it, but he turned out to be OK. The trip through Starr Valley was pretty. Lots of trees, grass, and flowers, hay meadows and pastures. Went on down the highway to a junction for our noon change. Red had taken the camper into town; so we ate what sandwiches were left in the coach. Red came back with the Dodge and some more sandwich stuff and doughnuts. We hooked up his hitch and took off down the power line road. I rode on the box with him and Wendy was inside. Kip rode Muskrat. Tam drove the Ford.

About half way in, we came to where a couple pickups were parked in front of a small Basque beer joint. There as we rolled up, a fellow stepped to the door, and yelled to us, "If you'll tie up that hitch and come in, I'll buy you all a cool drink." The afternoon had been pretty warm so that sure sounded like a winner. We spent a good half hour there. It was a little old square building of wood and adobe, with a flat topped roof. Inside was an old bar and some round tables, old lamps and relics of other bygone days. It was like walking into a Max Brand book. Several men were cooling their heels, as well as their throats. The proprietor was short and stout, and spoke with a thick accent. It turned out, he was a barkeep I'd known in Elko years before.

In checking the road out that morning, I'd come up a "little hill". Before getting back up on the box, I checked over the brakes of the coach, and adjusted them a little tighter. Then with a "Thanks!" and a wave, we took off.

Marge wrote her description of that "little hill". She exaggerated a bit, but it makes good reading. Here's what she thought of it. "After a half hour or so across country, we started up a gradual slope. At the top was a ridge which was a break in the cliff. This was our "little hill".

It wasn't long, maybe a quarter mile, but she was steep. We could see the bottom right straight down, with the flat stretching out in front just waiting for us. I got good holds with both hands on the side railings as I was on the box with Red. Wendy was on the inside and said she was ready. Red set the brake, gathered the lines, and started off, holding the horses down to a slow walk. Within thirty feet, he had to let them out to keep them ahead of the coach, as it was starting to slide. The further we went, the faster the horses had to go. Halfway down, the coach was skidding sideways as Red had the brake on full to hold it back as much as possible. *By then, he had to throw 'em the slack and let 'em out!* We went down the last half in a full gallop and hit the bottom in a flat out run! With the straight-away in the front, it took Red a quarter mile to pull them up!"

We bounced over the sagebrush until the dips got too wild. After taking one pretty fast, we drove over to a better road. Tam drove the pickup ahead and got into a steep place. Finally came out on a frontage road and stopped by a little square building with a couple old pumps in front! One of the local men offered to buy drinks for all and since it was awfully hot, and we were all thirsty, we all trooped in and got pop. Inside as Kip put it, "was like a page out of a Max Brand book." We talked horses until the pop was gone. Red checked the brakes as he said it felt squeaky. Then we went on to another dirt road. This one was not too bad except for one hill. It was a gradual pull to the top, and then we got set as Red said. Wendy and I got good holds. He set his brake and gathered the lines, and we started down with the horses in a slow walk.

He looked around at me with a big grin from ear to ear. "Scared?" "Well, not exactly, but if I had any butterflies in my stomach when we started, I lost them about half way down!" Then Wendy stuck her head out the window with her eyes gleaming, and said, "Boy that was fun!" About then Tammie came bouncing down behind us in the pickup, and we proceeded out to the highway and on into town.

> *Marge and I both thought that was one of the best rides on the whole trip!*

We were met by the Bicentennial chairman quite a ways out of town that afternoon. He said there were some other people who wanted to ride in with us, and the Elko newspaper was sending a photographer out to meet us. He suggested we should drive on towards town until we came to the roadside rest area where he'd have the other people come meet us. He would return to town and tell them where to come, and he would also meet us there. When we got there, our man was there, but no one else had shown up. We waited and waited and waited. Finally we all agreed that something must have gone wrong; so we headed for town. We met one carload of people waiting up the road a couple miles for us, but no newspaper man. We loaded everybody on and had a good ride on into the fairgrounds.

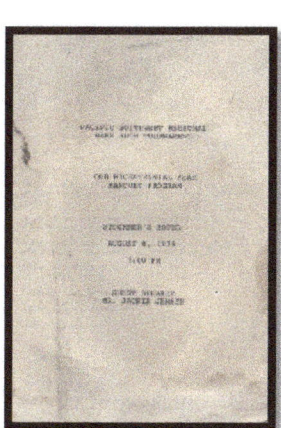

The Little League Baseball Association was holding their regional playoffs in Elko that weekend, and were having a banquet at the Stockman's Hotel that evening. We were really thrilled and honored when the city and Bicentennial officials presented us with tickets to the doings that night.

Then Red took rides out while I took a nap. Tam rode Heidi, and Wendy rode Bandito. Red met an old stagecoach driver in town, and sent him out to talk to me, so I could write down his story.
Joe and Pearl took him in their camper, and I didn't get to meet him. Red sent Tam home because she almost led him out in front of a car. Fixed supper after they came home.

Fixed rolls. Red shod horses. Later we went to town to make phone calls. Also took Wendy to the Western Store. She got purple reins and spurs. Stopped by the vet's, and he wasn't home. Went home and got mad because the girls hadn't fixed supper. Went to the store and bought pizza. When we got back, Holly had fixed hamburgers and corn too. Slept outside under a tree by the camper. There were lots of birds in the tree, and their droppings hit the tarp all night.

There were around 450 people attending the dinner. The program afterwards included a number of prominent people and baseball heroes giving talks. Each ball team and its officials were introduced. We felt highly honored also, to be introduced that evening. It was an excellent meal, with a lot of gourmet foods not usually found on the ordinary cowboy's diet. We enjoyed eating "like kings" that night. The speakers were all good too. We particularly liked one, the main speaker, who was a very well known ball player. He really gave an interesting talk.

DAY SEVENTY FIVE/SIX AUGUST 7-8th

DAYS SEVENTY-FIVE/SIX AUGUST 7th-8th

The ball club had a parade scheduled for Elko on Saturday, which we were invited to attend with our stagecoach. Of course, we accepted. When we drove downtown to the assembly area that morning, we were ushered right up to the lead position, behind the police escort car. The whole bunch of baseball officials loaded up with us for the trip to the ball park. We stayed in Elko from Friday until Monday.

Within 20 or 30 feet, he had to let the horses out a little to keep ahead of the coach, and by half way down, the coach was skidding sideways. They were in a stiff gallop when we hit the bottom and we had a good run for a quarter of a mile. Came into a frontage road and later met Morris Gallagher, the Bicentennial Chairman of Elko. Drove on into Elko with a police escort, and went to the fairgrounds. It was smorgasbord, and a good one. Ate at great long tables, and there were probably 300 people there. It was the Babe Ruth Baseball Finals and Centennial Celebration. After the dinner, there were speeches, and our group was introduced.

8/7-8 ELKO LAYOVER
Got up early. We went downtown and led off the baseball parade. Carried all the State Directors on the stage. They enjoyed the ride.

East of Carlin. Rowdy on Bandera. Wendy on the brake, Marge - shotgun.

That gave us a chance to catch up on our horse shoeing again. I don't recall all the horses I tacked shoes on there, but I do remember one that got them. That was old Muskrat, the mustang I'd caught out of a wild band 21 years ago. What made his shoeing so spectacular was this. With his age, this was only the third pair of shoes he'd had on in his life, and they were the first ones for him on this trip! According to his daily log, he had been ridden 509 miles on this trip since leaving St. Joe, Missouri, barefoot! And this didn't count all the times the kids had ridden him around one of our camps, or the times they had loped a half mile off to the side of the trail to inspect some interesting obstacle. His feet weren't what you'd call short or sore then; but we'd had quite a few miles of rocky or sandy shoulders as well, and I'd got to feeling sorry for him so decided he'd wear some irons. I'd pull those shoes off him in the fall after we got home, before turning him out to pasture.

We had one other horse that made the entire trip on two sets of shoes. I used cold cowboy plates – plain -- with no hard surface welded to them. One or two of the horses were on their fourth set when we ended the trip, but the average seemed to be three. With the distances that the various horses traveled, I'd say we probably averaged 300 miles to a set of shoes. We had very little problem with lameness, only two horses on the entire trip, and one of those was our old Quarterhorse mare.

In spite of the hard pounding on the pavement, day after day, the horses didn't get tired, and never got leg-weary. The main reason for this is the built in "shock absorbers" in the Morgan horse. They have extreme flex in their ankles and hocks, which gives them a springy action. This cushions the shock and prevents the leg injuries so common to some of the other breeds. This "Action" also makes the gaits very smooth, which is one reason why a Morgan is so comfortable to ride. This can be demonstrated by watching the harness on a horse's back. On the Morgans, the harness stays right in place, even when galloping. On other breeds, it will work to one side or the other, sometimes letting the "britching" slide almost off.

He had worked on the line from Elko to Twin Falls, Idaho from 1918 to 1923. He said the company had six coaches at the time. Four of them were on the road all the time, and made three round tips a week between the two towns. I had several good visits with another "never sweat buckaroo from Nevada", when I ran into an old friend of mine there in Elko. He was George Downing, and I was surprised to learn he was a direct descendant of the Downing family of Abbott-& Downing Company of Concord, New Hampshire, who made the Concord stagecoach famous. He told me his family also traced back to Downing Street in London, England. George was born in Iowa in 1901 and moved west in 1919.

While driving down the street in Elko, I saw an old crippled fellow on the corner. His eyes lit up when he saw that coach and horses. I just had to stop, and he told me he was an old stagecoach driver.

He went to Oregon in 1938 and worked the country from Pendleton to Burns and east of Steens Mountain. He also worked west of Steens at Roaring Springs. He rode ahorseback, with his bedroll on a second horse, across the desert to Daugherty Valley in Guano Basia where he hired out to the MC wagon. He stayed there until he was drafted in the army. Afterwards, he returned to the MC for a couple years, then worked for Brattains and the ZX until 1946. From there he went to Baker and returned to Elko County in September 1949. George was one of my friends from my cowboy days in that country, and I sure was glad to get to visit with him there in Elko. California, and up to Montana.

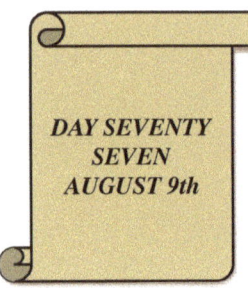

DAY SEVENTY SEVEN AUGUST 9th

DAY SEVENTY-SEVEN- AUGUST 9th

Monday saw us heading west again, with Joe ahold of the lines. He drove as far as the turn off, where we bypassed the tunnel. Joe didn't want to stop there that day, but Margie finally convinced him that was the spot where I'd said we'd have our noon camp.

From there on into Carlin was the afternoon when we made the trip down along the train tracks, running between the two trains.

They had quite a feast in the park that night. A good many more people showed up than were expected, and they just about ran out of food. That day was the birthday of one of the firemen. After the picnic was over, and all my chores were done, he and the city cop and I went down to one of the honkytonks and celebrated the occasion with a couple "pieces of snort".

8/9 – ELKO to CARLIN
Joe drove out. I drove the pilot car. Tam and Wendy were ahorseback. Wendy rode Heidi. We got up to the tunnel where we turned off on the old frontage road. The highway patrol unlocked the gate so we went through. We had a nice ride winding through the canyon. One place we came to a long curving hill on the side, and it was just like an old stage road. As we came into the yards, there were trains parked on sidings to our right, and the moving one on our left. Rowdy discovered he'd lost his canteen so we sent the two boys back to look for it, and told them to follow their horses' tracks. They finally found it. Supper was set for 6:30. There were lots of people. It was the biggest celebration Carlin had seen in a long time, and there were probably 200 to 300 people and more coming in from outlying areas and ranches.

DAY SEVENTY- EIGHT
AUGUST 10th

I mentioned a ways back down the road about not wanting our mares to have colts on the trip. For some time there had been quite a bit of discussion as to whether Sunny Ann was pregnant. The next morning, there at Carlin, when I went down to grain the horses, we had a new colt, up nursing. We hadn't driven Sunny for the past week. One week after the colt was born, we put her back in harness and back to work, without any ill effects on her or the colt.

I had been told there was a good place to camp at a highway underpass about 20 miles out. There was a good place there, but there weren't any gates in the fence leading from the highway to it. All we could do was keep going until we found a place that suited us. We finally came to an exit off the interstate, about 27 miles out. It had been pretty hot, and was kind of a long hard day, with mile after mile up one long hill and down another.

The TS Ranch had a good fenced in holding lot of about two acres just off the interstate exit a ways. We turned our horses in there and camped in the sagebrush. Marge cooked supper over a camp fire that evening, while the rest of us all went

8/10 – CARLIN TO DESERT
It was cool and damp with heavy dew when we got up, but a lovely morning. Red came back from feeding, and said Sunny had a black Appaloosa colt! The colt was a dark smoky-gray-black. After the trip was over and we got back to Colorado, we found out that the neighbor boys thought it would be a good joke to turn their Appaloosa stud in with our mare. Red and I were both very unhappy over that. Joe drove the coach, Tam rode, and I drove the Ford. Had some long hills that day. Red and Wallace went ahead on a frontage road and set up camp at a wire water trap. Wallace had to climb on the truck and hold up wires while Holly drove under them. After the horses were fed, Wallace built a sagebrush fire. I made slumgullion stew out of all the canned goods.

swimming in the river. The cold water was too much of a change for Tammie, who had been outriding all day. She was pretty well burned from the sun and the wind. She got sick right after supper, and hit the sack early. The rest of us sat around the campfire and drank coffee 'till late that night, with the foreman of the TS who stopped by.

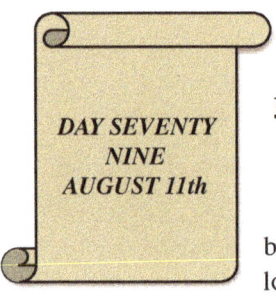

**DAY SEVENTY NINE
AUGUST 11th**

DAY SEVENTY-NINE
AUGUST 11th

The next morning he brought us over a large load of hay. He and his boys rode with us that morning for four or five miles, back down to his ranch gate. We stayed on a frontage road all the way into Battle Mountain. About ten miles out from town, we were met by an old time cowboy buckaroo friend of mine. I'd cowboyed with Harry Price on the ZX up in Oregon in the 40's and in Nevada after that. Harry had been wagon boss there on the TS for several years.

Awhile before we traveled through there, he'd quit and moved to town. He went to driving a truck in the copper mines. A heck of a way for a good cowboy to go. Harry's whole family was with him that morning. He climbed up on the shotgun seat with me for the ride into town. The kids got on somewhere.

I tried to talk his wife into parking her car and riding with us, telling her we'd bring her back after it, but she just smiled and said she'd meet us in town. We all had supper together in the park that evening.

I slept. Everyone else went swimming in the river. They came back wet and cold, and Tam was sick. She'd had too much sun, and then too much cold water. We sat and had coffee over the campfire, and the kids all roasted marshmallows. We rolled the beds out on the sagebrush. Had a full moon, and it was a beautiful night on the Nevada desert.

8/11 – DESERT to BATTLE MOUNTAIN

We cooked breakfast over the campfire. Red drove his hitch out. I rode inside with the boys and Wendy.
Tam drove the pickup on with the truck. Kip and Rowdy rode Muskrat and Bandera. Later a car met us. It was Harry Price. We drove on to the fairgrounds, then decided to "drag Main", then drove back to the fairgrounds and unhitched.

DAY EIGHTY
AUGUST 12th

We stayed in Battle Mountain two nights so we hitched up the next afternoon and took several loads of kids around town. While we were there at the fairgrounds, I took advantage of the extra time to harness Holly's and Wallace's palomino mares up and drive them. I drove each one separately for about an hour; then hooked them together and drove them for quite awhile. All of this driving took place in a big corral with me driving them on foot. They really gave to the driving quick and easy.

It sure is rewarding when you can accomplish something like breaking that team of mares to drive in one easy lesson. They still had lots to learn and needed worked, but the hard part was over. They didn't fight the harness and they'd learned to gee and haw real easy.

8/12 – BATTLE MOUNTAIN LAYOVER
After breakfast, we took a load of diapers to wash. Should have done the whole laundry because it was cheap, but didn't. Went shopping. Got Rowdy new boots, sox, and shorts with his money he'd earned, and what Darla had given me. Then bought Kip 2 shirts: a white with green plaid, and an orange one, and got Rowdy a tan one. We found a real pretty brown blouse, but we didn't get it because it was $5.00. Kip found a bugle in a store, and asked about it. It was the one that was found at the site of "Battle Mountain". Wasn't for sale. Fixed hamburgers for lunch. Then Red hooked up, and took rides all afternoon. It got pretty hot for awhile. When they came in, they'd all had ice cream at the "Happy Ox" at the owner's invitation. Two reporters took a bunch of pictures of Joe shoeing horses.

Battle Mountain on the Road to Fame See page 4

"The Old West Was Gone When I Got There"

By Andria Daley and
Marc Keyser-Cooper

Stagecoach '76 is one man's dream come true in celebration of our American Western heritage in the Bicentennial Year.

Red Wolverton and his family are retracing the old Overland Stagecoach route in a bright red stagecoach and teams of Morgan horses.

The red stagecoach was built in Oklahoma City at the cost of over $28,000.00. Red Wolverton is a cattleman and a trucker by profession, and Stagecoach '76 has been a two and half year project.

Insurance cost $4,000.00 and travel expenses will be around $15,000.00. It will end up costing around $48,000.00. According to Red, they were expecting financial assistance, but everything fell through at the last minute. The Wolvertons are paying for the trip themselves.

When asked why he was doing this, Red said, "It needed to be done. I have buckarooed all through this country. I guess I always felt slighted because the Old West was sort of gone when I got there."

The Overland Stages ran in 1857 until the railroad was completed at Promontory, Utah. The old stagecoach route began in St. Joseph, Missouri and terminated in Placerville, California. It took 21 days in 1859 to make the trip, depending on flood, Indians or other problems. The record time for a stage run was 17 days and 8 hours.

Red and his family started from St. Joe on May 25th and will complete their journey at Sacramento... just in time for the State Fair.

There are ten people in the group: Red, his wife Marge, and their children, Tammi, Kip and Wendy; and their son-in-law, Wallace Cotton and his wife, Holly. Ron McComb is the choreboy and Joe and Peal Heran are helping.

Red said, "Here in Battle Mountain, the TS Ranch gave us a load of hay and my old friend, Harry Price, had us over for a picnic in the park. We are proud of our American heritage and we enjoy seeing the old timers along the trail

DAY EIGHTY-ONE - AUGUST 13th

Wendy and I rode the palomino mares again the morning we left Battle Mountain. After noon that day when we hitched up, I put one of them Misty, in the off swing position and drove her on to Golconda. We had quite a large group of people to haul when we got there; so I had Wallace bring a fresh horse to replace Misty, as I didn't want to sour her by too much driving on the first time. Golconda is a small town, but they never celebrate in a small way. Sometimes one celebration there spills over into the next one.

One of my very interesting passengers that afternoon was old Huey Bane, a rancher from up north of Golconda about a full day's gallop. I wasn't real sure about Huey when he climbed up on the seat beside me. I was kind of afraid he would want to drive. He'd been partying quite awhile, but I sure didn't want to insult him. The Banes had been one of the last old time freighting families in Nevada, and I was sure Huey had done his share of it. And some of them had been my friends in the past. When he climbed up beside me he said, "If you think I don't know how to drive a six horse hitch, just tell me your leaders' names, and I'll show you how to start that hitch when we're all loaded." I replied, "The near leader is Romeo and the off leader is Rebel." He went on to tell me he could drive eight head too; that he'd freighted many a mile across Nevada with eight head back in the 20's and 30's. He said, "I've also had one of the wildest wrecks you've ever seen with eight head." To my great disappointment, he was interrupted before he got far enough into his story for me to figure out what must have happened.

About this time, all our passengers were aboard. Huey turned to me, says, now we're ready to go? I nodded yes, and fingered my lines up to a little better balance, waiting to see his next move.

8/13 – BATTLE MOUNTAIN to GOLCONDA
We were invited for breakfast at the "Happy Ox" Got down there about 7:30. I had a shawl over my dress, but it was cold as the air conditioner was on. I ordered a strawberry waffle, and it came with 2 inches of whipped cream in a heart-shape around the edge of the waffle, and the whole center full of berries. Scrumptious! And I didn't need any syrup. Asked the manager to join us for coffee, but he was too busy. We got the bill, and our gift breakfast cost us $22.00.
Wendy rode Holly Ann. Red rode Mistie out of town, Joe drove the coach, and I drove the Ford. Talked to an old man with 2 boys who had come out to buy a ranch and raise Quarter horses. Tried to talk them into riding on the coach, but they were in too much of a hurry. They did buy some buttons from the kids.

Whereupon he calls out in a good strong, clear voice, "Romeo! Rebel! Get up!", and our horses lifted their heads, and the hitch moved out as even as if I had called them myself. Huey, as proud as a kid with a new hat, grinned up towards me and says, "See thar, I told you I knew how to start out a stagecoach hitch!"

I did get down one of Huey's stories that day:

It was about Butch Cassidy, who held up the bank in Winnemucca along about 1902. It wasn't a haphazard robbery; Butch had it planned to the last detail for quite awhile. Money was pretty hard to come by in some of the ranch country then, like it still is today; so who was to look a gift horse in the mouth when this band of cowboys stopped at an isolated ranch one day. They told the rancher they would pay a good fee if he would take care of their extra horses, feed them a good helping of grain and exercise them each day until they returned. They said they'd have a long hard ride ahead of them when they came back by, and would need some good mounts to carry them on. The outlaw band then rode leisurely on down close to Winnemucca to await the proper time for their robbery. They pulled their holdup off without a hitch, and made their escape out of town with no trouble. Soon afterwards the news was spread to the outside world via the telegraph. One of the ranches that headquartered on the rails up the country about 25 miles, picked up the story along with the rest of the country. The men folks all saddled up and galloped out into the hills to try to apprehend the villains on the most likely of the hidden trails. About 4:30 that afternoon, a 15 year old boy who had been left behind to take care of the ranch, looked out across the meadow. Five horsemen were approaching from the direction of Winnemucca. That was the right number, and they were traveling in the right direction. Also they were riding the right colored horses according to the news they'd heard; one of them being a magnificent big grey. The boy bristled up immediately. He grabbed his old shotgun, mounted his horse, and rode out to capture the whole "wild bunch'. Before he reached the outlaw group, the fellow on the big grey horse turned from the others, and rode to meet the boy. When he rode up he said, "What do you say, boy?" in a friendly greeting. At this, the boy's mouth dropped open, and all he could think of to say was, "That sure is a good looking horse you're riding." Butch Cassidy sat there grinning at him for a spell. Then he asked, "Boy, don't you have some chores that need taken care of back at the ranch?" The boy gulped once or twice, and agreed, "I sure do," "Then you better get on home and get them done." "I sure had," the boy blurted out, as he whirled his horse around and galloped back to the ranch. Butch and his wild bunch moseyed on up to the isolated ranch where they'd left their horses. They had a good meal and a little rest before galloping on into that wild free Humbolt country to the northeast. Before they left the ranch, Butch left explicit instructions for the rancher to take that "magnificent grey hoss" down to the "boy with the shotgun", and give it to him as a present from Butch Cassidy. The boy and "grey hoss" lived the rest of their lives there on that ranch, with many fond feelings towards Butch, I'm sure.

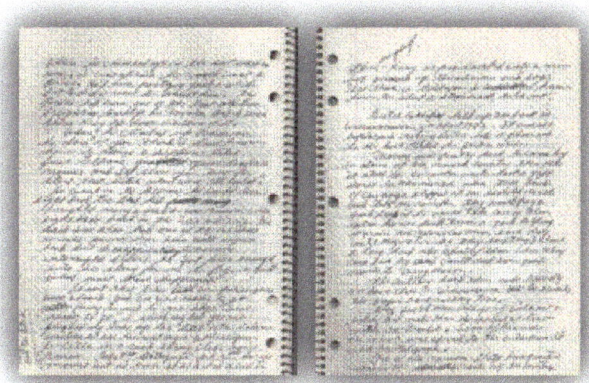

Mark's Waterhole #1 was our camp at Golconda. We joined all there in a great meal, this time a western barbecue. Afterwards the rest of the community swung their celebrating into high gear at the waterhole. Since we'd been up since 5 am, we declined further invitations and turned in. We slept outside, as we had done most of the trip. We were closer to the corrals than usual. The wind came up during the night, and we could feel something dropping on the tarp from time to time. Next morning we found dry cow chips all over us.

Tammie spent the day with Mike so I drove the Ford again. Red drove the coach over Golconda Summit. Kip rode Muskrat, and Wendy rode part way with me, and the rest with Red. Tam and Mike went to Winnemucca and brought back 2 picnic hams for supper. I hadn't bought any in Battle Mountain because they were too high priced. Got into Golconda, and Red gave rides for a couple hours. They had a barbecue. Had grilled wienies as the rest of the meat was already gone. Holly said she'd given them one ham and they'd put it in the beans. The food was good, but we didn't find much ham in the beans. The 4H Club was doing this all for us, not for the town, and they weren't making any money. The people took up a collection for rides on the stagecoach and it was donated to the 4H Club. Slept that night beside the truck. The wind came up and blew manure chips all over our bed.

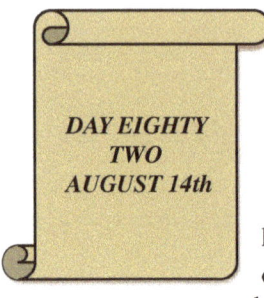

DAY EIGHTY-TWO
AUGUST 14th

That morning as we were hitching up, one of the local celebrants came out and said he hadn't gotten his ride the night before. I promised him if he'd stay out of our way while we hooked up, I'd haul him back up to the Waterhole. When we pulled around in front of the building, we found the celebration was still going on.

Instead of our not-so-dry friend getting off when we got there, he talked another fellow into riding on to Winnemucca with us. Fella #1 rode inside the coach with Marge and the kids. He sang awhile, slept awhile, and chattered awhile; then slept some more. Marge told me that once, when I pulled off in the bar pit and we hit a really bad bump, he slid half way off the seat and banged his head on the window. She figured if he had a colossal headache when he sobered up, he probably never knew it was more than just a hangover.

8/14 GOLCONDA to WINNEMUCCA
Was cool, cloudy, and threatening rain. Red drove the coach. Holly, Wallace, and Rowdy were ahorseback. I had Cody and Wendy in the coach, and Lisa rode in the Ford with Tam. Kip was on top, Shoshone Tom rode shotgun, and "the drunk" rode inside. It was cold so we put down the curtains. The drunk jabbered for about 5 miles, then fell asleep. A reporter from Winnemucca met us on the highway, and took a bunch of pictures; then rode inside with us. When the drunk woke up, he did all the talking so I don't know if the reporter ever got any information or not. Once Red drove off the highway, and hit a real bad bump or washout. It threw all of us almost off the seats, and the drunk cracked his head on the window pane. Didn't wake him up though. I wondered if it knocked him out.

... the last Indian massacre that occurred in the U.S. was right there in Nevada, a half day's gallop to the north. It was a long story, but ended with the fact that a bunch of white men had hunted and tracked down 18 of his Shoshone ancestors, surrounded them, and killed every man and woman in the bunch. The massacre was of the Indians, not by them. This took place in 1915.

My second passenger was "Shoshone Tom", a full blooded Shoshone Indian, born and raised right there in Nevada. One of the interesting accounts of local history he told me was the fact that…

It was raining lightly that morning as we rolled on towards Winnemucca. We were flagged down by a man and woman in a yellow car with a "press" tag on their license plate. They were from Winnemucca and didn't seem to be very thrilled to be sent out to film a stagecoach in the rain. They also weren't interested in riding on it either, but we finally convinced one of them he ought to give it a try. How could he write a story about it if he hadn't tried it? After catching up with the car again in a couple miles, the one who had ridden with us, talked the other one into trading off and trying out the coach.

By the time we got to the fairgrounds, they had changed their minds so much **that I had to make several circles around the horse barns to satisfy their sudden desire to ride and photograph a real live authentic stagecoach.** We arrived in Winnemucca on August 14, what should be fairly warm weather.

(8/14) We turned off the main highway, then turned into the fairgrounds. When we got there Red did some figure 8's at a gallop that had the coach leaning. Cody was awake. Put the horses in pole stalls built in a long line. They were neat, and western looking. Then we all climbed into the Ford, and went back to Mark's Waterhole to get the camper and truck. By then, Jay, the drunk, had sobered up some. He bought lunch for us. Went to the movie that night. It was a western that was half funny and half nasty. "The Gunfighter and the Stranger".

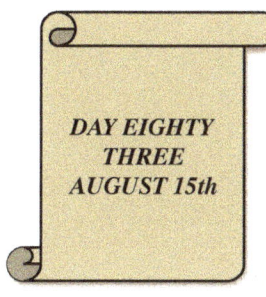

DAY EIGHTY THREE AUGUST 15th

DAY EIGHTY- THREE
AUGUST 15th

The next morning when we went to feed the horses, there was snow down on the mountains sides, to just a few feet over our heads. It shore was pretty, but pretty near more than we could stand. We laid over that weekend.

Sunday night when a car drove up to our camp, I was delighted to see another of my old cowboy friends get out. It was "Lopey, the Bandit, from up in Oregon. It had been about 23 years since I'd last seen him. I couldn't see he looked a day older.

8/15 WINNEMUCCA LAYOVER

Fixed rolls for breakfast. Holly and I took the laundry in, about ½ block from the movie. Tam took Lisa and went with Red to make calls and look around town. It was awfully hot in the laundry, but turned cool later in the day. Was downright cold that night, and felt like the middle of November. Had wind and rain, and a little bit of snow.

Lopey had been…

...the jigger boss on the ZX wagon for a good many years before finally working up to wagon boss for awhile. We'd spent a good many long hard days ahorseback together, and not a few nights celebrating in town together, trying to forget all the other. I don't do much 'elbow bendin' now days, but sometimes I keep a bottle around for just such emergencies like an old buddy dropping in unexpected. It didn't take long for us to outmaneuver the other, each swapping lies. Finally that night Lopey and I were at it again. I dug out a good story and we all got a laugh out of it when I asked, "Lopey, do you remember the night in the Corral Bar that I kept bragging on how good a singer you were?" "Yeah, you almost got both of us throwed in jail that night," he laughed. It had all happened because I was becoming very bored from having a broken leg. I'd already had it in a cast about five months and had a long ways to go yet. I did have a walking cast and heel on it and could get around pretty good with the help of a hickory cane.

I'd come to town that day to see the doctor and had decided to stay for awhile, when I saw Lopey and some of the other crew come in about dark. It was getting pretty late when I strolled in the Corral Bar and sidled up beside Lopey and ordered an orange pop. Lopey was in a good mood so I started in on him to sing me a song. It didn't take much urging; he was feeling so good he was more than willing to answer my request. The only thing is, Lopey isn't, nor never was any kind of a "canary", but what he lacked in quality, he tried to make up in quantity. I don't think the bartender appreciated his crooning either, for he'd keep telling Lopey to "Shut up". As soon as he'd turn his back, I'd get Lopey started again. Finally after quite awhile, the bartender told Lope to shut up or he'd throw him out. I ducked my head and whispered under my arm, "You're not man enough to do it". Lopey repeated what I said, only said it loud enough that the barkeep heard it. It irritated him no limit. He came right around the bar and grabbed old Lopey and started marching him towards the door.

All the while I'm setting back there giving Lopey instructions on how not to leave. When they get to the door before going out, I yells, "Hey Lopey, here's your coat," holding it out. "Come and get it". When he got away from the barkeep and came over to get his coat, I wouldn't give it to him, and we got into a big squabble. About this time, the bartender finally figured out that I was the one that had been causing all the trouble all along. Furious then, he orders me out. I answered that just because he could throw out a half-tanked up cowboy didn't mean he was man enough to throw me out. "Like H---!, he says, as he yells for reinforcements from another barkeep and starts after me. I could see I was fast becoming outnumbered, so started giving way and backing towards the door. I was just about ready to give in and leave when some brave soul punched me right square in the nose.

Fun is fun, but when they start punching me in the nose, it ceases to be funny. For a minute there, I forgot I was standing on only one leg, but I never forgot about that hickory cane. I about had things evened out when I heard a voice behind which I recognized as one of the crew. "Red, if you'll settle down and get out of town, the city cop out here says he'll let you go. But if you don't he's going to throw you in jail." That struck me as being funny. Just how in the dickens was he going to throw me in jail if he couldn't get ahold of me? Anyhow, I answered that sounded good to me. Waving at the bartender, I turned to the sidewalk. I gathered Lopey up and poured him in my old pickup; then headed out of town.

Those were the "good old days" when a cowboy could come to town and raise a little "cane" and let off steam without getting into much trouble. That was the type of tales that filled our camper that evening until my little bottle dried up. It sure was good to see old Lopey again.

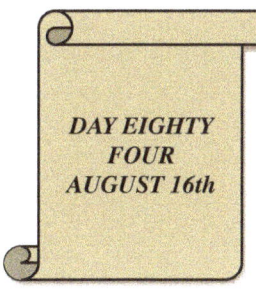

DAY EIGHTY FOUR AUGUST 16th

CHAPTER THIRTEEN
Eyes on the horizon

DAY EIGHTY-FOUR
AUGUST 16th

Joe drove out through Winnemucca that Monday morning. We put Sunny Ann back in the hitch as the off leader, her first day's work after having her colt. She sure was acting like it felt good to get out and stretch her legs again. Even though she was 15 years old and had raised 7 or 8 colts for us, she still had lots of class and go left in her. In the bright morning sunlight, she stepped out with her head and tail high, leading proudly that matched hitch of six shining chestnut horses. There were lots of comments on how pretty they looked that morning. Joe had to circle east, then south, before coming out on the road that headed west through town. It shore was a sight to see as everyone stopped to watch that hitch stepping out. We had our noon camp at a highway rest area about half way to Imlay. I took the coach on to Imlay. We were able to follow a frontage road partways for a few miles. We made several passes through

town, picking up people, before heading out to the Highway Maintenance Shop where we had our portable corrals set up for the night. It was a wonderful friendly group of people that set out a western potluck meal before us that evening.

8/16 WINNEMUCCA to IMLAY

Put Sunny back in harness, and she was raring to go. The six really looked good out in the sun, going around the curve. The air was cool, and there was fresh snow on the mountaintops. We were supposed to stop at a rest area. Tam got up to the exit, and turned. Joe started to turn, but went past the exit. I figured I'd better follow him; so then he turned and went over the curb and down across a steep bank. I had to go between the sign and the curb. It was a real bad maneuver. After changing horses, I rode with Red, and Tam drove. Kip and Rowdy rode in the afternoon. Bandera was pretty lame. When we were ready to go to the Maintenance Depot, we had to cross a cattle guard. Tam discovered she'd lost one plywood panel. The people of Imlay fixed a potluck for us there. It was so nice.

DAY EIGHTY-FIVE
AUGUST 17th

We'd been going steady, and our luck was holding real good too good. Marge and I had talked about it, and she was getting a little uneasy. It's awfully hard to prepare for something you don't know what, nor when it might happen. All we could do was try to be more careful than usual, and hope that everyone else would take equal care. When trouble came, it came sudden, --- as it always does with horses.

I got Joe started out with the coach. It was quite awhile before the rest of us were ready to leave with the horse van and campers. It was almost noon before I caught up to the coach.

Marge hollered on the CB to find the first spot possible and pull over **as they'd had an awful wreck.**

*****This is what she told me when they got in:

'I was driving the pickup behind the coach. Joe was driving pretty slow. Slower than usual it seemed to me. It was awful hot, and I was starting to get logy. Since running the pilot car was a monotonous job, especially in the heat, I'd figured out all kinds of things to do to keep alert. Of course, the CB provided all kinds of interesting conversations as people asked questions, commented on the outfit, or as often happened among the truckers, told us where they'd seen us last. Some of them met us several times through the summer.

Another thing I did when the driving got too boring was to clock the horses; up hill or down, on the level, walking, trotting, or loping; it didn't matter. This morning, when I noticed how slow it seemed we were going, I checked, and we were just barely going four miles per hour.

8/17 – IMLAY to LOVELOCK

Joe drove out in the morning. Had the Imlay people with him. Tam and Wendy rode ahorseback. I drove the Ford. Went on a frontage road for about 8 miles. I brought the passengers back to Imlay in the Ford. Then we went on out on the freeway. We'd been going quite awhile. I looked in the rear view mirror for traffic, then looked ahead, and there were horses all over the road! Checked the mirror and pulled past the coach and in front of the horses. They were down, and it looked like an awful mess. I yelled on the CB for RED, then started to get out and my door was jammed. I tried several times to open it. Finally had to kick it to get out.** Nothing seemed to be hurt, so we changed horses, ate lunch, and left. I rode on the box with Red. Tam drove the pickup, and Kip rode Muskrat.

Ordinarily Joe drove just over seven MPH. We were on the interstate west of Imlay, and as usual for interstate driving, I was in back of the coach, keeping a close watch on the rear-view mirror for traffic to come up behind. Tammie was riding big Max so I had no worries about the outriding, as I sometimes did if one of the younger kids was riding alone. Wendy was also riding that morning. Everything was fine up ahead, going along slow. I checked the mirror again, and it was clear a long ways back. When I looked back up front again toward the coach, **there were horses all over the highway!**

I quickly checked all around for traffic, hit the gas pedal and charged up past the coach and horses. I swung around in front of them and backed up as close to the leaders as I could. I was "breaking 19" for Red who was driving the truck, to tell him we'd had a wreck with the horses. I made two quick calls, then went to jump out of the pickup, and my door was jammed because the pickup was on a slant. I almost panicked, but finally swung around in the seat and holding the handle down with one hand, kicked with both feet, and the door flew open. By the time I got out, Tammie had bailed off Max, and Wendy was holding him. What we saw was an awful mess.

The near leader, Houlihan, was down flat, unmoving, with the swing tongue on top of him. Roulette, the near swing horse, was laid out flat on top of the swing tongue, almost obliterating Houlihan. Sunny Ann, the off leader, was standing over the two of them, with her line under Houlihan, and her head and neck bent way off to the side. Robby, the off swing horse, was clear out of the hitch, off the right side. The only good thing was that both wheel horses were still standing up and in place, and so was the coach.

Tammie and I had both untangled a good many wrecks throughout the years; so it only took a minute to size up the situation. I grabbed Sunny's head and talked to her, holding her steady while Tam reached underneath Houlihan and unsnapped the caught line. As soon as her head came free, we unbuckled her harness, and pulled her back off the other two horses. You can bet we didn't waste any time either as we were terribly worried about Houlihan on the bottom. Got Sunny's tugs undone and pulled the other end of her line loose. Then we tied her up to the side of the pickup. By then Tammie was unbuckling Roulette's harness as she lay there. I pulled Robby's line loose, unhitched him, and tied him next to Sunny. Tam finally got Roulette loose. She started struggling, finally got her feet under her and lunged up. She was shaking all over. I held her while Tam untangled her harness; then tied her to the pickup also. We unhooked the tugs on the wheelers and tied them right to the wheel tongue, which was our usual way of unhitching. Then we were finally able to move the swing pole and get if off Houlihan. He had never moved.

(8/17 p.2) The country between Inlay and Lovelock was pretty. Lots of trees, and there were small places as we got closer to Lovelock, with trees and grass, and the river valley with the stacks of hay. At the outskirts of town, the sheriff we'd met at Imlay escorted us through town. We turned off the freeway on a 2 lane street. There was lots of traffic. There were huge trees at the side of the road. They made welcome shade as the day was hot. Kip kept getting mad at Muskrat and yanking him around. He wasn't looking and ran smack into a tree limb that poked him in the eye. The people on top of the coach had to duck branches. Red ran over one road marker trying to keep off the street. Then a motorized stagecoach came out from town. We came back to the fairgrounds. Had to cross an old bridge. I fixed supper.

I couldn't see him breathing, and I thought he was dead. Tammie leaned across and unbuckled his harness. She poked him and prodded him and we kept calling him. Finally he opened his eyes. She prodded again, and he raised his head; then fell back again and didn't move. Now that we knew he was alive, she pushed, and I pulled. We finally got his legs out in front of him and his head up. He started struggling, and with our help finally made it up on his feet, but just stood there swaying. We went all over him. Miraculously, we could find nothing wrong. After making sure he was alright, we checked the others over too. We'd been in too much of a hurry to do it before. Nothing but a few scrapes and bruises.

We were so thankful, as we both knew what we'd have had to do if a leg or neck had gotten broken in the pileup. When you've raised and trained and lived with horses as we had with these, that thought is hard to face.

The calm, gentle nature of our horses had helped, as there'd been no kicking or struggling until we'd gotten them untangled and were able to help them up on their feet. We walked Houlihan around until he stopped shaking. Then we put Roulette and Robby back in place in the swing. Then Houlihan and Sunny back in the lead. When we went to harness up, we found the only thing we'd done in the whole wreck was to break the rope between the hames of the leaders! We hitched up, Joe got back on the box, Tam and Wendy remounted. I moved the pickup back out on the highway, and we started up. The horses were a little sore at first, but soon were back trotting again.

The traffic had been very light and only a few vehicles went by. I picked up Red on the CB about 15 minutes later, and he stopped as soon as he could find a place wide enough for the horse van. While talking it over, as near as he and I could ever figure out, the pace that morning had been too slow, and the weather too warm. Drowsiness had set in. Roulette must have stepped over Houlihan's singletree. This caused him to fall down and pulled Roulette's feet out from under her. She went over too as the momentum from the wheel horses pushed the swing pole over Houlihan. When the coach pulled in beside the truck, and we were unhitching, Joe told Red, "We had a little trouble back there." Red said, "Yeah, what happened?"

(8/17 p.3)

Afterwards Red and I went downtown to check on bus schedules to see if Keith would get in. Decided he couldn't make it before midnight. Went over to a little roadside store to get groceries, diapers and ice. Found a cute stagecoach bank and got it for Lisa. Went on home and went to bed. About 2:00 A.M. a police car brought Keith out so we bedded him down on the floor of the camper, as it had been raining and was cold and wet.

Joe replied, "An Injun shot the near leader!'

Back up the country a ways, I mentioned about putting Misty, one of the palomino mares in the hitch. Well, the very next day, I put them both in the swing team position and had been using them there regularly ever since. The afternoon after Joe's wreck I had both palominos in again, heading on into Lovelock, Nevada.

We were met out about five miles by a group of the Lovelock town fathers and officials. The sheriff also met us and escorted us all the way to town. He acted to me like he was in a hurry so I let the horses out to a pretty good clip, even though I had already driven over 20 miles that afternoon. He told me afterwards that he had timed and clocked us, and that we had averaged exactly 13½ miles for the five miles he led us. That's not real rapid, but is moving right along.

We camped at the edge of the arena at the fairgrounds that night. It was a good thing we didn't plan on leaving early the next day as it snowed on the hills and rained in the valley again all night.

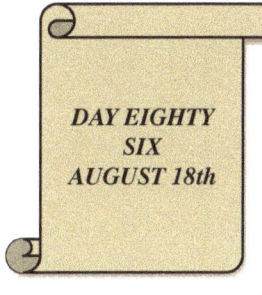

DAY EIGHTY-SIX
AUGUST 18th

We were camped in a sea of mud by morning. The sun came out though, and by noon things were dried up enough that we were able to get away. We were planning on spending that night at a highway rest area out about 22 miles, so we decided to leave late and make the whole run on my hitch. Wallace said that he and Holly could load the horses and break camp OK by themselves so we hitched up and drove out. Joe was riding shotgun beside me. We'd just gotten a few miles out of town when Joe's wife caught up with us and flagged us to a stop. She said Sunny Ann had slipped in the truck when they were loading her and had run a hind leg through a hole and almost cut it off. There wasn't a veterinarian anywhere around Lovelock, and Wallace was about scared to death and wasn't sure what to do.

8/18 LOVELOCK to REST CAMP/BRADY HOT SPRINGS
Some fellows came out that had cheaper hay for sale, so Red got two pickup loads. We hitched up Red's hitch and he and Joe and Keith went on the stage. I drove the Ford, Tam and Rowdy outriding. Hadn't been gone over about ½ hour when Pearl drove up on the freeway. Told us Sunny Ann had gotten cut up real bad loading, and needed a vet, and there wasn't one nearer than Fallon. Red gave Joe the lines and told them not to go any further than the end of the frontage road, as we had to cross a cattle guard there. Then Red and I went back to town. Picked up Holly on the CB going through town. Went out to the fairgrounds. Wallace had Sunny out and he was washing her leg. She'd fallen through the stairway. It was cut to the bone, and a vein was ruptured. He tied it off. Leg looked terrible.

Well, we held a quick pow-wow and decided it would be best for Joe to take the coach on, and I'd go back and see about Sunny Ann. Her right hind leg was skinned clear to the bone below the knee for about a foot.

Wallace had finally pulled the end of the vein out and tied a string around it. The bleeding stopped shortly after I got there. It looked pretty bad. We got it washed good and doctored her. We had a supply of medicine and also got some from the sheriff who came by. He had horses of his own. Since there was nothing else we could do, we reloaded the horses and headed out.

We caught up with Joe about seven or eight miles from the rest area where we'd planned our night camp. Everything looked OK so I took over the coach. Wallace went on to camp with the horse van. We

hadn't gone far until I sure wished the van was back there with us. Romeo was real sick with as bad a case of the diarrhea as I'd ever seen. I thought about unhitching him and tying him on behind but decided that wouldn't be any different than where he was. He wasn't doing any pulling there in the lead. We finally finished the afternoon at a slow walk to accommodate his feelings. I never figured for sure what had made him sick, whether it was the water, or possibly some new alfalfa hay that I'd bought there in Lovelock. It was several days before he completely got over whatever kind of bug it was that he had.

8/18 (p.2)

The sheriff and a deputy both came out. They got some medicine for us and helped Red doctor her and wrap it. Then he fixed a stall in one end and loaded her and the colt in it. Loaded everything else and got the camper ready, and we all left. We went to a rest camp where Wallace had a corral set up by a fence. Stayed there that night. Several tourists came over to visit, including a doctor from California. Juliet and Romeo were both sick, had the scours, and were lame on the front end. The doctor gave us some scours pills for Romeo. Red had driven real slow because Romeo was feeling so bad.

DAY EIGHTY-SEVEN
AUGUST 19th

Nothing much exciting happened all that day from the rest area on into Fernley, unless you think it's exciting to be fighting mosquitoes with both hands, while you're driving a six horse hitch. It does keep you some busy. That afternoon as we crept slowly past the Humbolt Sinks, we were about eaten alive. We were in a high trot much of the time, but it sure felt like we'd just as well be staked out spead-eagled the way the mosquitoes were getting to us. It reminded me so much of the Nevada mosquito story, that I almost over-strained my eyes searching for the scars up on the rimrocks where they whetted their bills.

The Indians used to chase the coaches to the stations. Well, we stopped out on the highway and talked several Indian kids into riding in with us. They liked it so well that they came down the next morning and rode all the way to Reno with us.

[We pulled a switch on the old time customs when we rolled into Fernley.]

There at Fernley, I had written and phoned ahead as usual to advise them when we'd be in. The local ladies prepared a lovely picnic for us in the park, but nobody else showed up.

This seemed rather unusual to us, as most of the little towns were quite enthused. After visiting awhile, I learned a local newspaper had printed the wrong date, and advertised we'd be there the day before. It seems a good many people drove out to meet us and were quite disappointed when we didn't show up.

Besides Romeo getting sick, we'd also doctored Juliet. She hadn't really been sick, just wasn't up to her usually high-spirited nature.

8/19 – REST CAMP/ BRADY HOT SPRINGS to FERNLEY

Mistie got a bad bite on her withers during the night. Took a ride around the campground for the tourists. Changed horses late, and had lunch. Red drove and I rode on the box. Tam drove the Ford. Wendy rode Holly Ann. The mosquitoes were terrible, and got in our hair. Very bad. Even bothered the horses. The marshes and lakes were off to the side with hills in the background. We went on an overpass and down into Fernley at a park and roping area. Wallace and Holly said the caretaker wouldn't let them have water for awhile. We got in about 4:30 and unhitched. The Bicentennial committee of women brought out dinner at 5:00 and wouldn't eat with us. We got to visit with them, and they finally thawed out, and ate a little. Bandera and Romeo were both sick.

Then when we got to Fernley, Bandera, our Quarterhorse mare, got **down. She was in pretty bad shape and I think we all were pretty worried about her.**

DAY EIGHTY-EIGHT
AUGUST 20th

In the morning, Marge went out to see about her. Walked right up to her and Bandera never moved. She didn't move until Marge touched her on the neck. She'd been thrashing around on the ground quite a bit during the night, and still didn't want to get up. Marge finally got her up and moving around a bit. She seemed awfully stiff, but was better than the night before.

We had a whole load of people come out to ride with us through town before we left. At least some of them got over being peeved at us. We had a lot of interesting things happen that morning. Joe was driving. I was riding shotgun. Tammie hadn't ridden on the coach all summer; so when she offered to trade with me for a ways I took her up on it. I was ahead of the coach when a man driving an oncoming semi stuck his head out of the window and yelled over to me. He asked if we'd stop and wait for him to get his camera out of his suitcase in the side compartment of his truck so he could take a picture. "Sure", I answered, pulling Max up and signaling Joe to stop. The trucker finally got his camera and snapped a couple or three pictures. Grinning as big as you please, he called his thanks, climbed back in his truck and moved on. We seldom stopped right on the highway like that, but

---

8/20 – FERNLEY to RENO

Truckers roaring by on the highway bothered us during the night. Got up fairly early. Went out to see about Bandera.

The Fernley people gave us all the leftover food. Had the refrigerator full. When we left, a couple of them and 2 Indian kids rode with us. I rode in the stage with Wendy and Red on top. Tam on Max, and Keith in the Ford. It was pretty coming out of Fernley. Real green with the river and trees. One of the women told me there was a Morgan breeder there. Changed horses at the side of the freeway. Fixed sandwiches. Camper smelled so bad from the toilet. I drained it, and then discovered the valve was open. Kip had to dig a hole and bury it. Kip thought Shag was lost. I went back to the camper and found Shag underneath it.

I've done enough trucking. I knew just how he felt, when he saw something like that, and his camera was out of reach.

Later on I was riding on the coach. Keith was driving the pickup behind when I heard a screeching sound, then what sounded like a crash. Two old cars shot around us and whipped right across in front of us to the highway shoulder to park. There was juice spilling out of the one in behind, and its radiator looked smashed. Keith said they were angry and tried to cut in front of him to stop him when he came along, but he just buzzed further out and went on around them and kept going. He had seen what happened. The car in the lead had come roaring around the corner real fast, with the second car right close behind him. They were probably racing. Instead of pulling out around, the lead car had slammed on his brakes first and the second one had crashed into it. They were yelling to Keith that it was his fault when he came by. Later on they passed us with a tow chain between the two junkers. **We were thankful they hadn't bumped into Keith. Guys like that, who can't see those rotating lights and flashing blinkers, usually don't have any insurance either.**

We had been told there was a good camp area about the right mileage for our noon camp. When Wallace got there, he missed the exit so he pulled off in a big wide sandy barpit. I decided that afternoon, when we went to hook up that it was about time to put Mr. Red Horse up in the lead since Romeo still had the "punies". Just about the time we were hooked up and ready to give him a try, a TV cameraman showed up to do a series of road shots for Reno and Sacramento. That was fine, but when I tried to pull out of that sandy barpit, I couldn't get going. Red Horse had been one of our best dependable pullers on the wheel, but he wouldn't tighten a trace there in the lead. Also, I had the palomino mares in the swing, which really hadn't learned anything about pulling or at least not enough to .know how to start a load. That should have been embarrassing and probably was, but I've had worse things happen. Anyhow, I didn't get excited.

(8/20 p. 2)

Red drove out. Had the palominos in the swing. I rode on top with him. The reporter from the paper was there. He took lots of pictures and should have gotten some good ones. Rowdy was riding Muskrat, and Tam was driving the Ford. The TV guys came out too and rode with us. They drove alongside and filmed; and one place Red drove on a dirt road while they were driving on the freeway. Traffic into Sparks and Reno got real bad. Wendy traded with Rowdy and we had to put her behind the coach and in front of the pickup because of the traffic. Finally got to the right exit and went to the fairgrounds. A Little Britches Rodeo was coming in, so we had to move our horses and move the camper and truck. Had an electrical storm that night, but not much rain.

I just had our pickup pull up ahead of us and run a lass rope back down between the leaders to the end of the swing tongue and tied on. We pulled the coach back up that slant to the blacktop before unhooking the pickup. That time we got started alright.

As we moved along, the photographer got some really good shots from all sides. One place there was quite a large area alongside the highway, uncluttered by phone lines, fences or anything else manmade. I was able to make a big half circle in crossing it that he seemed to like exceptionally well. A reporter from the Reno newspaper caught up with us and shot some pictures. He got one of us from an overpass, with traffic on all sides, and a semi right next to the coach. Rowdy had been riding Muskrat. He got tired so traded with Wendy. The traffic between Sparks and Reno got so bad, we had to put Wendy behind the coach and in front of our pickup to protect her. It got pretty hairy there for awhile.

DAY EIGHTY-NINE
AUGUST 21st

The next day at the county fairgrounds, we were pleasantly surprised to have some old friends from Paisley, Oregon drop in on us. I had known the Brattains for 30 years. They had read about us in the paper and come up to see us. I had gone to work in the Paisley area when I was 16 years old. I worked with the Brattains and their crews a good many times through the years. We think a lot of them and had a good visit that afternoon.

Pony Boy Days is Reno's own private kids' rodeo. It was in full swing the weekend we stopped over there. We were asked to show the stagecoach in the arena during the show. The kids all seemed to like it, which made us all feel good.

Tammie had to leave us at Reno. She was entered in the Miss Rodeo Colorado contest back at Pueblo, which would start the following weekend. We fixed stock racks on the flat stagecoach trailer, and loaded up Max and Bandera. Max was her rodeo horse and we decided Bandera needed to rest. Late Saturday, Tammie, Keith, and Rowdy headed back for Colorado. We sure hated to see them go.

8/21 – RENO LAYOVER

After breakfast Red and Tammie went hunting for a horse trailer. Didn't find one so came back about noon with lumber and plywood to build racks on the coach trailer. Morning was hot and muggy, but afternoon showers came up. Almost rained out the rodeo.

Holly and I did laundry. Got back late. Got all the clothes taken care of, and helped Tam pack her things and Rowdy his. The men worked on the trailer all afternoon. Finished it after supper. Then Red took the pickup and gassed it up and greased it.

Finally got all loaded and Tam, Keith, and Rowdy left about 10:30.

DAY NINETY
AUGUST 22nd

We originally planned our trip schedule to include the trip up through Virginia City, Nevada. We hadn't received an answer from them so decided to drive there in our pickup on Sunday and check the town out before attempting to run the stagecoach up there.

It's a long steep hill both up to and down from Virginia City, but I think we could have managed that alright. However the amount of traffic on the highway and in the town was more than I cared to tangle with. I couldn't see a vacant level spot large enough in the city to set our camp up so we decided to forget about running the coach up there.

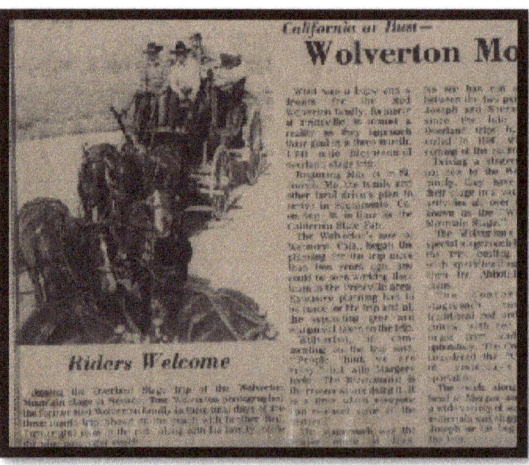

8/22 RENO LAYOVER 2ND DAY
Late breakfast. Red hitched up the coach and drove in the arena at 12:30. Almost was late as we couldn't hear the loud speaker. I had Cody and Lisa in the coach with me. Holly and Wendy rode ahorseback. Came back and unhitched, and were getting ready to go eat when Paul and Dulcie Brattain came out. Talked to them. They said Helen Bradbury had died on the 10th.

Got in the pickup and drove to Virginia City. Decided it was too much a tourist town. The stage road was steep and full of traffic. Went on out to Carson City and had supper at a Taco Bell. I got sick from sitting cramped in the pickup, but finally got over it OK. Made arrangements for our next night's stop. Ate supper, took care of the horses, and went to bed. Joe and Pearl never came around all weekend.

DAY NINETY-ONE
AUGUST 23rd

I rode shotgun out of Reno, with Joe driving the coach. Wallace went on further than what I'd planned for our noon camp so it was past noon when we got in. After lunch, we visited with a Carson area rancher and a state brand inspector who both happened by. Being horsemen, they had to stop and look us over.

I had contacted the officials at Carson City several times, and each time things were changed a little, so I wasn't sure of anything when we entered town. I had told them we would arrive there at 4 PM. When we started out that afternoon I thought we had quite a ways further to go than what we actually did have; so suddenly we arrived at Carson an hour too soon. If I would have stopped at the first wide place we came to and waited, it would have worked out just right, but I didn't. I drove by it, and then never found another place large enough to park in town.

After pulling over and tying up in this large lot by a store and office building, we discovered the state Bicentennial office was there. They came out and talked awhile; then informed me the local chairman had a delegation of city officials who planned on meeting us at the north edge of town at exactly 4PM. They climbed on and drove back out to where we were supposed to be to meet the group. I don't remember if we were five minutes early or five minutes late, but I do recall getting quite a lecture from one lady for not being exactly on the dot at the exact route I was supposed to be. It seems she had driven half way to Reno looking for us. She hadn't noticed us parked by the highway when she drove past on her way out to meet us. Nobody else seemed to be very worked up about it, so I smiled and promised to be more punctual when we reran the route again on the TriCentennial celebration. **You do know we are planning on rerunning this Overland Stage trip every 100 years ?**

8/23 RENO to CARSON CITY

Herins showed up early with their pickup. Joe drove the stage out and Red rode with him. Wendy outrode. Pearl used her pickup for a pilot car. I stayed behind and helped Holly get the camper ready to go. Wallace had to get a permit so we drove out to Boomtown "Stage Stop" and fueled up. Holly backed out of the gas pumps and got turned wrong. While we were getting horses out and fixing lunch, Mr. Foote and his family stopped to visit. They owned the ranch next to Fuji Park, where we would be staying, and also the Ponderosa. He was real interested in the hitch. He said his dad had had polio two years earlier, and their harness was hung up in the barn as it had come in from the fields. He stayed until Joe and Red came in with the stage.

DAY NINETY TWO
AUGUST 24th

CHAPTER FOURTEEN
THE WESTERN SLOPES

DAY NINETY-TWO
AUGUST 24th

The history books tell about the stages "pulling the hill". The hill was between Carson City and Placerville, and was actually two hills. This was the run made famous by Hank Monk.

Hank Monk was to the stage-coaching fashions what Babe Ruth was to the ballplayers, or what Jack Dempsey was to Manassa, Colorado and the prizefighting ring.

Hank's average time for coming off that grade was 45 minutes or 13.33 MPH. That's about the same speed we followed the sheriff into Lovelock, only we were on flat ground and had a straight road.

Joe drove that morning out of Carson valley, going up Spooner. We never made it in 45 minutes either. It's a little different going up than coming down. We stayed on the new highway, but could have traveled the old route. I wish now we would have taken it. We might have met old Hank coming down the grade. I rode on the coach quite a ways up the hill that morning.

Hank became quite popular throughout the West when he hauled Horace Greeley over the hump about 1859 in record breaking time to make an appointment. When Hank pulled out, you had better be setting down and hanging on tight, for he most always "went from a standstill to a dead run in six jumps". Hank drove with his fingers mostly, with his hands resting lightly on the insides of his knees. He was such an expert at creeping running, and slipping the lines between his fingers that he could circle a six horse hitch at a full gallop in a U-turn in a street without any apparent movement of his arms.

8/24 – CARSON CITY to S. LAKE TAHOE, CA. (STATELINE STABLES)
It was bright and sunny. Our camper was parked by a creek with grass and trees, and it was pretty. Red said afterwards the water wasn't too good, and we might get the scours.

Joe drove with Red on top. Wendy rode, I drove the Dodge, and we left the camper. Joe had started out at his usual trot. And Red told him to walk up the hill. It was steep and long.

Heavy traffic, and hot and slow. Dodge heated quite a bit. About half way up, Red didn't like my driving so he drove. It was very tiresome in spite of the country being so pretty with pines and rocky cliffs. Took us about four hours to get to the top. Had sandwiches for lunch.

It was said, "he was such a skilled driver that very few people could believe what they saw". They thought he drove with some kind of magic or was just plain lucky. Most of Hank's driving was on the western division, with much of it back and forth over the hump, as Spooner and Echo Summit, were called. It was a 10 mile run from the top of Spooner into Carson valley on the east side in the old days.

The back seat on top of the coach was an excellent place to sit and watch the endless miles of Nevada recede into the distance. I have lots of fond memories of Nevada, both from this summer and of years ago.

I hated to see Nevada pull away into the distance. When we rounded a corner that cut off my view of the distant peaks and deserts, I climbed back to the shotgun seat.

(8/24 p. 2) While we were stopped a vet came by. Red got shots for Heidi and Mistie. Then had him clean Sunny's leg. He tranquilized her, and she fell down kicking, and broke his tail light. Lay there and shook. For a while he thought he was going to lose her. He wrapped her leg, and she finally got OK. Changed horses and I rode with Red. Kip was on Muskrat. Holly drove the Dodge. It was beautiful coming down Spooner Summit. Tall pines and Lake Tahoe showing blue over the horses' ears. We went down at a pretty good clip. Had the coach sliding. When we came to the tunnel, Red loped them out with Kip ahead and they went right through. Traffic was very heavy. A patrolman pulled us over. Said we were running the horses too fast. Convinced him the horses weren't hurting, and we went trotting away.

It was time to look ahead; to think and plan what we might bring to California with our page of yesterday's history.

After all, we only had a few more days left. Instead of nearing a mental state of satisfaction that we were nearing the end of our goal, we became more remorseful each day.

> *I had the feeling like I was closing the door to a chapter of life that had been very dear to me.*

It was like a person who knows he must soon leave a place or a very dear old friend that he hates to think of leaving. The end was getting close, and we hated to see it get here. Perhaps if we could have realized that this was a presentiment of coming disaster or tragedy instead of feeling that it was due to the nearing end of the trip, things might have been better.

As it was, all we could do was to be more careful, more on guard and take no chances, but we were too close to the finish to let up now.

It took us over three hours to reach the summit. We'd traveled in a slow walk and had rested several times. We were in no hurry anyhow, as nobody would believe we could pull from Carson valley to Stateline in any less than a long hard day.

(8/24 p. 3)
In South Tahoe we were running in the center lane of traffic and bumper to bumper all around. Pedestrians thick as fleas walking across streets. Casinos all full of slot machines, and slots all full of crowds waiting in line to throw their money away.

Started to turn left one block early so a fellow in a pickup let us go ahead and ran interference in the other lane, with Holly behind us until we got to our turn. Had the lane empty ahead of us. At the turn, it was a sharp left with 2 lanes of traffic on a narrow street, and the 4th lane with construction up. Just barely had room to get through, and had the leaders' noses in the sign posts. Then had to dodge around traffic and up around a shopping center; and across a street where a car ran a STOP sign and just missed us.

I had even changed our schedule, taking advantage of the day that we didn't use going to Virginia City. We put it in here and stayed overnight at State Line Stables in South Lake Tahoe. We made our noon camp that day right on the summit of Spooner. That seemed like a fitting place to change horses, change drivers, and change paces.

While we were there, the Carson valley veterinarian happened to drive by and decided to stop and see if we needed his help in any way. The only problem we had was Sunny Ann's leg. We had been doctoring it regularly; and it had been healing and draining pretty good, so we didn't call a veterinary for her when we were in Reno. This fellow wanted to do something for us so bad, that I finally had him look at her leg. He thought it should be scraped and cleaned and bandaged; so we proceeded to go to work on her. It is surprising how touchy such a gentle-natured animal can be sometimes.

It became apparent quickly that we were going to have to tranquilize Sunny to work on her. She is such a good mother, that mostly due to her concern over her colt, she was able to fight the effects of the first shot the vet gave her and whip it; so the vet gave her some more. This was almost too much and caused her to go into a fighting spasm, and kick out a tail light on his pickup. She fell over then, kicking and twitching, and finally passed clear out. We were all quite worried for a while, even the vet. I think even then, the only reason she finally settled down was that someone thought to bring the colt and stand it right by her head. She had blinked her eyes at it a couple times before passing into a peaceful sleep. She was easy enough to doctor then, but had to be walked around quite awhile after she woke up before we could load her once more in the horse van and move on.

I put a fast hitch on the coach, with big, long-legged Buddy in the lead with Rebel. I took the lines that afternoon, and we headed down the west side of Spooner, on towards California. I had made some contact with the South Lake Tahoe newspaper. They said they would like to get our story and some pictures; so would send their reporter to meet us outside of town around 4:30. I could see by the clock when we started off Spooner that if I didn't drive about half slow that we would be way too early for that appointment. We had driven at a trot and gallop all summer; so the jog trot I was holding down the grade seemed pretty slow to me. We still went down at a pretty fast clip though, as the grade was steep enough that when I'd apply the brake, the coach would skid sideways on the blacktop.

It was beautiful country. The sight of Lake Tahoe shining through the pines was as spectacular as we'd always heard. We appreciated every time the road curved around to give us a different view of it. Marge got one snapshot of me outlined against the sunset over the lake.

When we came to the tunnel, I sent Kip out in front of us. He was riding old Muskrat, who would go almost anywhere. Almost all our horses were used to following a saddle horse through bad places, when it was needed. Kip led right out, and I kicked those horses into a lope, as we curved down and around, heading for the tunnel. We went right through it like tumbleweeds rolling in the wind. Those horses didn't hardly have time to think about the dark shadows on all sides before we were coming out the other end into the sunlight again. I pulled them up some and we slowed down to a trot again.

Down and around, and up again and down some more. It was quite a few miles from the top down, but hardly any pull on the horses; so they hardly even had the edge worn off when we got to the edge of town. You can understand my surprise, when a sheriff's car stopped and the officer motioned me over to the side of the road. He jumped right in the middle of me for driving my horses so fast and hard. It took me a minute or two to

figure what he was getting at. I said, "We've just been trotting, mostly." He cut in, "Well, I've passed you several times coming down off Spooner, and you're running them pretty fast. It's too hard on horses." I answered, "These horses have been going like this steady for three whole months." The officer looked them over and said, "Maybe so, but this country is steep and it's a high altitude here." I replied, "Our horses are accustomed to being at a high

elevation. These guys were trained in high country." I was biting my tongue by this time, and Marge was snickering beside me. Kip, sitting on Muskrat by the hitch, was grinning like a possum, and Wendy behind us, sat there with her eyes just dancing. The horses weren't even blowing; they were kind of stamping their feet impatiently, saying, "What's the matter back there, let's get going." About this time, the officer informed me we were at an elevation of over 5,000 feet. I said the ranch where our horses have lived and were trained for several years was over 6,000 feet. Here again we were presumed to be from Missouri.

That deputy reared back and said, "Not in St. Joe they weren't at 5,000 feet. There aren't any mountains back there." I couldn't keep from grinning as I said, "We may have started this trip from St. Joe, but that's not where we're from. We live in Colorado, and these horses have to climb a mile and a half up and down the mountain every time we go in or out of the ranch. At this, he just threw his

hands up in the air and went muttering back to his car. It sure must have looked comical to any passerby as we went trotting down the highway. Marge busted out laughing, and me with a dumbfounded look on my face at the thought of that cop stopping us for **"speeding"**!

Driving through Stateline and South Tahoe in the summer is about like threading your way through a Midway in a large carnival.

The traffic was bumper to bumper on all sides, and the pedestrians were "bumper to bumper" on the sidewalks and overflowing into the street. I almost turned one block too soon, which would have really complicated things, as it led right in under a hotel veranda which was not nearly high enough to let the coach pass under.

> *I realized the mistake just barely in time, and was able to maneuver the leaders back into the street, with the help of some understanding motorists.*

We had to wait at a red light at the next block where we needed to make a left turn. Just before we were ready to start, the off lead horse swung his head around and rubbed it against the near leader. We were already moving through the intersection when I discovered he had hooked his bridle on the near leader's harness and couldn't get loose. The lead team were beginning to have a little quarrel by this time, but I was able to keep them under control, and continue on until we cleared the traffic. At the same time, we had to thread our way between an open manhole, some construction signs, and a couple of sawhorses, while trying to swing wide to make the sharp corner with the coach, and still keep out of the way of the oncoming traffic. As soon as we were out of the hole, I stopped and got Kip to come over and untangle the leaders. We spent that night at the State Line Stables and drove on down to Meyers the next day just before noon.

(8/24 p. 4)

Drove up to the State Line Stables and unhitched. Red took the Dodge and went back to Carson for the camper.

Wallace had the horses turned out. Holly said Herins came by and told her they were invited to stay at a motel with a pool and have supper and breakfast all free. Afterwards we found out their friends were the motel owners.

"State Line" had tall pines and cold clean air. Had Fortune in a stall next to a Llama.

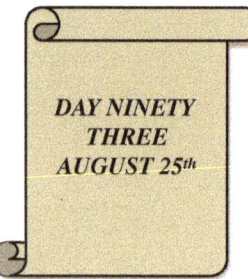

DAY NINETY –THREE
AUGUST 25th

DAY NINETY THREE AUGUST 25th

8/25 - SOUTH LAKE TAHOE to MEYERS

Had breakfast and Red went to call Police. City cop came out and advised he'd get ahold of State Patrol. Reporter from came out. We hitched up late as it was a short trip to Meyers. I helped catch the horses down in the pines. They broke twice and ran around the pasture. Red drove the stage out with Joe and the reporter, and their friends riding. We took the old road and it was a beautiful morning, curving road with pines and little houses. Kip was riding and almost got blocked by a lake and mountain meadow. Horses out in pasture ran along with us. Got to Meyers early, and Red took several rides. Bruce Weisman had arranged a supper party by the Saddle Club. It was almost dark when we ate. It turned cold and the wind was chilly.

The reporter showed up that morning while we were messing around camp, and got his story. They had already run one on us the week before about our approach; so we had quite a few visitors while there. We had a full load that morning going to Meyers, one of whom was Bruce, who we got quite well acquainted with. He rode on top of the coach with us. We traveled most of the ways over the same ground as where the original trail had been over 100 years ago. Bruce showed us a couple places where it had run a short way in a different location.

Again, we spent a couple hours in the afternoon hauling local people around town. The day was finished off with a good ranch cooked supper served at the back door of the local entertainment center. We were asked to park the coach where everybody could inspect it, so we moved it close by for the evening, then moved it back to camp for the night. There was a dance going on and the kids wanted to go so I took them up to it for awhile.

When I returned to our camper, there were three full grown young men standing up on the driver's box of the stagecoach, swaying up and down. They really had it bucking, almost enough to pick the front wheels off the ground.

When I walked up there and saw that, I asked, in words loud enough to cause all action to cease immediately, "Just what do you fellows think you're doing?" In a very meek, soft voice, this big, hairy faced fellow answered me, "I think we're just fixing to get down off here and get lost." Which they immediately proceeded to do. I wondered afterwards if perhaps they had climbed up there to get the strongbox. Upon finding it chained to the top railing they had decided to just go for a stagecoach ride instead. Quien sabe?

DAY NINETY-FOUR
AUGUST 26th

The next morning, Bruce and his wife invited all of us over to their house for a most delicious breakfast of sourdough pancakes, with all the trimmings. What a treat! I can still taste them.

We kind of hated to quit feasting and get back to work, but we did. Just before leaving Meyers, Bruce and the other officials presented us with a large Bicentennial flag and an AREA satin banner. We placed that flag on the back corner of the stagecoach and have flown it proudly ever since. Everyone there was so friendly, it was hard to go on.

> **We never considered it, but that sure seemed like it would have been a good place to have ended the trip.**

The California State Police escorted us all the way from the State Line to Sacramento, with two police cars, one in front and one behind. We sure needed and appreciated them as the road is narrow, steep, and winding most of the way, and the traffic was heavy. We consider them a great bunch of guys, and well deserving of all the credit we can give them. Without their skilled help, I'm sure we would have gotten clobbered.

Joe drove up Echo that morning. It was the last part of the "hump" between Carson and Placerville. It is a two lane, two-way traffic highway. I rode shotgun that morning, which is sometimes very rewarding if you like to observe the surrounding country. It's very scenic and quite a thrill pulling up Echo. We climbed steeply with the horses working hard and all traces were tight. Whenever possible, we pulled off to the side with our police escorts, and let traffic pass.

8/26 – MEYERS to KYBURZ (over ECHO SUMMIT) Weismans had us over for breakfast. Lots of bacon, sourdough hotcakes. After breakfast we hitched up and the Bicentennial Committee presented us with the 76 Bicentennial Flag, and took pictures. Joe drove the coach. Red on top.

At some time during the morning, Red chewed Joe out for sloppy driving, and Joe got mad. I rode inside with Rhoda Sherman, the cop's daughter. He was our lead car (John Sherman), and McFarland was in behind; so didn't have to use our own. They had both escorted the Highway 50 Wagon Train to Placerville several years and were experienced. Wendy rode. We left Meyers and started over Echo. It was a 2 lane, 2 way road that climbed steeply with sharp curves.

Pretty soon, the road rises right up on the mountain side high enough to look out across the tops of the pine trees down below. We could see Lake Tahoe far out in the distance and a long way down. About a mile or two from the summit, the main highway circles around the mountain to the south, while the old road pulls off to the right, climbing a steep uphill grade with two 70° turns and one 90° turn just as it topped out, which was only about ¼ mile from where it left the main highway,

Our police escort pulled off to the side again and asked me which way I wanted to go. When I said I'd never been over either one, he said, "Get in, then, and we'll go look them over". The short cut was the three switchbacks listed above; the main road is almost as breathtaking the way it's carved out of the face of a cliff for quite a ways, just two good lanes wide with no shoulders. The traffic was becoming quite heavy which didn't seem to bother our patrolmen escort any. It really didn't bother me much either, although I prefer more open country. But I really liked the looks of that old road. After all, the old time coaches pulled it before it was even paved. This was good and bad. The dirt roads gave the horses better footing, but made the coaches pull harder when it was soft. The black top on the old road was the only thing that bothered me. It was that black, shiny kind and sure looked like it wouldn't hold a horse's iron shod hoof very good. Well, we took the old road.

The hairpin curves were really steep and sharp, with no extra turning room. The leaders had to be swung clear to the far side, and then brought sharply back just as the swings were crowding close on their heels. I sure thought Joe hadn't led the outside of the first enough when we got into it. I had been back-seat driving in my head for quite a ways, mentally trying to get him further over to the left side of the road coming into it, but just couldn't get him over quite as far as I wanted. We made the turn, but with the front inside wheel kissing the side of the coach all the way. When we were on the straight away again, Joe shook his head and let his breath out in a rush.

(8/26 p. 2)

Weather was beautiful, and so was the country. Tall pines and rocky cliffs. Traffic very heavy. Whenever we could, we pulled aside to let it pass. At times, we could look down and see the road below, or look up and see it above us. We went up at a walk, and it was slow. The horses really had to work. As we climbed higher, it got colder and a breeze came up. We could see the lake down below.
Left the highway, and followed the old road to the top. It was 3 switchbacks that just barely allowed room for the hitch to turn, and it took the whole road. It was quite a thrill to hang on the edge of the road, and look down 50 feet to the curve below, and 100 to 150 feet to the next one below that. Finally got to the summit. We stopped at the Alpine Club. They brought out chocolate milk, coffee, and homemade zucchini bread.

"Those curves are pretty tight, aren't they?" He said. I just grinned at him, thinking, "That they are, Joe, that they are!" Joe got over the extra foot needed on the next curve, and we made it much easier.

Marge was riding on the inside of the coach. She said it was quite a thrill hanging on the edge of the road, as the horses swung around, and looking back and down. It was fifty feet to the curve below which we had just come around, and then 100-150 feet to the next level down below the middle one. With thirty-six feet of horses out in front, on a road not over half that wide, it didn't leave much room for the coach to turn in, so it hugged the outside edge.

When we pulled on over the top, we stopped to get our breath and look the country over before going off the west side. The heat of summer in the valley below gave way to clouds and a cold wind up here. There was a Swiss Chalet private clubhouse at the top of the mountain. When we pulled up and stopped, they demonstrated true Swiss hospitality and brought out coffee and cakes for all of us, while we rested the horses. It really went over good in that pure cold, fresh mountain air.

I let Joe drive on down the west side and on into Strawberry Lodge.

(8/26 p. 3)

Started down over the hill and trotted. It wasn't quite as steep as coming up. Trees were beautiful. Some of the largest pines I've ever seen. They looked 4 or 5 feet in diameter, and 100 feet tall. We stopped at Strawberry for lunch. A beautiful old lodge with stone steps. Red and Joe took turns holding horses and eating. High priced. Wendy was pouting about where to sit, so I ordered hamburgers to go for her and Red. On the way out, Lisa stumbled and fell down the steps. Cut her forehead and bruised it; bloodied her nose. Set up camp at Kyburz. We were surprised by the Apple Hill Gang. They were all in costume and ready to party. They insisted we go back up to Strawberry. To our amazement, they staged a shootout at the bar, complete with fights and dead bodies. It was quite an evening. We finally got everyone rounded up and went back to camp.

This also was an original old stage station, the first relay station coming down the west side of Echo. When we drove up to Strawberry, it was to see a large illuminated sign hanging out in front of the lodge, reading, "Welcome Stagecoach 76". It sure made us

feel welcome. We had a late lunch there inside the lodge. It's a large old log building with big fireplaces and wide stone steps. Our two-year old granddaughter, little Lisa, tumbled down these, resulting in a real goose-egg on her forehead and a scraped and bleeding nose. After packing it with cold wet cloths, we were soon ready to go again. We didn't change horses that afternoon; just trotted on down to the Forest Service camp at Kyburz and set up camp. It was a tingling feeling to know we had crossed the "hump" as the old timers called it, and were on the west side, coming down the home stretch.

That evening, just after dark, we were invaded by the "Apple Hill Gang, a group of gunmen from Hangtown (Placerville). They were all in complete costume, Indians to Sheriffs, to madams. They are one of those groups that have a lot of fun and really enjoy

putting on their melodrama shootouts. That night, nothing would do, but we had to go back up to Strawberry with them for some entertainment. One of their specialties is to infiltrate a crowded bar; then get into an argument which rapidly develops into a shootout. This is what they did that night at Strawberry, to the owner's astonishment and our incredulous delight. We had a good time that

evening and went back to camp fairly early, telling the Gang we'd see them the next afternoon in Hangtown.

DAY NINETY-FIVE
AUGUST 27th

Many things happened the next day. It was the next to the last day scheduled for our trip. It was the day we rolled into Hangtown.

> Maybe we shouldn't have stopped there overnight.

We certainly had a hard time getting in there and getting set up, and then even a worse time after we got there.

```
On the other hand, maybe the Hand of Fate
that awaited us would have dealt with us
regardless of where we stopped. Who knows?
```

8/27 – KYBURZ to PLACERVILLE

Pollock Pines. Stopped here awhile. Somehow, Wendy's little dog, Flint, got loose. He wasn't comfortable with strangers, so when a lot of people came around, he would hide out somewhere. When we left here, he was nowhere to be found. We called and called but he never showed up; so we finally had to leave. We went on down through Pacific House and into Placerville.

The whole day was an odd one, all muddled up, much activity, both good and bad.

The road down out of Kyburz is a winding narrow canyon road with no shoulders most of the way. There are a few steep down pitches, but for the most part it is a pretty gentle slope. There is lots of traffic that time of year so I wanted to get there as quickly as possible. The highway patrol was ten miles behind us down to where we came to the divided freeway highway so as to lessen the chance of some impatient motorist causing serious trouble. I took the lines on Joe's hitch that morning, and when we started down the canyon it was in a gallop.

It was a good run, but made in spurts from one turn-out to another. Each time, we'd come to a wide place, I'd pull over and hold up until the cars that had built up behind us could move on by. One time when we were coming around a curve that was hacked out of a rock bluff, I heard an awful screeching sound behind us, like rubber tires sliding on blacktop highway. When we got to the next turnout, our rear escort patrolman got out of his car, still a little nervous. He wanted to know if we'd heard the "screeching back up the canyon". We asked him what happened. "Well I heard this noise and looked in my rear view mirror," said the patrolman. "Here he came, sideways, heading right for the rear end of my patrol car."

Pacific House had also been one of the original stage relay stations, and again we enjoyed the historical significance of the place with its peace and beauty and age-old memories.

"Then at the last instant before he crashed into me, he must have released his brake and shot out into the other lane and slid on around us. It's a good thing nobody was coming." We could all agree on that.

We galloped around another curve and were dropping right on down a pretty good grade, when an empty logging truck coming towards us started to duck between our lead patrol car and our horses. He was signaling for his turn and was looking right towards us. I never considered under the circumstances that he would do anything other than stop or slow up just a trifle until we

got by, before he turned. Suddenly, after our lead car rolled past him, he started to cut between us. I couldn't see any way in that instant I could keep from piling into him with some part of my outfit. Luckily for all of us, as quickly as he

had started to duck between us, just as sudden, he jumped on his brake and was still locked up in a bounding skid as we shot across in front of him. Boy, I sure swallowed a couple times then before my breathing smoothed out again.

It wasn't much farther until we rolled on to the four lane highway, and our escort pulled up for a powwow as one of them had to go back up the country to tend to something. We went a short ways with just one pilot car. At this stop, I gave the lines to Joe for awhile. It would be his last turn to drive on the trip. We pulled in at Pacific House and rested for a little while. The proprietor had coffee and pop "on the house" for us.

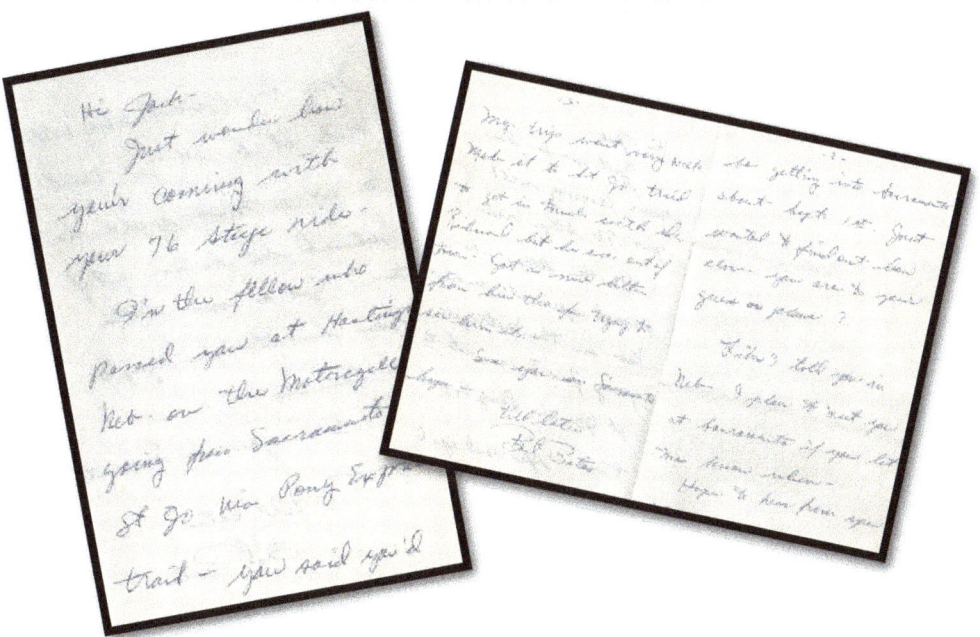

    While we were stopped there a fellow came in whom we had met a long while earlier on the trip. He was the one who had been riding a motorcycle across country from west to east, following the Pony Express Trail. We had met him just west of Hastings, Nebraska and enjoyed seeing and visiting with him again.

Wallace had been waiting for us at Pacific House and had some bad news for us. Flint, our youngest watch dog, had jerked away from Wallace when he'd started to load him in the horse van with the others. He ran off, and though they stayed there a long time trying to call him back, it was to no avail. Margie figured he'd come back to her and Wendy; so they took the pickup and went back to try to find him, while we stopped for lunch at Pollock Pines. They finally returned without him. He was nowhere to be found. After lunch we had to go on without him.

The people at Pollock Pines were a real friendly bunch and couldn't do enough for us. One dry goods store gave us a whole pile of bandanna handkerchiefs, and a grocery store handed us a large box of ripe fruit. We hauled a sizable load of Pollock Pines people down the road with us for quite a spell. Our state police picked out the route and led us down a backwoods road much of the way into Placerville that afternoon. It was great for stagecoaching, but it did cause a mix-up because it was a different route than what our waiting mounted escort had anticipated; and they missed us, or we missed them, I don't know which. It was only by coincidence, at the last moment almost, that we were stopping in Placerville anyhow, as we had sure gotten the run around before finally making any definite plans to stop there. Only two days before, I had told their Chamber of Commerce to forget the whole thing; we'd just camp by the road or at a ranch along the way.

(8/27 – p. 2)
PLACERVILLE

When we got there, they had their sprinkler system running full blast, and the grassy pasture was soaked good. I even got sprinkled on in my long dress and hat. Red took several rides around for people. Wendy had been outriding, but the local horse club people wanted to escort the coach around, and said, "Let the little girl get down, we can outride for her." There were from 5 to 10 of them, so it seemed OK, as we were just going around in the pasture.

I guess the trouble all started when we wrote to the wrong Chamber of Commerce in Placerville in February, when we were making arrangements for every town scheduled on the trip. You see, Placerville has two Chambers of Commerce; something I guess I had never heard of or thought about before.

Placerville has a regular Chamber of Commerce which apparently handles all the business dealings for the town, and the Hangtown Chamber of Commerce handles many of the festivities; or maybe it is one town within another, I'm not sure. Anyhow, the Placerville COC must have gotten our first letter. They were not too excited about our coming to their town; so if we wanted to use their fairgrounds it would cost us $5.00 per horse per night, plus a camping fee to stay there. Since ours was a non-profit, non-sponsored Bicentennial project, we couldn't afford to pay for services like that, especially if it didn't actually cost anybody any money if we used their fairgrounds. At $5.00 per horse for 20 horses, for the 100 days scheduled for the trip, it sure figures close to $10,000.00 to me.

After writing to them again and calling them after we got into California and talking to them, I still got the same kind of answer. That's when I told them to skip it; we'd just forget about Placerville. Nobody told me about the Hangtown Chamber until the day before, when I got a message to call a number and they said they had it all set up, to come on to town. They were expecting us and had plans for a ceremony to come off downtown when we arrived; so I said OK. Meanwhile, 'back at the edge of town', our mounted escort finally located us and proceeded to lead us down town at a very slow snail's pace walk. We finally arrived in a most congested area, a narrow street with heavy traffic and lots of pedestrians. It created no problems we couldn't cope with, but when they asked me to get off the coach and come up to the announcer's stand, one did arise. We had a set of stagecoaching rules which I laid out. One was that the driver would never get off the driver's box while the horses were hooked to the coach when it was in a place like that unless enough others of our crew were present to hold the lines while other crew members stood at the horses' heads.

Wallace and Holly were supposed to be down here for the ceremony. They had left Pollock Pines in plenty of time to have set up camp and driven on down town.

(8/27 - p. 3)
PLACERVILLE
Finally it seemed like everyone had ridden, some even got on a second time on the last ride around. We unloaded. I got out. Joe stood in front of the hitch, and was soon surrounded by people asking questions, and wanting to know all about our trip. He was standing there holding onto the bridle of the off lead horse. The kids were getting ready to unhitch, when this woman came up and said she hadn't gotten to ride. I said we were through for the night, but she got in my face, and got loud and offensive. Insisted she had a right to ride. Finally, Red said he'd take one more ride, so I had to show her how to get in. She was big boned with a few extra pounds, and not agile. Two or three other people got on top. I don't remember anyone else being inside.

Later, we learned they had been directed away from the fairgrounds by someone who sent them up the wrong road. It was one that was too narrow for the horse van, and it took them almost an hour to get it turned around and back out of the bad place. When they finally did get to the fairgrounds, the caretakers there had tried to run them off, before they gave in with a squabble. All of this caused them to arrive at the fairgrounds after we did. I looked around the crowd downtown again. Not finding Wallace,
I finally agreed to get down if Mac, one of the Apple Hill Gang, would hold the lines, and a couple others would stand by the horses. They had quite an elaborate ceremony, and presented Marge and me with several mementoes and small presents. Afterwards, I climbed back on the coach, threaded my way through a very tight zigzag opening, and headed for the fairgrounds.

After figuring where they wanted us, I finally got the coach pulled up there, on the beautiful lawn-covered parade grounds. There was some discussion whether or not they wanted us on there, as the grass was thick and green and spongy, and they had the sprinklers going on it all day; but the supper was to be there and all the crowd was waiting for their stagecoach rides around the grounds. As there were quite a few people who wanted to get in, Marge got out, and went over to talk with some of the ladies. I hauled one load of people around in a circle for a ride; then came back, unloaded and took on the second load. Joe was standing at the lead horses' heads, a spot we always had someone in when loading or unloading.

We were all loaded. I looked to my lines and checked them all out. I was ready to pull out when a lady came up to my front wheel and handed up a note pad asking for my autograph. It was hard to refuse; so I crossed the three right hand lines over to my left hand, which forms an X with the lines in your hand, a maneuver which keeps thelines frombeingmixedup. After signing the pad, I handed it back to her, refilled my right fist with its lines. I checked both lead lines to make sure they were still free. I glanced to my right side to make sure there was noone in the way, and asked the passenger sitting on the left side to check the left side at the same time.

Quickly he said we're all clear, and I nodded to Joe which meant, if it all looked good to him from where he was standing, that I was ready to go. He turned loose of the lead horses and stepped back out of the way; so I called my leaders, "Romeo, Rebel, Get up", and we started out.

Marge had gotten a cup of coffee, and was walking back toward the coach with some of the ladies when she noticed Wendy, who was outriding that afternoon, was off her horse. She commented that she'd better hurry over and get Wendy back on again, as the coach was about ready to pull out. One of the ladies said to her, there was no need of that. There were plenty of horseback riders around, and there was no need for the little girl to ride when there were several grown men who could take her place. By this time, they were over to Wendy, and when the grownups nearby offered to take her place, she remained on the ground. We had to curve a little to the left before straightening out to cross the parade ground.

> We made the curve fine, but when I pulled my off lead line to straighten them up, it was hung---as solid as if it were buckled to the lead horses' hames.

A stagecoach as large as ours will not turn as sharp as 25°. If you turn sharper than that, the front wheel will rub against the side of the coach body. If you continue to turn sharper than that, that side of the body is picked up by the front wheel. If you don't get straightened out in a hurry, you're in trouble---bad trouble, real quick.

When I felt the lead line hung up, I immediately jabbed the brake lever down as far as I could, and hauled in hard on all the lines, trying to stop the hitch. At the same time, I reached across with my left hand and grabbed the right lead line and yanked on it, but it wouldn't come completely free. Twice I almost got the hitch straightened out, but I couldn't get the lead team freed up enough to get them back in front of me. Each time I tried to pull all the horses up to stop, it would only pull the lead team in a tighter circle. Finally the swing team ducked over to the left after the leaders, and that pulled the tongue around farther than was permissible. The ground was so soft, the extra weight on the right hand wheels caused them to sink into the ground six or more inches. The combination of everything was too much.

(8/27 - p. 4)
PLACERVILLE

Red started off, and something was very wrong. His off lead line was hung up, and he had no way to straighten out the hitch. It immediately caused them to swing hard to the left, which the coach was not designed for. With the wet grass, and the ruts the wheels had already made in the ground, the coach couldn't turn sharp enough, and it fell over on its side.

It pulled the coach past its center of balance, and over we went!

Marge was watching as we started out making that first curve. She knew approximately how I was going to go, and saw the hitch start to straighten out. Then she saw the horses swing left again, and thought, "What is he going to do now?" Then the hitch started to straighten back out again, and then started circling hard left again. By then, she knew something was wrong, and she started running for the horses, to try to catch Romeo or Rebel. As the coach had turned away from her at the start she was close to 100 feet away. She ran as fast as a long dress and high-heeled shoes would permit. She noticed that everyone in the crowd was just standing, watching the coach. It was almost as if they were under a hypnotic spell. The horses were not running up to that time. They were still in a walk. If I could have held them a few more steps, I'm sure I would have gotten them stopped. All this happened in less time than it takes to tell about it; probably less than five seconds.

When the coach went over, the front axle dropped free from the rest of the chassie. I had whirled and stepped over on the ground just at the last minute, and landed on my feet with the lines still in my hands. Although the horses were stopped just for an instant, the commotion of the coach going over and the noise it created with the front axle dropping back to the ground, spooked them, and it didn't take them long to light out again. Marge said she missed the horses by ten feet. Rebel went by her, stepping high. She said Joe was in front of her and made a grab at Rebel's bridle, but he missed it, either from the horses still circling left away from him, or from Rebel shaking his head away from an out stretched arm.

Marge said when I went by them, I was scooting along on my rear end, with both feet braced out in front of me, trying to dig my heels into the ground, and with the lines tight in both fists. By this time, the leaders were doubled right back into the swing team.

(8/27 – p. 5)
PLACERVILLE

Red and the others who were on top just stepped off. The pin holding the horses to the coach came out, turning the horses loose from it. When I turned away from the people around me, I see Red being pulled by the hitch, scooting along on his rear with his legs out in front of him, but he still had all the lines in his hands, holding onto the horses. Of course, pandemonium reined! People were running everywhere. Somebody opened the door of the coach. The woman was just lying there. Guess she was in shock.

Some of the men ran out in front of them, and we got them stopped almost in the exact same spot they had been standing in, six or eight seconds earlier, hooked to the coach.

While we were untangling and unhitching the horses, some of the other men had immediately run over and set the coach back up on its wheels, rear wheels that is. There had been only four or five people inside the coach on that ride. When they got them out, two women and one young girl were shook up pretty bad. They were laid out on the ground, waiting for the ambulance that had been called. Marge had been helping untangle the horses and holding lines until the men got them fairly straightened out, and took the extra lines. She then went over to see about the women who were hurt; to see if there was anything she could do to help. She would have given almost anything right then if she could have been the one hurt instead of the passengers. She said one of the spectators came over and told her not to worry, everything was being taken care of that could be done. It could have been much worse; and that the horses didn't seem to be hurt at all. She said she replied that, "The one thing we didn't ever want to happen was to hurt anybody." She said all she could think of was, "Oh God, please don't let them be hurt" and "How did it happen, what went wrong?" Everybody that was on top of the coach just stepped off as it went over.

(8/27 - p. 6)
PLACERVILLE

They helped her out, and I think laid her on the ground. Someone called the ambulance. None of the other people seemed to be hurt, but the medics insisted they should all go to the hospital to be checked out. Several of the younger guys swooped in and stopped the horses. Red got up, and all of our crew who were there, unhitched, and helped put them up. Red and the others put the coach back up on its wheels. It didn't seem to be damaged at all.

The people that were watching said that the coach went over slowly, it was just like slow-motion on a film. It just leaned further and further, and noone really believed it could go, until it was clear on the ground.

After we got the women on the way to the hospital, several of us picked the front end of the coach up and rolled the front wheels back under it and in place. The damage to the coach looked pretty serious. Apparently the glue holding the back of the coach to the side had lost its bonding properties.

When it tipped over, that corner popped loose, and that put all the strain on the window and door uprights and popped them loose at their tops and bottoms. One door hinge was broken, and the king pin was bent in a curve. The swing pole got broke when the horses got fouled up after the front axle came loose. The jagged end of it apparently poked Romeo in the tussle, as he was lame the next day. He was the only horse injured in the wreck, and we weren't able to use him again for almost six months.

Things looked pretty black to all of us that night. Noone could hardly touch the big fancy supper they'd fixed, and almost everybody except the Apple Hill Gang went home early that night. We sat there and discussed it with them until late. Marge said she'd even asked George, one of the leaders of the Highway 50 Annual Wagon Train, if he'd seen anything wrong that had caused the wreck. He said, "No, he hadn't seen anything wrong." The only thing he could think of was that with the wagon train, sometimes they had extra horseback riders that got in the way of the teams, causing them to turn the wrong way or get messed up because they didn't get out of the way of the harness horses. He noticed there had been quite a few horseback riders milling around, but he really didn't know if that had anything to do with it or not. We discussed the best way to repair the coach the next morning so we could get on with our trip. We were told that all arrangements had been made to care for the injured women; in fact the one girl came back that evening, I believe. Since it had happened at the fairgrounds, the County was taking care of everything.

(8/27 – p. 7)
PLACERVILLE

Devastation! Go 1,800 plus miles and then have this happen 2 days before the end of the journey.

Right after this, Wallace and Holly arrived with the truck and camper. They had been given wrong directions by someone in town, so they weren't there when everything went wrong.

That also could have made the difference as both of them might have prevented the disaster.

Horses were watered, fed, and put up for the night.

We all hit the soogans as soon as possible.

Everyone felt we should continue the trip,
as we were just one day's journey from the end.
We finally went to camp, but it was
a bad night on the western slopes for us.

CHAPTER FIFTEEN
TRAGEDY – TO TRIUMPH:
THE END OF A JOURNEY

DAY NINETY-SIX
AUGUST 28th

Early the next morning, several members of the Gang met me at the coach, and we went to work. It wasn't long until we had everything glued back together and repaired. We had an early lunch, harnessed the horses, hitched up, loaded quite a bunch of passengers (including one young girl who had been inside when it tipped over the night before), and headed for Folsom. We also had several others climb back up with me, who had either been on top or had seen it go over. Holly, Wallace, and the kids all rode horseback, and Marge had the two grandkids inside with her. There was a downhill grade just a short ways out of town which they said was so steep that they had to tie a pickup to the rear of their big freight wagons when they went off it on their yearly treks. They were sure I would need some help, but when I looked down the grade, it didn't look near as steep to me as what Main Street in Salt Lake City had, coming back from the Capitol. They were surprised I was able to hold the coach back with its brake. *I had one of the best drives that afternoon that I'd had all summer.*

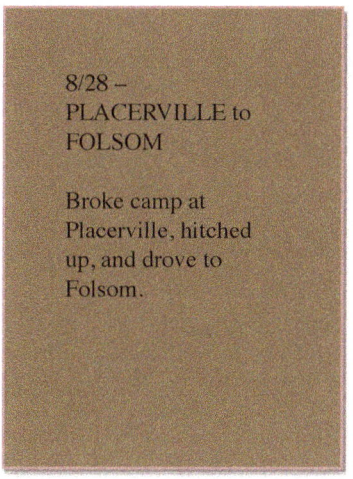

8/28 –
PLACERVILLE to FOLSOM

Broke camp at Placerville, hitched up, and drove to Folsom.

One good downhill slope after another, and our police escort was always willing to speed up a little if I crowded them any. I got the idea that maybe we might make it on to Sacramento after all. Quien Sabe?

When we got unhitched at Folsom without any problems, we had to go back to get the horse van. We decided that Marge, Kip, Wendy, and I would take Wallace back to the truck, and then we'd run back up to Kyburz to see if we could find our Flint dog. Somebody at Placerville told us that they had seen him after Marge and Wendy had left the campground that afternoon. We took Kila, Tammie's Australian Shepherd dog, along as bait, hoping she might bark and attract him. It was about dark when we got back up there, but Flint was nowhere around.

About that time, we realized we'd forgotten about supper. Since it was about the same distance down the canyon or up to a restaurant, we decided to go back up to Strawberry and have supper, and then check the campground again when we came back down. Jerry and his partner met us at the door and insisted that we be their guests. It's a real treat to eat out like that after a good many meals in our little camper. When we got back to the campground, we still couldn't find Flint. We had a pretty good bedroll in the shell on the back of the pickup so we turned Kila loose outside, and the four of us crowded into that one bed. It was cold enough up there that night that we could appreciate being cuddled up. Along in the middle of the night, I heard a lonesome wolf-dog howl, and Kila barked a couple times in answer. A short while later, I heard a noise outside the pickup. On peaking out, I could see we had two dogs. Flint had come back to camp. I was far too comfortable and tired to get up and welcome him back. He would stay now. **Good night Flint.**

DAY NINETY-SEVEN
AUGUST 29th

He was sure a happy dog the next morning when he saw his people. A stranger can't get close to him, and that's how he'd come to get lost to start with. He didn't know Wallace and Holly well enough, and wouldn't let them get close to him. He sure gets carried away though when he sees someone he knows. I put him in the back of the pickup with Marge and the kids and I drove on down to Folsom to be there in time to hitch up. That Flint crawled up on the bed between Marge and Wendy and howled and cried and 'talked' to them for half an hour, telling them all about being lost and alone, and how he'd hunted all over the country for them. He didn't settle down from his tale of woe until we were almost back to camp, and then he started in all over again when he met Kip's dog Shaggy and the other members of the crew.

We got back to Folsom that morning before the rest of them were through with breakfast, but there wasn't any big rush. We had 22 miles more to go to the California State Fair Grounds, and 7¾ more after that to complete the trip. We wanted to get it finished now, but we hated to see it end. If nothing else went wrong, it looked like we were going to make it.

I started to swing a gate around out of the way so we could hitch up, just as a car drove up in my way. I said to the fellow in it, "Would you mind moving your car so I can open this gate?" Whereupon he climbs out, slams the door, turns to me with an odd expression across his face, and says, "Move it yourself if you want it moved."

Then he looks at me, busts out laughing, jabs his hand out towards me and says, "Stan". It had been 30 years since I'd seen him. He was a little heavier now, and a little bald, but otherwise he was the same.

Well, he moved his car and helped us hook up. Then he climbed up on the coach beside me, and rode half way to Sacramento with us. He had seen on TV that we were

---

8/29 – FOLSOM to SACRAMENTO

Then on to the State Fairgrounds in Sacramento. All kinds of problems there. No communication between the police, the Bicentennial committee, county officials, or anyone else. After waiting in the heat (it was way over 100 degrees that day) and we waited over 3 hours for the Manager to show up, Red finally got permission to set up our truck and vehicles to make a corral for our horses.

We had planned on being there for the ceremony that day, but the Patrol said the traffic would be way too heavy Sunday and requested we wait until Monday. Everyone was hot, tired, and disgusted, so we bedded down early.

coming west and had been hunting me for 24 hours. Now, here he had tracked us down just two hours before he had a plane reservation to fly back south, but we had two hours of good visiting first. The last time I'd seen him was when we went to work on the ZX together. I saw him once in Fresno during the Korea shindig. We had thought a lot of each other when we were young, and had lots of experiences. Once, when we were about 15, we fought and wrestled each other out in a horse corral, from right after noon until after sundown. Neither one ever whipped the other. Finally we were both so tired and give out, we just lay there in the corral and laughed at each other, still friends. It was good to see him, and I wished he could stay longer,

Mac of the Apple Hill Gang drove Stan's car until he had to leave for the airport. That afternoon about 2 PM we drove up to the State Fair grounds, almost at the end of the trip. Then for a couple hours, it looked like we might not make it after all. I was about ready to turn around and head back for Folsom. The California State Fair was one of the first places we wrote to inquiring what other people thought about our proposed trip, and if they would want to include it in their plans for the 1976 Fair. Their sincere and spontaneous enthusiastic response to our plans was one of the determining factors that convinced us to go ahead with our trip.

In the two years before we arrived there, we had written them numerous times, answered all questions and sent all the information they had requested, advising them of the number of horses we had, and the type of set up, vehicles, etc. In the month previous to our arrival, I had called them four or five times to let them know exactly when we'd be there. When we arrived, the only outfit that knew we were coming was the TV Station who picked us up coming through town. They met us at the gate and filmed our 'grand' entry - noone to meet us, nobody to direct us where to go, and a guard that wouldn't let us go on in because nobody knew we were coming. We sat outside the gate for over half an hour.

Finally we were told to drive on up by the dairy barn. They set up a small corral of bright red pipe sections about 16 feet in diameter and told us we could put our horses in it. We put nine horses in that pen, out in the blazing sun, with no shade or water, after driving them for 22 miles. It was only 105° that day. We felt like a bunch of prize hyenas in a cage there at that corral. They sent in

a call for their head man to find out what to do with us. Two hours later I was just about ready to hook up and go back to Folsom, when Mr. Jim finally came by. He said he planned on us camping across the levee in the slough.

I was willing to go look at it with him. It did have a certain appeal as there were quite a few big shade trees and some grass, and they sure looked good after sitting out in that sun all afternoon, especially when he said we'd be the only people down there and there'd be no traffic by our camp. When I asked him what activities they had planned for us to take part in, he answered he thought he'd have us drive into the arena to show the coach before the draft horse contest started on Friday night, and then again on Sunday. Big Deal. This was Sunday when we were talking; so what do we do until Friday night? "Well," he says, "I guess you can put the horses up in that round corral and park the coach beside it each day if you want to show it."

> I sure was thinking about what a way to end a 2,000 mile historical reenactment stagecoach trip ---spending the week hid over behind the levee down in a slough.

Also he said we could drive the hitch in the inter-fairgrounds parade each evening if we wanted to, but they didn't feel it was a safe place to drive a six horse hitch around in. I was getting about fed up with things and was just about to say something, when he comes back with, "Maybe he could get with the other directors the next morning, and work something else out for us."

I was tired, and that shady slough looked inviting right then, so I said it would be OK, and we headed back to the pen to get the horses. About this time, Wallace showed up without the horse van. It had taken a balky streak and Wallace couldn't get it started. He thought maybe I knew it better than he did. I've driven that old KW truck so many miles, that I know most of it's chronic ailments. After I got back up there and had a little chat with it, it fired right up and ran like a top; so we loaded up the extra horses and headed back to the slough at the fairgrounds.

We still had 7-¼ miles more to go to drive to the real "end of the trail"; maybe we could put up with the slough until we got that accomplished. Little did we know, that the closer we got to the finish, the more difficult it would become for us to get there.

When we went back to the slough, we set up a corral with our own panels that was big enough for our 18 head of horses. The evening parade that Mr. Jim mentioned wasn't a big one; a few floats, a couple bands, and a clown or two; nothing at all like I expected. It just wound around down the midway and through the barn area. It was alright to liven up the spirits of the spectators, but it wasn't made up from the exhibitors' items.

We'd never been there before; so didn't know what to expect, so we decided to take part in their parade. The people organizing the activities were very nice and friendly, and made sure we knew what time to be ready and where to go to get in the lineup. The area back behind the midway was too small for us to get in with the coach; so we sat just outside the gate, ready to fall in line. The paraders filed by us in a joyous atmosphere, and then it was our turn to pull in line. Right then, one of the most embarrassing things of the whole trip happened,

I called out softly to my leaders, "Roulette, Rebel, get up." They took up the slack in the lead bars, the swing team stepped out in line, and the wheel team picked up the slack almost immediately. There was a crackling sound, and I had problems. The wheel tongue simply pulled straight apart into two pieces, back about two feet from the front end! That left the front end of the tongue completely free. The swing team and leaders were still fastened to the wheel team, but only by their pull-back chains, and you can't go far like that, with a loose tongue. Of course, I pulled my horses to a stop immediately, and called my outriders back to stand by the horses. We just sat there and watched the parade pass by. I was thinking about that tongue. It was brand new, and made from the best possible piece of wood the Frizzells could locate.

Young John tested each tongue by jumping up and down on its middle, and he's a pretty fair sized man, big enough that Little Joe had to look up at him. When I examined it later, it was broken almost straight across the grain, and had the look of a piece of crystallized iron or dry-rotted wood. It was totally disgusting, to say the least. I sent one of the outriders to camp after the pickup, and after we unhitched the horses, we chained the coach to it, and pulled it back to camp. That turned out to be our one and only attempt to show in their evening parade. We planned to try it again, with a new tongue, but circumstances prevented it. When we had sent the Santa Fe coach back to Oklahoma City, we kept the tongue with us, just in case. It was lucky for us we did. The front hounds on the two coaches weren't made to the exact same specifications; so I had to rework the end of the Santa Fe tongue a little to make it fit properly in our coach. At that, we had it fixed and ready to go again before dark.

   That day when we had entered the fairgrounds, one of the questions I was asked in front of the TV camera was what time did I expect we would arrive in 'Old Town' the next day? 'Old Town' is the downtown part of Sacramento that was there in 1860. It was sort of a triangle where the river boats, steam engines, and the stagecoaches all came together to trade passengers and freight. It was the "hub", not only of the town, but of the country for miles and miles around in all directions.

It was where the Overland Trail ended, and where the original stage station had stood. It was our final destination.

   Throughout the years, that part of the town became very run down and finally degenerated into one of the worst slum areas imaginable. When the interstate highways came through, about a six square block area containing that old "hub", was cut off from the rest of the town, boxed in by the river on one side, and the new highway on the other. It was an eyesore from that new elevated highway. Something had to be done, but the area was too full of history and romance of the gold rush to just simply demolish it.

   A group of enterprising citizens, with much determination and faith in the future, formed a Citizens Improvement Commission for "Old Town", as the area had become known, and they went to work restoring the area to 1860 vintage, bringing in new businesses and reestablishing old ones in the renovated buildings. The restoration wasn't finished, but they were doing a tremendous job, and we certainly enjoyed visiting there.

When the TV crew asked when we'd be there, I said, definitely, "by 12:30 noon tomorrow!" Little did I know that after $100 worth of long distance phone calls in the past few days, still nothing was set up.

We had been unable to make any contacts with the Bicentennial Commission in Sacramento; they just didn't answer our letters. When we were informed that the

Northern California Morgan Horse Club would like to take over arrangements for our stay and journey on to Old Town, we were delighted. A gal named Marian was elected to the job and she put out a lot of effort and did a great job, but she kept getting the run around by the city officials, like we were getting at the fairgrounds. It began to look like the downtown officials didn't care to go out of their way to see an event go smoothly at Old Town. Politics again.

DAY NINETY-EIGHT
AUGUST 30th

That Monday morning when I called Marian, she said she had just talked to the City Hall, and they informed her we didn't have a permit to drive our horses to Old Town. We couldn't go without one, and it would take at least three days to get one----! I was flabbergasted.

Here we were, all hitched up, the crew was ready and waiting, and our extra outriders from the Morgan Horse Club were there and ready to escort us through town. Marian gave me the phone number to call so I did. He not only confirmed all of the above, *but added if they caught us on the street without a permit, we would be arrested and our outfit impounded.*

He did say that he guessed if I insisted, he might be able to get us a permit to load the horses and coach on our truck, and haul them down to Old Town. I answered "No Thanks" and hung up. **After almost 2000 miles of pulling that coach with the horses, we were not going to load them on a truck to go the last 7½ miles across town!**

I doubted they would carry out their threat to impound our outfit, and I was trying to figure out just what to do next. I was standing there scratching my head and kicking at an imaginary cloud of dirt, when a messenger found me and delivered a note asking to call a man in Old Town. Well, what would it hurt? I had to do something. When I called, I discovered he was the head of the Improvement association. His words were, "Am I ever glad to finally get ahold of you. I've been out of town, and only last night at midnight when I turned on the TV news, did I learn of your coming down to Old Town today.

I have quite a program lined up for your arrival, but I need to know the exact time you'll get here so I can call the newspapers and TV stations again." I hadn't been able to get a word in edgewise, and I sure hated to have to tell him that the way things looked at the present we might not be able to make it, because of the police permit. He wanted to know all the details. After listening to my story, he asked if I would hold the line for a few minutes. I had nothing else pressing to do, so shrugged my shoulders and answered, "Sure, go ahead."

8/30–
SACRAMENTO to OLD TOWN SACRAMENTO (The End of our Journey)

Old Town. Original Stage Station.

Our excitement that morning was hard to contain, but with the normal routine of harnessing and hooking up to the coach, we were soon on our way. Sacramento, here we come!

We arrived with 2 minutes to spare from the time Red had told them we'd be there.

With TV cameras rolling, and our flags flying, we rolled up to the Welcoming Committee at 12:28. Romeo, Rebel, Whoa!

He called City Hall, and I don't know what he said, but when he came back on my line, he joyously stated, "It's all set, you can come on down today, but stay where you're at until a policeman shows up to tell you what route to take." I felt much better. When he asked me again if I thought we could still make it by 12:30, I answered, "We'll be there right on the dot."

We were waiting by the gate at the fairgrounds long before our policeman showed up. I didn't know the town so I let our local escort riders do all the talking. It was 11:30 before the cop got there. We had 7½ miles to go, and it was city all the way. When he got through, I shouted "Let's go", and shook a whole bunch of slack to my hitch. We were in a high trot pounding at the hip pockets of our escort riders in nothing flat, heading out on our last leg of the trip. Once I got slightly nervous when our escort leaders became unsure of the route and had to stop and ask some workmen on the street about directions, but when they informed us we were right on course, it began to look like we might make it yet. It was 107° and a bright, sunny day, but I kept those Morgans pounding right on down the street; and they didn't need any urging, they knew they were going somewhere. If we didn't make it, it wasn't going to be because I couldn't drive fast enough. Had I known the route, I'm sure our escort riders would have been riding for all they were worth to keep up behind us, instead of barely keeping ahead out in front.

Finally we curved into another street, and there was the overhead interstate highway. We ducked under it, curved to the left, and we were in Old Town. Just two or three blocks more now. In a high trot, we jingled up that cobblestone street, and curved to the right.

There at the end of the block stood a large crowd of waiting people. Our horses have learned that they are the center of attention during parades. This always brings out the "ham" in them. They could feel the excitement in the air and they decided this was a parade. With their ears pricked forward, and their necks arched, they were stepping out high and stylish. With the TV cameras rolling, we threaded our way between the parked vehicles, the crowds of people making an opening for us as we trotted up to the waiting committee.

Only a 3-month trip
Missouri stagecoach rolls into Sacramento

(8/30 p. 2)
OLD TOWN SACRAMENTO

With TV cameras rolling, and our flags flying, we rolled up to the Welcoming Committee at 12:28. Whoa!

After the ceremony, we went back to our camp. Unhitched. Unharnessed. Watered and fed the horses. Relaxed and talked it over.

We had done it. What we started with an idea, had become a reality, and we had done it.

At exactly 28 minutes past 12 o'clock noon, Monday, August 30, 1976, I pulled in on the lines, jabbed the brake lever home, and called out loudly, "Roulette, Rebel, Whooaa! The clip-clop of shod feet stopped, the wheels of the coach stopped rolling.

Our journey was over!

We were finished, and all else could fall in place in due time. The Judge presented the California Bear Flag to us, and we were presented a plaque with a large old key almost 7 inches long mounted on it. It was the "Key to Old Sacramento" which was found in the rubble of the old stage station building. We had rerun the Overland Trail every inch of the way, from the original starting point at the Pony Express Stables in St. Joseph Missouri, to the very spot in the old cobblestone street where the first Overland Stage might have stopped. We were highly elated! Of one hundred days scheduled for the trip, we had traveled seventy-one. Over 49 miles of farmlands, grassy prairies, steep mountain peaks, sun-bleached deserts, and finally, the orchards of California. Through wind, sun, rain, and storm; through joyous memories and tragedy, we had made it.

We had accomplished what seemed impossible ---driven from St. Joe Missouri to Sacramento California with a Concord stagecoach and a six horse hitch!

1977 Presidential Inaugural Parade

Plymouth Horse Show - Sept. 1976 after the trip

Apache Junction, Arizona 1978

Fiddletown, California 1984

"STAGECOACH" 1986
JOHNNY CASH   KRIS KRISTOFFERSON
JOHN SCHNEIDER
RED

'Desperado' 1989

Highway 50 Wagon Train - Placerville, Ca.1984

Sacramento 2000

Western Horseman
Magazine

Holly and Red

Tammie

Wendy

Kip driving in Old Sacramento - photo by Dianne Queirolo

EPILOGUE

    We went back to Colorado. After three years of planning and three months on the road in a stagecoach, our life was never to be the same. In many ways, the end of our trip was anti-climactic; because it was touched by sorrow from our wreck and lack of enthusiasm from the city of Sacramento, after all of the wonderful people and towns along the way. But our happy ending came in a big way, several months later, when we were invited to represent the entire American West in the presidential inauguration parade for Jimmy Carter. January 1977 found us caravanning the horses and stagecoach across country through rain and snow, to parade down Pennsylvania Avenue. It was a proud moment for all of us, including our devoted extended family and close friends who accompanied us. When the Wolverton Stagecoach was announced, the cheers from the crowds lining the streets made us proud and made it all seem worthwhile.

    From that point on, the stagecoach became our livelihood and our life. My father decided he would make his living with it. We hauled tourists in Colorado, then performed nationwide with Monty Montana Jr's Buffalo Bill Wild West show. This brought the history of our stagecoach full circle, since the iron-work on our coach had come from an original stagecoach used by Buffalo Bill in the 1890s. We moved to Arizona and began using the coach and six-up in movies. From 'Stagecoach" with Johnny Cash and Kris Kristofferson; to the "Desperado" Tv movies, to "Posse", and "Tombstone", the Wolverton coach criss-crossed the silver screen. It carried legends. It created legacy.

    Looking back now, from a future perspective of unimaginable events, including a worldwide pandemic, and a nation struggling to find hope while divided by racism and violence; our stagecoach trip in 1976 was a phenomenon. It brought people together. It brought communities together. It spread hope. We traveled across country to promote and celebrate the Bicentennial promise that was America. We saw 200 years of history and freedom rolling along at a stagecoach trot. And it was a beautiful sight. Never to be forgotten, no matter how dusty the road.

Wendy Wolverton – 2022

*AC*KNOWLEDGEMENTS

We had many newspaper reporters, journalists, radio people, and photographers take pictures, do interviews, and write articles throughout the 7 states. Where possible, the person was given their credit. For those that weren't credited, we acknowledge your contribution and interest in our history project, and wish to thank you for your part in documenting our journey in a time before the internet, cell phones, and even home video cameras. We also acknowledge all the people along the way who appeared in or took photos, and helped us have a record of this trip with your letters, cards, and pictures.

We couldn't have done it without you. THANK YOU.

Wolverton extended family 2019

www.ingramcontent.com/pod-product-compliance
Lightning Source LLC
Chambersburg PA
CBHW040106120526
44589CB00039B/2757